Palgrave Macmillan

Series Editors: **Andrew H**

International Advisory Board: **Mary Carruthers**, New York University, USA, **Astrid Erll**, University of Wuppertal, Germany, **Jürgen Habermas**, University of Frankfurt am Main, **Jeffrey Olick**, Virginia, USA, **Susannah Radstone**, University of Utrecht, the Netherlands.

The nascent field of Memory Studies emerges from contemporary trends that include a shift from concern with historical knowledge of events to that of memory, from 'what we know' to 'how we remember it'; changes in generational memory; the rapid advance of technologies of memory; panic over declining powers of memory, which mirrors our fascination with the possibilities of memory enhancement; and the development of trauma narratives in reshaping the past.

These factors have contributed to an intensification of public discourses on our past over the last thirty years. Technological, political, interpersonal, social and cultural shifts affect what, how and why people and societies remember and forget. This groundbreaking series tackles questions such as: What is 'memory' under these conditions? What are its prospects, and also the prospects for its interdisciplinary and systematic study? What are the conceptual, theoretical and methodological tools for its investigation and illumination?

Silke Arnold-de Simine
MEDIATING MEMORY IN THE MUSEUM
Empathy, Trauma, Nostalgia

Rebecca Bramall
THE CULTURAL POLITICS OF AUSTERITY
Past and Present in Austere Times

Irit Dekel
MEDIATION AT THE HOLOCAUST MEMORIAL IN BERLIN

Anne Fuchs
AFTER THE DRESDEN BOMBING
Pathways of Memory 1945 to the Present

Irial Glynn and J. Olaf Kleist (*editors*)
HISTORY, MEMORY AND MIGRATION
Perceptions of the Past and the Politics of Incorporation

Andrea Hajek
NEGOTIATING MEMORIES OF PROTEST IN WESTERN EUROPE
The Case of Italy

Amy Holdsworth
TELEVISION, MEMORY AND NOSTALGIA

Jason James
PRESERVATION AND NATIONAL BELONGING IN EASTERN GERMANY
Heritage Fetishism and Redeeming Germanness

Sara Jones
THE MEDIA OF TESTOMONY
Remembering the East German Stasi in the Berlin Republic

Emily Keightley and Michael Pickering
THE MNEMONIC IMAGINATION
Remembering as Creative Practice

Amanda Lagerkvist
MEDIA AND MEMORY IN NEW SHANGHAI
Western Performances of Futures Past

Philip Lee and Pradip Ninan Thomas (*editors*)
PUBLIC MEMORY, PUBLIC MEDIA AND THE POLITICS OF JUSTICE

Erica Lehrer, Cynthia E. Milton and Monica Eileen Patterson (*editors*)
CURATING DIFFICULT KNOWLEDGE
Violent Pasts in Public Places

Oren Meyers, Eyal Zandberg and Motti Neiger
COMMUNICATING AWE
Media, Memory and Holocaust Commemoration

Anne Marie Monchamp
AUTOBIOGRAPHICAL MEMORY IN AN ABORIGINAL AUSTRALIAN COMMUNITY
Culture, Place and Narrative

Motti Neiger, Oren Meyers and Eyal Zandberg (*editors*)
ON MEDIA MEMORY
Collective Memory in a New Media Age

Katharina Niemeyer (*editor*)
MEDIA AND NOSTALGIA
Yearning for the Past, Present and Future

Margarita Saona
MEMORY MATTERS IN TRANSITIONAL PERU

Anna Saunders and Debbie Pinfold (*editors*)
REMEMBERING AND RETHINKING THE GDR
Multiple Perspectives and Plural Authenticities

V. Seidler
REMEMBERING DIANA
Cultural Memory and the Reinvention of Authority

Bryoni Trezise
PERFORMING FEELING IN CULTURES OF MEMORY

Evelyn B. Tribble and Nicholas Keene
COGNITIVE ECOLOGIES AND THE HISTORY OF REMEMBERING
Religion, Education and Memory in Early Modern England

Barbie Zelizer and Keren Tenenboim-Weinblatt (*editors*)
JOURNALISM AND MEMORY

Palgrave Macmillan Memory Studies
Series Standing Order ISBN 978–0–230–23851–0 (hardback)
978–0–230–23852–7 (paperback)
(*outside North America only*)

You can receive future titles in this series as they are published by placing a standing order. Please contact your bookseller or, in case of difficulty, write to us at the address below with your name and address, the title of the series and the ISBN quoted above.

Customer Services Department, Macmillan Distribution Ltd, Houndmills, Basingstoke, Hampshire RG21 6XS, England

Media and Nostalgia
Yearning for the Past, Present and Future

Edited by

Katharina Niemeyer
The French Press Institute/CARISM, Pantheon-Assas University, Paris 2, France

palgrave
macmillan

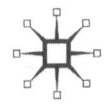

Introduction, selection and editorial matter © Katharina Niemeyer 2014
Individual chapters © Respective authors 2014
Cover photograph © Marlène Dorgny (textile and graphic designer)
Softcover reprint of the hardcover 1st edition 2014 978-1-137-37587-2
Corrected Printing 2014

All rights reserved. No reproduction, copy or transmission of this publication may be made without written permission.

No portion of this publication may be reproduced, copied or transmitted save with written permission or in accordance with the provisions of the Copyright, Designs and Patents Act 1988, or under the terms of any licence permitting limited copying issued by the Copyright Licensing Agency, Saffron House, 6–10 Kirby Street, London EC1N 8TS.

Any person who does any unauthorized act in relation to this publication may be liable to criminal prosecution and civil claims for damages.

The authors have asserted their rights to be identified as the authors of this work in accordance with the Copyright, Designs and Patents Act 1988.

First published 2014 by
PALGRAVE MACMILLAN

Palgrave Macmillan in the UK is an imprint of Macmillan Publishers Limited, registered in England, company number 785998, of Houndmills, Basingstoke, Hampshire RG21 6XS.

Palgrave Macmillan in the US is a division of St Martin's Press LLC, 175 Fifth Avenue, New York, NY 10010.

Palgrave Macmillan is the global academic imprint of the above companies and has companies and representatives throughout the world.

Palgrave® and Macmillan® are registered trademarks in the United States, the United Kingdom, Europe and other countries.

ISBN 978-1-349-47750-0   ISBN 978-1-137-37588-9 (eBook)
DOI 10.1057/9781137375889

A catalogue record for this book is available from the British Library.

Library of Congress Cataloging-in-Publication Data
Media and nostalgia : yearning for the past, present and future / edited
   by Katharina Niemeyer.
       pages cm — (Palgrave Macmillan memory studies)
   Summary: "Media and Nostalgia takes a closer look at the recent nostalgia boom and the relationship between media and nostalgia more generally; for example, digital photography that adopts a vintage style, the success of films such as The Artist and television series such as Mad Men, revivals of past music, fashion, and video games. However, this boom is not simply a fascination with the past; rather, it hints at something more profound. Expressions of nostalgia indicate a double helix type phenomenon with slower reactions to ever-faster technologies, and the possibility of an escape from the current crisis into a middle status of wanderlust (Fernweh) and a specific form of nostalgia such as homesickness. This collection explores, with a critical lens, the ways in which various media produce narratives of nostalgia, how they trigger nostalgic emotions and how they can in fact be a creative projection space in themselves"—Provided by publisher.
   ISBN 978-1-349-47750-0
   1. Mass media—Social aspects.   2. Nostalgia—Social aspects.
   3. Collective memory.   4. Media—psychological aspects.
   I. Niemeyer, Katharina, 1980– editor of compilation.
   HM1206.M3874 2014
   302.23—dc23   2014016793

Transferred to Digital Printing in 2014

Contents

List of Figures — vii

Acknowledgements — viii

Notes on Contributors — ix

Introduction: Media and Nostalgia — 1
Katharina Niemeyer

Part I Analogue Nostalgias

1 Analogue Nostalgia and the Aesthetics of Digital Remediation — 27
Dominik Schrey

2 Homesick for Aged Home Movies: Why Do We Shoot Contemporary Family Videos in Old-Fashioned Ways? — 39
Giuseppina Sapio

3 The Instant Past: Nostalgia and Digital Retro Photography — 51
Gil Bartholeyns

4 Retromania: Crisis of the Progressive Ideal and Pop Music Spectrality — 70
Maël Guesdon and Philippe Le Guern

Part II Exploited Nostalgias

5 Retrotyping and the Marketing of Nostalgia — 83
Michael Pickering and Emily Keightley

6 Anti-nostalgia in Citroën's Advertising Campaign — 95
Emmanuelle Fantin

7 Networks as Media for Nostalgia in an Organisational Context — 105
Thibaut Bardon, Emmanuel Josserand and Florence Villesèche

8 Media and the Closure of the Memory Boom — 118
Andrew Hoskins

Part III Screened Nostalgias

9   Nostalgia Is Not What It Used to Be: Serial Nostalgia and
    Nostalgic Television Series   129
    Katharina Niemeyer and Daniela Wentz

10 AMC's *Mad Men* and the Politics of Nostalgia   139
    David Pierson

11 The Television Channel ARTE as a Time Machine and
    Matrix for European Identity   152
    Aline Hartemann

12 Nostalgia, Tinted Memories and Cinematic
    Historiography: On Otto Preminger's
    Bonjour Tristesse (1958)   160
    Ute Holl

Part IV Creative Nostalgias

13 Creative Nostalgia for an Imagined Better Future: *Il treno
    del Sud* by the Migrant Filmmaker Alvaro Bizzarri   179
    Morena La Barba

14 Nostalgia and Postcolonial Utopia in Senghor's *Négritude*   191
    Nadia Yala Kisukidi

15 Impossible Nostalgia   203
    Itzhak Goldberg

16 Journeys through the Past: Contempt, Nostalgia, Enigma   212
    John Potts

Poetic Transfer of a (Serious) Situation   223
Marine Baudrillard

Index   229

Figures

3.1 The apps replicate the look produced by old technical processes. They reveal the materiality of photographs and how images age   53
3.2 Little Tripping Nostalgia by Vlad Lunin, 27 December 2010   56
3.3 Screenshot of the list of WeHeartIt.com, 3 May 2013   57
3.4 Covers and analogue simulations of old digital photos. Top and bottom: *Gak, halfway up Mt McKay circa the early 1980's*, 18 February 2011, by Gary A. K.; *Cousins*, 26 April 2010, by Anne H.   59
3.5 To photograph ancient artefacts and environments, to disclose their historicity. Top and bottom: *Coastal drive*, 10 October 2012; *The Allure. Vintage photo booth vendor at the San Bernardino County Fair*, 5 May 2011   61
3.6 Restoring the visual aesthetics of their time to things. Top and bottom: *Got the deck hooked up*, 10 July 2011, by John Common; *Nostalgia in Snow*, 5 January 2011, by Tanja Taube   63
3.7 The virtual materiality of cameras and films. 'Past meets present meets you'   64
3.8 Between the subject matter and ourselves: the 'image'. Arcana 1996/2008, Cambridge, March 1992 by Joachim Schmid   66
5.1 Hovis print ad from 1993: 'Sunday Best'   84
12.1 Direct gaze of Seberg into the camera (Bonjour Tristesse, screenshot)   168
16.1 Installation View: Thomas Demand, 'The Dailyies', Kaldor Public Art Project 25, Sydney, 2012. Photo: Kaldor Public Art Projects/Paul Green (caption 1)   221
16.2 Installation View: Thomas Demand, 'The Dailyies', Kaldor Public Art Project 25, Sydney, 2012. Photo: Kaldor Public Art Projects/Paul Green (caption 2)   221

Acknowledgements

In the winter of 2011, I was sitting with Céline and Olivier in a living room somewhere in Quebec and our conversations were filled with nostalgic thoughts of past times and distant places. We began talking about the incredible boom of these longings in media, and that very evening I decided to organise an international conference on the topic. It eventually took place in September of the following year at the University of Geneva under the name 'Flashbacks – Nostalgic Media and Other Mediated Forms of Nostalgia'. Most of the chapters in this volume are based on papers from the conference. I would thus like to first thank the Faculty of Economic and Social Sciences, especially the Dean, Bernard Morard; the Administrative Commission and the Institute for Communication, Media and Journalism Studies at the University of Geneva, as well as the Swiss National Science Foundation for their support. Thanks also go to my former colleagues Patrick Amey, Marie-Antoinette Belloccio, Luc Gauthier, Chloé Rosselet, Sandra Zanelli and Virginie Zimmerli, as well as to my former students for their intellectual and organisational assistance. I am grateful to each of the contributors to this book for their passionate and reflective work on media and nostalgia, and many thanks to Marine Baudrillard for 'the letter', Emilie Camacho for dancing thoughts and Marlène Dorgny for the cover picture. I am indebted to Felicity Plester, Chris Penfold and the staff of Palgrave Macmillan for their extraordinarily professional help in producing this book. I would also like to thank Andrew Hoskins and John Sutton, the editors of the Palgrave Macmillan Memory Studies Series, as well as the reviewers for their interest and confidence in the project. I express my gratitude to all translators and correctors of the chapters, Jane Linekar for her help concerning the book proposal, and especially Peter Clayburn for his thoughtful work correcting the Introduction and several chapters. I would also like to thank my students and colleagues at the French Press Institute (Pantheon-Assas University, Paris 2) for the many lively and rather controversial discussions on the topic. Lastly, thank you Daniela, for your endless support and helpful critiques. This volume is dedicated to my beloved grandparents, to my parents, to Kerstin for the reasons she knows and, last but not least, to Olivier who is always on my side.

Contributors

Thibaut Bardon is an assistant professor and head of the consulting major at Audencia Nantes School of Management, France. He received a PhD double diploma from the University of Geneva, HEC, Switzerland, and Université Paris-Dauphine, DRM-CREPA, France. His main research interests are identity, management practices and epistemology, from a critical and post-structuralist perspective. His work has been published in *Organisation* and *M@n@gement*.

Gil Bartholeyns holds the chair in visual culture studies at the University Lille III, France. He has received degrees and held positions at the universities of Brussels and Oxford, the École des Hautes Études en Sciences Sociales and the Musée du Quai Branly in Paris. After working on the visual construction of medieval society, he has focused on issues of materiality, the value of objects and norms of visual production in pre-industrial Europe. Regarding images, his work explores the anthropological aspects of their efficacy. His research encompasses the representations and uses of the past in the visual arts and scientific discourse. He is a member of the editorial boards of *Techniques & Culture*, *Civilisations*, EditionsPapiers.org and CultureVisuelle.org. He has authored or co-edited *Image et Transgression au Moyen Âge* (2008), *La Performance des Images* (2010), 'Les Apparences de l'Homme' (*Civilisations*, 59/2, 2011) and *Cultures matérielles, une Anthologie* (2011, 2 vols).

Marine Baudrillard is Jean Baudrillard's wife. In 2009 she created the association Cool Memories, Jean Baudrillard's Friends (http://coolmemories.fr/), an association that aims at contributing to the development and transmission of Jean Baudrillard's work in France and elsewhere. Marine Baudrillard organises conferences that explore the philosopher's work. In 2012, the association participated in a conference in Nankin (13–14 October, International Seminar on Studies of Baudrillard, Nanjing University). She recently introduced several exhibitions dedicated to Jean Baudrillard's photographic work in China (Times Museum of Canton, CAFA Art Museum of Peking, Tap Seac Gallery in Macao) and organised a one-day conference at the National Library of France (BNF) in Paris (November 2013).

Emmanuelle Fantin is a PhD candidate at CELSA, Paris IV Sorbonne, and member of the Group of Interdisciplinary Researches on Information and Communication Process (GRIPIC). Her forthcoming doctoral thesis will analyse the rewriting of the past through advertising. Her research focuses on knowledge circulations and media communications of history, memory and time. She has received a master's degree in French literature from La Sorbonne and, prior to beginning her PhD, held roles in marketing development and strategic planning for L'Oréal and Aegis Media.

Itzhak Goldberg is an art history professor at the University of Saint-Etienne in France and a member of the Centre Interdisciplinaire d'Etudes et de Recherches sur l'Expression Contemporaine (CIEREC). His main research interests are in the field of fine arts and aesthetics with a special focus on portraiture, expressionism, abstraction and Middle Eastern art.

Maël Guesdon is a PhD candidate and graduate student instructor at the Ecole des Hautes Etudes en Sciences Sociales, Paris. He is currently preparing a doctoral dissertation, under the direction of Anne Sauvagnargues and Esteban Buch, on music in the thought of Gilles Deleuze and Félix Guattari. His research focuses on the relationships between philosophy, music and social science in the twentieth century. He is a member of the board of editors of the journals *Chimères* and *Transposition, Musique et Sciences Sociales*.

Aline Hartemann is a PhD candidate in sociology at the Ecole des Hautes Etudes en Sciences Sociales, Paris and at the Centre Marc Bloch in Berlin (Franco-German Research Centre for the Social Sciences). She facilitates the cooperation between the German and French departments at the European television channel Arte. She studied politics at Sciences Po in Paris and art history at the Ecole du Louvre as well as at the Sorbonne in Paris. She is also curator and head librarian at the Invalides in Paris.

Ute Holl is a full professor of media studies at the University of Basel in Switzerland. She has taught in Weimar, Berlin and Cologne. Her main research interests are in film history with a focus on perception, media history of acoustic and film sounds, and ethnographic and experimental film. She has published three books, with Wolfgang Ernst and Stefan Heidenreich: *Suchbilde: Visuelle Kultur zwischen Algorithmen und*

Archiven (2003), *Kino, Trance und Kybernetik* (2002) and *Choreographie für eine Kamera. Maya Derens Schriften zum Film* (1995). She has published more than 50 articles in international journals and books.

Andrew Hoskins is an interdisciplinary research professor in global security at the University of Glasgow, UK. His research focuses on the theoretical and empirical investigation of today's 'new media ecology' and the nature of/challenges for security and individual, social and cultural memory in this environment. He is founding editor-in-chief of *Memory Studies*, founding co-editor of *Media, War & Conflict*, co-editor of the book series 'Memory Studies' and co-editor of the book series 'Media, War & Security'. His latest books are *War and Media: The Emergence of Diffused War* (2010) and *Radicalisation and Media: Connectivity and Terrorism in the New Media Ecology* (2011, with Awan and O'Loughlin).

Emmanuel Josserand is Professor of Management at the University of Geneva and the University of Technology, Sydney. His research has been published in numerous books and peer-reviewed journals. His current research interests relate to inter- and intra-organisational networks, identity and communities of practice. He serves as editor-in-chief of *M@n@gement*.

Emily Keightley is Senior Lecturer in Communication and Media Studies in the Department of Social Sciences at Loughborough University. She is currently working on the research project 'Media of Remembering: Photography and Phonography in Everyday Remembering' funded by the Leverhulme Trust. Recent books include *Time, Media and Modernity* (2012), which considers how time is structured by media technologies, how it is represented in cultural texts and how it is experienced in different social contexts and environments; *The Mnemonic Imagination* (2012, with Michael Pickering), which addresses areas that have been relatively ignored or overlooked in the study of memory and its mediation; and *Research Methods for Memory Studies* (2013, with Michael Pickering). Emily is also assistant editor of *Media, Culture and Society*.

Nadia Yala Kisukidi is a specialist on Henri Bergson. She received her doctorate in philosophy at the University of Lille, France, and works now as a lecturer and researcher in the Department of Theology and Ethics at the University of Geneva. She also obtained the French state examination (*aggrégation*) in philosophy in 2005. Her main research interests are in contemporary French philosophy, postcolonial studies, and ethics and theology. She has written articles in various books and journals, and she recently published *L'humanité créatrice: esthétique et politique chez Bergson*.

Morena La Barba is a lecturer and founding member of the Visual Sociology Unit at the University of Geneva. She received her training in political science and in women's studies at the University of Bologna and in documentary filmmaking and journalism at Dortmund/Bielefeld. She is currently researching the history and memory of Italian migration to Switzerland, with particular reference to migrant associations and cinema.

Philippe Le Guern is a full professor in the Department of Communication Science at the University of Nantes, where he teaches media sociology. He is a member of the Centre Atlantique de Philosophie and an affiliate researcher at the Research Center for Arts and Language (CRAL-EHESS). His work focuses on the digital turn and its different manifestations in the musical world, from the use of technology to the renewal of norms and aesthetic standards or the patrimonialisation of so-called contemporary music. He is currently developing a research programme centred on non-human ontologies (for example, animals, holograms and robots).

Katharina Niemeyer is an associate professor at the French Press Institute, Pantheon-Assas University, Paris 2. She is a member of the Centre for Interdisciplinary Research and Analysis of the Media (CARISM) as well as the International Association for Media and History (IAMHIST) council. Until July 2012, she worked as a lecturer and researcher at the University of Geneva, where she also obtained her PhD in media and communication studies. Her major areas of research are in the fields of media studies, memory studies, historical (media) events, semiotics, media philosophy and the philosophy of history. She is the author of *De la chute du mur de Berlin au 11 Septembre 2001* (2011) and *Die Mediasphären des Terrorismus* (2006). She has also translated texts by the French philosopher Jean Baudrillard.

Michael Pickering teaches in the Department of Social Sciences at Loughborough University. He has published in the areas of social and cultural history, the sociology of art and culture, and media and communication studies. Recent books include *History, Experience and Cultural Studies* (1997); *Researching Communications* (1999/2007), co-written with

David Deacon, Peter Golding and Graham Murdock; *Stereotyping: The Politics of Representation* (2001); *Creativity, Communication and Cultural Value* (2004), co-written with Keith Negus; *Beyond a Joke: The Limits of Humour* (2005/2009), co-edited with Sharon Lockyer; *Blackface Minstrelsy in Britain* (2008); *Research Methods for Cultural Studies* (2008); *Popular Culture*, a four-volume edited collection (2010); *The Mnemonic Imagination* (2012), co-written with Emily Keightley; *Research Methods for Memory Studies* (2013), co-edited with Emily Keightley; and *Rhythms of Labour: Music at Work in Britain* (2013), co-written with Marek Korczynski and Emma Robertson.

David Pierson is Associate Professor of Media Studies and Chair of the Department of Communication and Media Studies at the University of Southern Maine. His research interests are the aesthetic and discursive dimensions of cable and broadcast network programming, and the relationship between American television and history. He has published book chapters and articles in the *Journal of Communication Inquiry*, *Journal of Popular Culture* and *Film & History* on *C.S.I.: Crime Scene Investigation*, *Combat!*, *Mad Men*, *Seinfeld*, The Discovery Channel and Turner Network Television made-for-TV westerns. He has recently published a monograph on the 1960s TV series *The Fugitive*.

John Potts is Professor in Media at Macquarie University, Sydney. He has published five books, including *A History of Charisma* (2009) and *After the Event: New Perspectives on Art History* (edited with Charles Merewether, 2010). He has also published many articles and essays on media, cultural history, studies of technology, art history and intellectual history.

Giuseppina Sapio is a PhD student at IRCAV, the research centre in Cinema Studies at the University of Paris III (Sorbonne Nouvelle). Part of her research, entailing a study of the practice of home movies, was awarded the 2013 'Prix de l'Observatoire du Bonheur' (*ex-aequo*) by a jury made up of CNRS researchers in partnership with the Coca-Cola Company.

Dominik Schrey studied German literature and culture (with an emphasis on media studies) at Universität Karlsruhe, Germany. The thesis for his master's degree was on the motif of the time machine as a figuration of media epistemology. He is now a research assistant at the Karlsruhe Institute of Technology (KIT), where he teaches courses in media and cultural studies. Since December 2010 he has held a scholarship from the federal state of Baden-Württemberg, and is working on his PhD thesis, provisionally titled 'Analog Nostalgia in Digital Media Culture'.

Florence Villesèche holds a PhD and an MSc in business administration from HEC, University of Geneva, as well as an MA in anglophone studies from the University of Montpellier, France. Her main research interests are networks, gender, identity and discourse analysis methods. For her doctoral dissertation, she received an Emerald/EFMD Highly Commended Award 2012 for outstanding doctoral research. She is currently conducting postdoctoral research about women on boards at Copenhagen Business School as a recipient of Swiss and European grants.

Daniela Wentz works as a researcher in the research project 'TV-Series as Reflection and Projection of Change' at the Bauhaus-University Weimar, Germany. Her main research interests are seriality, diagrammatology, philosophy and epistemology of media, history and theory of television. Her most recent publications include 'Der Medienwandel der Serie' (*Navigationen*, January 2013, edited together with D. Maeder), 'Lost in Media' (forthcoming, edited together with. B. Beil and H. Schwaab) and issue 'Die Serie' (*Zeitschrift für Medienwissenschaft*, February 2012, edited together with B. Beil, L. Engell, J. Schröter and H. Schwaab). She recently obtained her PhD, which deals with the diagrammatology of television series.

Introduction: Media and Nostalgia

Katharina Niemeyer

Nostalgic times, once again

'Nostalgia' is the name we commonly give to a bittersweet longing for former times and spaces. This private or public return to the past, and sometimes to an interlinking imagination of the future, is, of course, not new. There has always been a fascination for the, as we often call them, 'good old times'. But who would have thought, given the 1990s' imagining of a future filled with technology, that the beginning of the new century would in fact be marked by an increase in expressions of nostalgia, and in nostalgic objects, media content and styles? This volume goes back to a simple observation of the current nostalgia boom, which is infiltrating various aspects of our lives. On social media sites like *Facebook*, groups and forums with titles like 'nostalgia', 'vintage' or 'retronaut' have emerged, videos and pictures with nostalgic statements are posted and the vintage fashion collection of the television series *Mad Men* (AMC, 2007–) is celebrated. Not to mention editing digital photographs on mobile phones to resemble Polaroids; retro design has become digitised. Indeed, part of the web could be seen as a huge attic or bric-a-brac market where individual and collective nostalgias converge and spread. Skeuomorphs invade our mobile phones using old-fashioned objects to represent new ones, even when the old objects are no longer necessary or relevant. An example could be the 'notes' application in which you can write things down in a digital imagined space designed to resemble 'real' yellow paper. Films like *The Artist* (Hazanavicius, 2001), *Populaire* (Roinsard, 2012) and *Hugo* (Scorcese, 2011), or television series like *Pan Am* (ABC, 2011–2012), *Magic City* (Starz, 2012–) or *Boardwalk Empire* (HBO, 2010–), exploring the aesthetics and social life of past decades, are also examples of this nostalgia wave. Similarly, several old television series, such as *Dallas*, have been revived, and numerous television and radio shows re-engage with the past by rediscovering and reproducing their own or other archives. Advertising for watches or cars is linked to nostalgic forms of family tradition. Fans of the 1950s organise parties and fashion events to feel part of the past while in the present. One can observe further revivals of past music, fashion, furniture, video games, food, drinks and other everyday objects. This is what we can superficially observe, but what is 'hidden' behind these longings? It would certainly be very 'in vogue' to ride this nostalgia wave by exclusively discussing this notion in terms of the retro styles, vintage moods and designs emerging in our environments. But nostalgia is not only a fashion or a trend. Rather, it very often expresses or hints at something more profound, as it deals with positive or negative relations to time and space. It is related to a way of living, imagining and sometimes exploiting or (re)inventing the past, present and future. With new components, the recent boom might join the concepts of media obsession with nostalgia (Hutcheon, 2000) or 'retromania' (Reynolds, 2011), and nostalgic cycles (Higson, 2003; Marcus, 2004), fevers (Panati, 1991), dreams and nightmares (Lowenthal, 2013), waves (Davis, 1977) and modes (Jameson, 1991). The boom could also be subject to the well-known argument that nostalgia is a traditional companion to progress (Boym, 2001). In our case, this last concept would refer primarily to the latest developments of new communication technologies as well as the increasing uses of social media that might activate nostalgia for the real (Baudrillard, 1981). This progress accompanies different types of crisis that affect economies and social structures, but as Boyer (2013) argues, a re-emergence of nostalgia mainly indicates a crisis of temporality. In this sense, nostalgic expressions or the creation of nostalgic worlds could indicate a twofold phenomenon: a reaction to fast technologies, despite using them, in desiring to slow down, and/or an escape from this crisis into a state of wanderlust (*Fernweh*) and nostalgia (in the sense of *Heimweh*) that could be 'cured', or encouraged, by media use and consumption. Nostalgia could consequently present a symptom of progress, but also of crisis. This volume is less interested in the symptoms or signs of these concepts, and will not deliver an empirical answer to the questions of causality. It might, however, present a first step to discovering nostalgia through new perspectives and thoughts that imply a wider approach: what is nostalgia *doing*, and what role *do* media play in this context of progress and crisis? On that score, 'Media and Nostalgia' is an invitation to reflect on nostalgia, its recent boom, its intrinsic and always existent relation to media, and its apparent contradictory position within the world of new technologies that view the experience and perception of time in terms of 'social acceleration' (Koselleck, 1979; Virilio, 1989; Rosa, 2005; Schnell, 2006). It is only an *apparent* contradictory position, because the nostalgia boom might join the memory boom that Andreas Huyssen explores in his work. He suggests that 'our obsessions with memory function as a reaction formation against the accelerating technical process that is transforming our Lebenswelt (lifeworld) in quite distinct ways' (1995, p. 7). Hartmut Rosa (2005) names this phenomenon *Entschleunigung* (deceleration, slowing down). In this sense, the mentioned 'acceleration' does not at all exclude the fact that media and media practice render different temporal experiences, time layers or 'timescapes' (Keightley, 2012) possible; nostalgia, along with its practices, might be one of them.

In order to discuss the mentioned elements properly, it will be necessary to put into a sharper perspective the modest attempts of this volume to engage with the fields of media, memory and nostalgia studies.

Memory and nostalgia

As Lowenthal argues, 'we crave evidence that the past endures in recoverable form. Some agency, some mechanism, some faith will enable us not just to know it, but to see and feel it' (1985, p. 14). What is gone can only be re-enacted, repeated, reconstructed, reshown, rethought and restored by an artificial act, by *mimesis* (Böhringer, 1989; Ricoeur, 1993). In other words, what is past comes along with the present, *via* re-presentation, a present that contracts parts of the past in its actualisation (Deleuze, 1997; Bergson, 2004/1939) and can also include imaginations of the future. This non-linear social understanding of time (Callender, 2011) and the concept of memory are closely correlated. Our ability to remember the past, and to actualise it, includes the imperfections of the human mind and endorses sometimes voluntarily embellished or falsified memories on an individual and collective level (Ricoeur, 2000; Candau, 2005). The scholarly reflection on this memory boom began in the 1980s with Pierre Nora's and Yosef Yerushalmi's (1982) works. According to Pierre Nora (1997), the old concept of memory was of its being vivid, subjective, emotional and 'fuzzy'. He argues that it has been replaced, becoming a type of history that is now 'archivistic'. Paul Ricoeur (2000) also regrets the abundance of systems of commemoration and suggests that they have begun to bring about the overwhelming demise of memory. Even if history and memory cannot be described as being the same, either epistemologically or socially, it becomes more and more difficult to confine their frontiers and their mutual exchange. Memory is not history, but it is one of its objects and is essential for 'historical elaboration' (Le Goff, 1988, p. 281). In his article about memory and its emergence in the historical discourse, Klein (2000) delivers a detailed reflection on this question, beginning with the so-called crisis of historicism in the early twentieth century and ending with the upcoming interrogations on postmodernist perspectives concerning historiography. In his conclusions, Klein argues that today 'memory can come to the fore in an age of historiographic crisis precisely because it figures as a therapeutic alternative to historical discourse' (2000, p. 145). This volume does not consider memory as being part of a therapy or as a dangerous counterpart of history, and this epistemological discussion is not directly its principal topic, but this short excursion is essential to introduce the question of media and their relation to nostalgia. Memory has often been considered as the 'bad twin' to history, especially when it comes to the notion of media that 'disrupt' memory and history (Nora, 1972; Le Goff, 1988; Hartog, 2003). Frederic Jameson describes media as agents and mechanisms that are responsible for historical amnesia (1998, pp. 19–20). Others assign the acceleration of history to media-narrated events (Gitlin, 1980), also creating a crisis of representation (Bougnoux, 2006) and of historiography. Altered by the world of news media, and live news broadcast in particular, the present takes a new place in critical historical reflection. François Hartog calls this phenomenon 'presentism' (*présentisme*), a contemporary experience of time. With reference to television, he states that the present would like to be regarded as being historical while it occurs (2011, p. 127). First, despite the problematic relationship of media, memory and history, it is important to say, without putting into question the work of historians, that media are platforms on which events are experienced as historical ones (Carr, 2010; Niemeyer, 2011). Second, media technologies have always been part of the historiographical processes, not only in the course of contemporary historical events (Crivellari et al., 2004). Third, media can activate, frame and render memory shareable. The relationship between media and memory has by now been largely and critically explored.[1] In respect to these reflections, the following contributions propose to understand media, nostalgia, memory and history as intrinsically related components without intermingling them arbitrarily.

Nostalgia is related to the concept of memory, since it recalls times and places that are no more, or are out of reach. This involves two different directions in which the relation of memory and nostalgia might lead. It can be seen as being essential and useful to maintaining identities (Wilson, 2005), and also as a factor of social amnesia (Doane and Hodges, 1987). In this sense, nostalgia offers a 'special significance for memory studies' (Attia and Davis, 2010, p. 181). Media are able to arouse two forms of memories, as defined by Ricoeur in relation to Aristotle: *mnēmē*, a simple recall by effect, and *anamnēsis*, a reminder, an active research that is related to temporal distance (Ricoeur, 2000, p. 22). Nostalgic expressions, feelings or creations can consequently be associated with the notion of memory and media, and, as we will see, media participate in this process of nostalgic remembering. Nostalgia, this mosaic-like phenomenon, engages and becomes entangled with memory and media in specific, ambivalent and intriguing ways.

Media: Spaces and times for nostalgia

The literature dealing with nostalgia is rich and covers a large spectrum of topics, methodological approaches and disciplines covering historical (Bolzinger, 2007), sociological (Davis, 1977; Keightley and Pickering, 2006), literary (Boym, 2001; Hochmann, 2004; Matt, 2011), semiotic (Greimas, 2002), ethnographic (Nash, 2012), gender (Doane and Hodges, 1987; Huang, 2006), psychological (Richard, 2004; Arndt el al., 2006; Viennet, 2009) and educational (Mitchell and Weber, 1999) perspectives. The notions of homeland and language (Robertson, 1997; Cassin, 2013), nature (Ladino, 2012) and heritage-making (Lowenthal, 1985; Berliner, 2012) appear in the research field, accompanied by the idea that ecological sustainability might indicate a nostalgia for the future (Davies, 2010). Very often, in the form of homesickness, nostalgia can concern individuals and groups on a very personal level, but, not necessarily separated from this, it can also be used or misused for larger political (Lasch, 1984; Duyvendak, 2011), commercial and consumer purposes (Jameson, 1991; Holbrook, 1993; Baer, 2001; Loveland, Smeesters and Mandel, 2010). Associated in nineteenth-century Europe with the idea of the nation state, the term 'nostalgia' was linked to the concepts of chauvinism and nationalism (Jankélévitch, 1974; Bolzinger, 2007). Daniel Marcus's (2004) recent work shows how members of the Republican Party took cultural symbols from the 1950s and 1960s to defend their political programmes in the 1970s and 1980s. The use of cultural products and symbols of the past for political issues is frequent. It is also a successful commercial strategy of the economic sector. The marketing of nostalgia is flourishing, playing with the nostalgic emotions of potential consumers (Kessous and Roux, 2012). Many historical locations have become touristic and merchandised (Goulding, 2001), and purposefully fabricated nostalgic goods and media productions are widespread. As Charles Panati states, 'Nostalgia was once a disease, today... selling a sweet image of the past brings big bucks' (1991, p. 4). Objects from the former German Democratic Republic (GDR) and Soviet Union that are sold in Berlin in the streets are one example, be they headwear, military decorations or gadgets. These fake consumer objects pervert what is frequently described as a very special type of nostalgia: *ostalgia*, the individual or collective yearning for the former GDR.[2]

But, considering the evolution in 'nostalgia studies', it would nowadays be overly simplistic to reduce nostalgia to the concept of a unique regressive, embellished social phenomenon of popular culture, historical amnesia or the consumer world. Instead, nostalgia has to be understood in the larger critical context of historical, social, political, economic and aesthetic considerations (see, for example, Tannock, 1995; Keightley and Pickering, 2006; Atia and Davies, 2010). This is what makes it a complex notion and an interesting subject for research. Paul Grainge (2002) defines the emotional and affective patterns of nostalgia as a 'nostalgia mood' mainly based on loss. Using Frederic Jameson's (1991) concept of 'nostalgia mode', he describes how it possesses a commodified and aesthetic style. Therefore, nostalgia could be described as being a liminal, ambiguous phenomenon that migrates into deep emotional and psychological structures as well as into larger cultural, social, economic and political ones. Even if Paul Grainge does not aim to schematise both mood and modes, they often melt together in his reflections (Keightley and Pickering, 2006).

In this sense, there is maybe no need to classify different types of nostalgia into distinct categories. Alternatively, it might be more useful to grant nostalgia its plural meanings by using the notion of *nostalgias*; especially when it comes to the question of media, where different nostalgias interact. It has to be emphasised that this volume engages with a concept of media within the idea of an existing media culture[3] (*Medienkultur*) or 'mediasphère' (Debray, 2000). Other technologies and devices as potential ways to express thoughts and feelings are conceived as being media. Even if they are considered essential to participate in our way of thinking and living, this is not an approach of technical determinism. These 'media devices' (*mediale Dispositive*) are always taken as being interwoven with social practices as well as historical and economic (production) conditions. Unfortunately, there is a lack of profound reflections on nostalgia and its relation to media. Keightley and Pickering suggest that 'where the negative sense of nostalgia prevails, there is a tendency to neglect the reciprocal relationship between audience and media in generating the conditions for making sense and meaning' (2006, p. 930). As a matter of fact, most of the scholarly works quoted in this Introduction refer to media or describe their narratives and aesthetics, without reflecting in detail on their functional relationship with nostalgia. Sometimes, nostalgia is mentioned as part of media changes (Thorburn and Jenkins, 2004; Bennett, Kendall and McDougall, 2011), but, even in the field of memory studies, works explicitly dealing with media focus on only one topic, such as television, film (Spigel, 1995; Dika, 2003; Milan, 2010; Holdsworth, 2011), video games (Suominen, 2007), camera phones (Schwarz, 2012) or museums (Arnold-de Simine, 2013).

Consequently, this volume aims to be the first modest contribution to consolidating a reflection on the recent nostalgia boom and the difficult task of demonstrating that nostalgia has always been an affair of mediated processes, within both literature and the arts. Media produce contents and narratives not only in the nostalgic style but also as triggers of nostalgia. Media, and new technologies in particular, can function as platforms, projection places and tools to express nostalgia. Furthermore, media are very often nostalgic for themselves, their own past, their structures and contents. Perpetual media changes render media nostalgic for their non-existent end. Nostalgia, in turn, offers a reflection on mediation, media and their related technologies. In this sense, media practice becomes an essential element of nostalgia, increasing with the recent development of new communication technologies.

Assuming this, the original meaning of nostalgia becomes interesting in association with media. The historical evolution of the notion serves to introduce numerous works on nostalgia, and is also a central element of Morena la Barba's contribution to this volume, which discusses nostalgia within an Italian-speaking context. My reminder here is, therefore, a synthetic one and goes back to the work of the French psychoanalyst André Bolzinger (2007). Nostalgia, a medical neologism signifying homesickness (from the German *Heimweh*), appears for the first time in a doctoral dissertation written by Johannes Hofer, published in Basel, Switzerland, in 1688. The notion is etymologically based on the Greek *nostos* (return home) and *algia* (longing), and refers in Hofer's case to a disease common among Swiss mercenaries at the time. At the beginning of the eighteenth century, soldiers' homesickness, beginning with the Swiss cases, was viewed as an issue of military discipline. Later, in 1793, it began to be seen as a massive health problem within the military. At the end of the nineteenth century, nostalgia was considered an excuse associated with the refusal to fight or defend the homeland. Meanwhile, doctoral dissertations on the subject were being ignored by authorities, contributing to a misunderstanding of the symptoms of nostalgia, a misunderstanding that Bolzinger (2007) tries to highlight by analysing systematically all existing medical dissertations on nostalgia in France and Switzerland. But only three scientific medical works on the topic had been written by the end of the twentieth century. Nostalgia as a word was not part of social vocabulary. Sick people were merely talked about as being nervous, homesick or 'having the blues'. Only curious doctors like Hofer, Zimmermann, and Percy related physical symptoms of nostalgia to mental or psychological conditions. As Bolzinger writes, 'homesickness always existed, but the concept of nostalgia was a lucky treasure. Hippocrates and Galion did not know anything about it. The invention of nostalgia was the result of a humanist effort to modernise the documentation of certain pathologies of the body and the brain' (2007, p. 13). The symptoms of nostalgia were varied. The sufferer did not eat or drink, and had fever or gastric illness. Hallucinations and schizophrenia were also described as symptoms of homesickness. All in all, nostalgia mostly led to death. In 1806, Castelnau related the power of imagination to the body. He described nostalgia as an excessive desire to return back to one's home and back to one's family. The mental appearance of nostalgia patients was analysed by Castelnau as their having an isolated soul and a neglected body. Then there were symptoms that suggested an excess of sensitivity, a particular vulnerability related to the young age of those concerned. Bolzinger, referring to Kant, also defines nostalgia as being a pathology of misery (p. 216), and nostalgia means here less the desire to go home, and more the desire to be young again. Kant's ideas (reaffirmed by Jaspers) contradicted those of Rousseau, who maintained the belief that nostalgia was related to the physical senses. Kant's explanations were less 'romantic', but, even if the idea of yearning for youth seems logical, it does not explain why sick people were healed upon coming home. According to Bolzinger, nostalgia was 'a melody of two voices' (p. 11), a young person dying and a doctor who was unable to explain why. The doctors who were really trying to understand the origins of the sickness underlined the importance of 'storytelling' in healing nostalgia. They described conversations and a mutual understanding via communication as the first step of the process. This is one of the reasons for the current psychoanalytical interest in nostalgia. The vocabulary of nostalgia, in the sense of a state of melancholia, is now rarely used. Instead, studies of the condition of depression have provided a new framework for rethinking nostalgia. But, as Bolzinger states, 'former centuries already tried to twin nostalgia and melancholia. The question deals with an ideological option: is nostalgia a special form of melancholia? Or could we consider that the nostalgic is simply a sensitive human being, too sensitive, but clearly not a fool?' (Bolzinger, 2007, p. 16). This type of nostalgia is no longer part of medical discourse, but it does still exist: the homesickness of immigrants and their descendants, for example, is analysed in many medical dissertations. These explore the same symptoms as those that studied nostalgia in the eighteenth or nineteenth century, but nobody uses the word any more. In the twentieth century, nostalgic symptoms have been present in medical discourse during the 1914–1918 war (in letters written by soldiers), among students in Paris, as well as in workers from North Africa who were far away from home.

Nostalgia can be cured. The main examples of cures given by Bolzinger, based on medical case studies between the eighteenth and twentieth centuries, are: returning home or having the promise of doing so; receiving a visit from family or a person with the same accent; and music that evokes images and memories of the homeland, for example, in the case of the Swiss mercenaries, *Ranz de Vaches*, a Swiss soldiers' song. Of course, it would be too easy to say that media products or practices could replace these old 'medicaments' which helped to heal nostalgia. But perhaps they do provide a sort of cure, temporarily comforting the homesick. The BBC recently reported on a few cases of extreme homesickness that led to an incapacity to work. The interviewed persons emphasise that their suffering can be calmed down by social media, or the use of Skype, but that this could also make it worse.[4] The current nostalgia boom might be more 'affected' or 'induced' by this 'old' form of nostalgia than we might think. According to Duyvendak (2011), leaving our home (if we have or had one) is more common in the age of globalisation and causes questions of belonging and homesickness. The uses of new technologies might also contribute to all of the nostalgias mentioned in this Introduction, as well as adding another 'false' nostalgia: a pleasure-seeking yearning for former times that we have not, in fact, lived. Comparing these two types of nostalgia perhaps suggests more of an emphasis on yearning, amnesia and artificial longing, and less on design, visuals, objects and clothes. Simultaneously, the clash between these nostalgias may recall, as Atia and Davies have noted, a 'self-consciousness' that shows 'how identity is entangled with difference' and portrays nostalgia as less of an 'unreflective form of memory' (2010, p. 184).

Finally, one might ask a very simple question: what is nostalgia good for? This is the title of an article written by John Tierney for the *New York Times* on 8 July 2013, and his answer is mainly based on the psychological aspects of nostalgia. He describes it as a two-sided feeling of both positive and negative bonds with the past (NYT, 2013). Tierney's conclusions reflect recent social-psychological research on the topic: as Arndt, Routledge, Sedikides and Wildschut (2006) outline, nostalgia is nowadays more often constructive than destructive. Tierney explains, then, that 'nostalgizing' would help to develop the feeling of being part of a community or a group.

According to different English dictionaries, the word 'nostalgize' does not exist, but it is used eight times in the *New York Times* article. This grammatical detail is very interesting, as nostalgia usually expresses a state of being and the adjective 'nostalgic' is, of course, more passive than the active participle 'nostalgizing'. A linguistic shift to employing the verb might, in this sense, indicate a social change. Nostalgia would be not only an expression of a feeling, but something you do, an act of speech (Austin, 1965) that can potentially turn into a pragmatic creative process. As Dames (2010) outlines, literature on nostalgia has been very much focused on diagnosis, which has left the concept in a petrified position. The contributors of the third volume (number three) of the *Memory Studies* journal, dedicated to nostalgia, offer a more complex approach: nostalgia is thought about in terms of its therapeutic and healing characteristics. Considering nostalgia with 'the freedom to treat it not as a symptom that *explains* something, but as a force that *does* something' (Dames, 2010, p. 271) is also the approach of this volume, but it takes the risk of going one step further: media could become spaces to 'nostalgize', including all kinds of imaginable temporal experiences of our contemporary world. This might, for example, indicate nostalgia for a past that has never been. Nostalgia becomes, consequently, a way to transform the past by imagination. A cinematographic example is the main character in the film *Good Bye Lenin* (Becker, 2003). Alexander creates in the present his ideal GDR. He does so through objects, media discourses and other rituals in order to hide what has changed since 1989 from his (apparently) socialist mother, who was in a coma during the fall of the Berlin Wall. At the end of the film, Alexander admits to himself how imaginative his nostalgia is: 'I was overwhelmed by my own strategy. The GDR I invented for my mother became more and more the GDR I would have dreamed of.'

In light of this, nostalgia would not only be something we are or feel like, and it would be more than only a cultural product we consume, admire or write about. It would, instead, be something we do actively, either superficially or profoundly, alone, with family or friends or, on a larger scale, with media.

Overview and discussion of the book

The following contributions engage in distinct ways with the question of nostalgia, media and mediated processes by putting dominant topics to the fore at different moments. The chapters provide a broad range of disciplinary perspectives, namely those of media studies, sociology, art history, history, political science, semiotics, philosophy and management. As a collection, this volume does not intend to deliver an overall and systematic answer to the relation of nostalgia and media. Some media are even missing here (the printed press, dance, theatre and radio, for example), but what follows might, with luck, be a source of inspiration for further work on the topic. What this volume does aim to do is bring together, for the first time, an international collection that offers critical approaches to nostalgia and its relation to different media. The contributors of this volume think and work in Europe, Australia and the US. By referring to film, photography, television, music, networks, literature, art works, home videos and printed advertising, they show that media do not only produce nostalgic narratives, but that they can be, in themselves, the creative projection spaces for nostalgia, as well as acting as the symptoms or triggers of nostalgia. They can also act as tools to manipulate nostalgia or to render it impossible. The arrangement of the collection into four parts is not designed to classify artificially different types of nostalgia, but it does help to separate several distinct, ambivalent and multi-layered patterns to which nostalgia is subject.

Part I addresses the use of analogue nostalgia in digitised environments. Within the wish to experience the (analogue) past constantly and immediately in the digitised 'present', we could ask whether the notion of nostalgia is still adequate, when, for example, a recently taken digital picture is labelled 'nostalgic'. Time passes, but we no longer have the patience to let our experiences become, silently or loudly, what we once called memories. The chapters of Part I suggest that both personal and commercial types of media production which attempt to mimic older aesthetic forms express a yearning not only for 'older' media or their period, but also for the temporal and social experiences that were related to them. The aesthetics of the past become in this sense a tool through which media can be used as an *ersatz* stand-in for former rituals, feelings or past, without actually replicating them exactly. The repetition and reiteration of past aesthetics in a digital practice might also indicate a new kind of ritual and the habits that come along with it. Whether there will be nostalgia for this in the future is another question.

Dominik Schrey discusses in the first chapter of this section the idea of 'analogue nostalgia' in relation to a media-inherent nostalgia for the past materials, noises and forms of media. In investigating this, he describes how the less welcomed traits of analogue media are now becoming interesting. He suggests that the 'mediality' of nostalgia itself should always be taken into account, and with this step underpins the idea that self-reference is a typical characteristic of media, which can lead to cyclic nostalgias within technological evolutions. His theoretical reflection leads to the argument that 'virtual ruins' are not orientated to witness absence, but instead try to consolidate and render eternally present the analogue, which, consequently, cannot get older or die. Parts of the analogue seem to survive, albeit in a simulated, digitised form, and these 'ruins' or 'archaeological items', if we think in Foucauldian terms, are the research topics of the three other contributions in Part I. Giuseppina Sapio's chapter is concerned with a very particular type of analogue media: the home video. She adds a social-historical aspect to the theoretical propositions of the first chapter by examining the practice of home movies. She looks at the relationship between the technologies and techniques of home by referring to their viewing, and goes on to address the changes that the French family has experienced over time. People add vintage effects to their home movies because they are nostalgic for traditional family rituals rather than for their aesthetics. Gil Bartholeyns's contribution focuses on digital photography and the aesthetics of its analogue ancestors. His reflection on photographs that can instantly be converted to old-fashioned souvenirs is accompanied by a discussion of vernacular photography that engages with new digital concepts. He develops the idea of an 'instant nostalgia' generated by the use of photographic 'apps' for mobile devices. Pictures look immediately old and will always look old. Other digitised processes might 'alter' them, but this would still be an artificial action. This chapter shows clearly the relationship between nostalgia and temporality by elaborating a detailed analysis of the 'self-induced' and 'biographical' nostalgias that characterise the sharing of digital photographs. It is not the experienced past that becomes present by viewing older-looking pictures. Instead, the present is 'nostalgized' by the aesthetics of the past that create a new method of engaging with the 'moment'. Once again, the predominance of so-called presentism, trying to find its meanings in media practice, can be seen. The idea that typical elements of the past can be simulated in the present without referring to something that really existed (for example, a digital photograph that has no 'real' connection with the past despite its simulated aesthetics) is also a topic of the last chapter. By referring to Simon Reynolds's work, Maël Guesdon and Philippe Le Guern analyse the retromaniac tendencies of pop music and the industrial patterns they are founded on. They aim to show 'how nostalgia in contemporary pop music bases itself on a staging of spectrality in the derridian sense'. 'Hypnagogic' aesthetics, 'rewriting collective memory' by using, for example, sounds intended to sound more '80s' than those actually produced in the period, are the focus of the fourth chapter. Guesdon and Le Guern show how this type of music corresponds to the ambivalent character of nostalgia: it can be a 'backward-looking renewal of a lost ideal' as well as a tool, using nostalgia as part of a creative process.

This ambivalence is inherent in all patterns of nostalgia analysed in this volume, especially when we deal with the eternal tension of vanishing and returning, but, when it comes to the interplay of various intense levels of yearning, dominant patterns of manipulated, faked or exploited nostalgia can emerge. Bartholeyns's chapter relates to the marketing process by demonstrating that 'apps' are merchandised on the basis of 'three selling points': nostalgia, personalisation and the ability to be used or viewed as analogue artefacts. Guesdon and Le Guern also point out that the revivals in music correspond to the economic and commercial interests of the pop industry.

Part II moves on to discuss in more detail the mentioned ambivalences and focuses on exploitations of nostalgia. What connects these four very different chapters is the notion of the manipulation, exploitation and petrifaction of nostalgia which is carried out in domains like marketing, advertising, corporate alumni networks and the news to produce effects, templates, feelings or purposes. Media are used here as tools to frame memory and the past in distinct ways. Emily Keightley and Michael Pickering reflect on the commodification of former times to show in what ways 'popular memory is exploited to enhance the market appeal of commodities'. Based on the example of one specific print advert, they demonstrate precisely how nostalgic feelings and values can be manipulated through a regressive nostalgia that is enabled by a process they name *retrotyping*. The only elements taken from the past are embellished or idealised and foreclose conflict or tension in their way of presenting former times. Retrotyping avoids and prevents approaching the more ambivalent elements of nostalgia. Retrotyped regressive nostalgia does, in this sense, something very special; it creates 'a consumerist packaging of the past'. The following chapter also deals with advertising and manipulated nostalgia. Emmanuelle Fantin explores the ways in which an apparent rejection of nostalgia can, in fact, be used to produce it. Her case study is based on the car brand Citroën, which surfs the current wave of nostalgia by claiming to reject it with the slogan 'anti-retro'. The semiotic interplays are analysed on an audio-visual narrative level and are then theoretically discussed with reference to the origins and forms of nostalgia: 'the contrasts and illusions that visually and semantically structure this ad reveal a precarious though audacious balance between a world rooted in memory and striving for progress'. Fantin's analysis of the 'anti-retro' advert is less concerned by the idea of retrotyping. It returns, instead, to the ambivalence of nostalgia and its relation to contemporary temporal experiences. The fascinating thing that emerges from this chapter is that even commercials seem to be stuck in vanishing and returning structures that exploit nostalgia to, once again, turn it into a commodity.

The fabrication of nostalgia does not only concern advertising. It is also important in an organisational context. Thibaut Bardon, Emmanuel Josserand and Florence Villesèche conceive networks as media for nostalgia, thus proposing a first joint exploration of media and nostalgia in organisation studies. Their case study, based on 21 semi-structured interviews of a corporate alumni network, reveals four interpretive repertoires that pinpoint how organisational nostalgia can be mediated through networks. The emotional justifications for the participation to the network are significant, and the chapter highlights precisely how organisational nostalgia is not only a matter of 'nostalgising' time that was given over to work, as, for alumni, their time at an organisation was a 'whole epoch of their lives' that is re-created and reiterated by the notions of share and transmission: a family concept within the business world. This chapter discloses three major elements. First, alumni networks are instrumental media that consolidate business networking. Second, they are media through which organisational nostalgia is both mediated and expressed. Third, the authors develop the idea that nostalgia can be leveraged through a variety of media to gain corporate influence, which seems to extend outside organisational boundaries, as with their example of the MultiCorp alumni network. Interestingly, this organisational nostalgia seems to exclude negative moments of the working experience. This is quite intriguing, as competition and conflicts are normally seen as key elements of life at work. A perceptible nostalgia-regressive manipulation of both business interests and the alumni-networkers' feelings of the past can thus be seen at play.

The last chapter of this section does not directly engage with nostalgia as a specific phenomenon, but offers a perspective on memorialisation and the media template serving nostalgic patterns. Andrew Hoskins engages with conflicts of memory and works specifically on uses of the notion of 'Blitz Spirit' in live news, with reference to the 2005 London bombings. These conflicted elements appear as the chapter tries to understand whether the clips and photographs of an occurring event that are broadcast over and over again are a matter of nostalgia and melancholia or are, in fact, more attributable to a perceived need for 'media templates' that is common in our digitally accelerated age. Media templates provide means of engaging with the past, but they also shape collective memory through the manner in which their images are edited and shown on television and by broadcast media in general. This particular type of screened memories leads directly to the next section.

Part III discusses nostalgias in television and film. Questions of identity, politics and homesickness are explored through diverse approaches that underpin one very rich character of media screens: they are projection spaces for nostalgias that flow into narratives, aesthetics, sounds, montages and structures absorbing and exuding simultaneously the creative and critical processes they are made of. Screened nostalgia consequently demands a great deal of analysis, as it concerns both the viewers and the makers of a given programme. All brought together, screened nostalgias exemplify and condense the critical and emotional meanings and functions of nostalgia as they point out its psychological, creative, historical and political layers. The first chapter of this section detects those layers by taking a very close look at television series and the televisual serial. Katharina Niemeyer and Daniela Wentz show in what ways the explicit and implicit narratives and aesthetics of homesickness can be found in American television series such as *Mad Men* (AMC, 2007–), *The Walking Dead* (AMC, 2010–), *The Newsroom* (HBO, 2012–) and *Homeland* (Showtime, 2011), touching on the political impact of the September 11 attacks and the reconceptualisation of the home in American popular culture. The chapter argues that most concepts of nostalgia fit the structural characteristics of televisual seriality. Similarly, the vanishing and returning character of nostalgia is apparent in television series. Television series can mutually provoke and heal by their very particular status of being ritual-makers and breakers, with the feeling of nostalgia as a ritual-breaker being of particular pertinence to the viewer. Besides these various nostalgic layers, the chapter reflects on the self-induced nostalgia that television series originate. Niemeyer and Wentz deconstruct the carousel scene of *Mad Men* in order to talk more generally about television series. In contrast, David Pierson's chapter takes a look behind the petrified and regressive nostalgic patterns that the series *Mad Men* as a whole seems to produce. His media-political and historical approach shows that this type of nostalgia can serve as a stimulus for progressive change, especially if it is used to question and critique social and economic conditions. The chapter shows in detail how *Mad Men* challenges popular notions of the early 1960s as an era defined by social conformity, upward mobility and unbridled optimism. As a product of popular culture, the television series certainly underlines the economic possibilities of the market for nostalgia and a yearning for 'the good old days'. But it is also a resource for critical inspiration and interrogation of the political present and future. By analysing the main characters, he shows that a fictional social resistance lies quietly beneath the surface, and this resistance brings to the forefront again the previously mentioned identity issue. But what happens when the search for identity meets with nostalgia and counter-nostalgia in less 'fictional' television formats? In her chapter, Aline Hartemann introduces the idea of 'policies of nostalgia' by analysing three different programmes of the European television channel ARTE. She examines the different structures of ARTE's screening policies, which are focused on painful historical recollections of the two world wars (and their different effects on France and Germany). Other programme items, such as *What I Miss* (ARTE, 2004–), are based on a yearning for specific objects: what kind of cultural products or types of cuisine were inaccessible when you lived on the other side of the Rhine, or even in other European countries? European identity cannot be a creation solely of past times, places and objects, and the analysis of a third programme shows that a sort of counter-nostalgia takes place when the identity question is looked at through the premise of 'presentism'. In the last chapter of Part III, Ute Holl examines Preminger's film *Bonjour Tristesse* (1958) and the use of the imagined or remembered colours that characterise its different imaginary flashbacks. The chapter also discusses nostalgic conceptions of the filmic past and the insistent presence of history. By discussing the historical perception of colour in cinema, Holl focuses on post-war strategies and discourses of colour, memory and filmic forms of remembering. *Bonjour Tristesse* might have a nostalgic tone, but, as Holl demonstrates, history inheres in the structure of colour in Preminger's film. In this context, her chapter reveals the struggle between the memories that the colours carry with them: 'the failed homecoming' of Preminger and the 'bitter comment on the Europe he finds ten years after the war'. Despite the historical and aesthetic implications, this observation of an unlucky homecoming further emphasises a personal yearning which infiltrates the film and creates an ambiguity in the colour play of this creative act of expressing suffering via mediated processes.

Part IV shifts more explicitly to the notion of creative nostalgias that has already accompanied most of the previous chapters. Prepared by the final part of Holl's contribution on *Bonjour Tristesse*, this last section aims to show how the notion of homesickness, the wish to construct a home and the ideas of impossible and freed nostalgias are related to creative processes, to philosophical and artistic creations that can help to imagine, dream or think of a better future. Within film, literature and arts, the chapters show through their specificities how creative nostalgias are interwoven with and triggered by media. Morena La Barba's chapter provides a deeper insight into migrant filmmaking by exploring different aspects of the production of the film *Il treno del Sud* (1970) and the film itself. Her approach is social-historical and assesses the psychological elements of homesickness. These elements are put into the perspective of Swiss nostalgia history and its relation to the filmmaker Alvaro Bizzarri, who experienced mass migration, a xenophobic atmosphere and political emancipation movements in 1960s Switzerland. The main character, Paolo, shows the classic symptoms of homesickness, and this influences the plot of the whole film. La Barba interviewed the filmmaker, and this not only gives hints of the difficult aspects of a suffering related to longing for home, but also shows touchingly how the feelings projected on Paolo were finally transformed into a creative process to change the present in order to be able to imagine and fight for a better future. The second chapter deals not with film, but with literature, and connects philosophically with the idea that the writing process can detect ethical and political uses of nostalgia. Yala Kisukidi explores the poetry of Léopold Sédar Senghor and the theory of *Négritude* in order to highlight the 'true cosmopolitical' purpose that is present in 'Senghorian' nostalgia. Despite Senghor's drawing of fantasised myths of Africa and Negro-African civilisations, his romantic legacy is not to be understood as a politically regressive or conservative return to the past, but instead as an attempt to help construct 'a post-colonial and cosmopolitical utopia'. The chapter emphasises a power of the writing and thinking process that is neither melancholic nor filled with an unbearable desire to return home. It suggests that Senghor's creative relation

18 *Introduction*

to nostalgia denotes the hope and wish to possess a space in which people can live side by side. Nostalgia can be regarded here as a wishful tool of relief, helping to transform the past into a way to invent the future. The idea of relief is also the topic of the third chapter of this section, but it shifts here to a very difficult historical subject: the Second World War and Nazi propaganda. Itzhak Goldberg develops the concept of 'impossible nostalgia' in relation to German artists such as Georg Baselitz, Anselm Kiefer and Markus Lüpertz. They attack the symbols of the glorious history they feel guilty for, a history that has become forever tainted by Nazism and Nazi propaganda. The chapter demonstrates that art as a medium can provoke false nostalgia and shows the impossibility of destroying it completely by new creative artistic propositions. Creative 'counter-nostalgia' reacting against a falsified and stolen past is finally devoted, as Goldberg states, to the exclusion of nostalgic tones in the recollection of tragic events. In contrast to this, John Potts, in the last chapter of this section, suggests that art can also be a 'relief' and create a memory zone free of 'sentiment, nostalgia and contempt', a connection with the past, a relation that frees the concept of nostalgia of its pejorative or regressive connotations. If the apparently instant present is already rendered nostalgic via aesthetic procedures and discursive markers, it becomes interesting to consider the idea that we are not confronted with a nostalgia for the past but with a nostalgia that includes the impossibility of becoming 'really' nostalgic for time passing. In other words, as Potts argues, nostalgia becomes an enigma. For him, contemporary art, using old and new communication technologies, allows us to escape the politics and economics of nostalgia by creating artwork that illustrates the emptiness of exploited nostalgia. Potts does not mean that the artwork renders you free from the possibility of feeling nostalgic in relation to it, but it does remove the sense of obligation to engage with consumer-oriented nostalgic products. The last chapter is, in this sense, contradictory to some of the other contributions, but the volume also intends to discuss ambivalences of both nostalgia and approaches to it.

With this volume I have tried to collect various chapters on nostalgia and media to offer researchers, lecturers, students and other interested readers critical, stimulating, divergent and diverse reflections on the contemporary nostalgia boom. I have aspired to show, in editing this volume, that nostalgia has always been an affair of different engagements with media. The chapters are heterogeneous, but all distinguish the vanishing and returning patterns of nostalgia. Starting with analogue nostalgia in the digital world, followed by manipulated and exploited nostalgias, the volume continues with on-screen nostalgias that introduce the idea of a projection space for nostalgias, a space that can also be occupied by contemporary art, literature and other forms of mediated and creative processes. Marine Baudrillard's poetical contribution, the last one of this volume, is a concrete example of this personal projection space for nostalgia, when she writes a letter to her husband Jean Baudrillard after he passed away.

Interestingly (and further works on other topics, epochs and media will have to add to these first results), the regressive–progressive doublesided nostalgia that emerges in the light of capitalist interests is not the only form nostalgia takes. In some chapters (2, 3, 5, 7, 13 and 14), the notion of family, along with its social images and developments, is raised, and alludes to a complex relationship with former times and identities. It also hints at the search for a place of belonging and recognition, not in the sense of a 'home, sweet home', a country, city or nationality, but in the sense of a solidarity and lessening of loneliness that might emerge by 'nostalgizing'. It may be a neologism, but it is not as new as we might have thought, and should be critically related to the concrete actions it can provoke and the objects it can create. Media occupy this delicate position of involving all varieties of nostalgias, a situation that further relates to the specific place of media within memory studies. I propose to introduce the notion of 'time studies' in this context, as the malaise with contemporary, seemingly accelerated, times is another constant theme of this volume. Resistant nostalgias could, in this sense, be elements of other opposing forms that create spaces for 'taking' and thinking about time, sometimes critically, sometimes joyfully and sometimes calmly.

Notes

1. See, for example, Keightley (2012); Niemeyer (2011); Engelen and Sterckx (2011); Gorin and Niemeyer (2009); Garde-Hansen, Hoskins and Reading (2009); Volkmer (2006); Arquembourg (2003); Casalegno (2001); Edgerton (2001); Merzeau and Weber (2001); Hoskins (2001); Assmann (1999); Barnhurts and Wartella (1998); Bourdon (1996); Dayan and Katz (1996).
2. This volume does not cover the notion of *ostalgia*, as numerous publications already exist in relation to this topic. See, for example, Allan, S. (2006) 'Good Bye, Lenin!: Ostalgie und Identität im wieder vereinigten Deutschland'. *gfl-journal*, 1, pp. 46–59; Twark, J. E. (ed.) (2011) *Strategies of Humor in Post-Unification German Literature, Film, and Other Media*. Newcastle: Cambridge Scholars Publishing.
3. Not primarily in a 'consumer culture' sense, but referring to the German approach of *Medienkultur*, which offers a philosophical and historical

approach to understanding the relation between media and culture. See, for example, Engell, L., Vogl, J., Pias, C., Fahle, O. and Neitzel, B. (1999) *Kursbuch Medienkultur – Die maßgeblichen Theorien von Brecht bis Baudrillard*. Stuttgart: DVA.
4. http://www.bbc.co.uk/news/magazine-22764986 (accessed 8 July 2013).

References

Arndt, J., Routledge, C., Sedikides, C. and Wildschut, T. (2006) 'Nostalgia: Content, Triggers, Functions'. *Journal of Personality and Social Psychology*, 91(5), pp. 975–993.
Arnold-de Simine, S. (2013) *Mediating Memory in the Museum – Trauma, Empathy, Nostalgia*. Basingstoke: Palgrave Macmillan.
Arquembourg, J. (2003) *Le temps des événements médiatiques*. Bruxelles: Éditions De Boeck Université, Institut National de l'Audiovisuel.
Assmann, A. (1999) *Erinnerungsräume. Formen und Wandlungen des kulturellen Gedächtnisses*. München: C. H. Beck.
Atia, N. and Davies, J. (2010) 'Nostalgia and the Shapes of History'. *Memory Studies*, 3(3), pp. 181–186.
Austin, J. L. (1965) *How to Do Things with Words*. Cambridge: Harvard University Press.
Baer, A. (2001) 'Consuming History and Memory through Mass Media Products'. *European Journal of Cultural Studies*, 4, pp. 491–501.
Barnhurts, K. G. and Wartella, E. (1998) 'Young Citizens, American TV Newscasts and the Collective Memory'. *Critical Studies in Mass Communication*, 15(13), pp. 279–305.
Baudrillard, J. (1981) *Simulacres et Simulation*. Paris: Galilée.
Bennett, P., Kendall, A. and Mcdougall, J. (2011) *After the Media – Culture and Identity in the 21st Century*. New York/Oxon: Routledge.
Bergson, H. (2004, 1939) *Matière et mémoire*. Paris: PUF.
Berliner, D. (2012) 'Multiple Nostalgias: The Fabric of Heritage in Luang Prabang (Lao PDR)'. *Journal of the Royal Anthropological Institute*, 18, pp. 769–786.
Böhringer, H. (1989) 'Das hölzerne Pferd', in ARS electronica (ed.) *Philosophien der neuen Technologie*. Berlin: Merve Verlag Berlin, pp. 7–26.
Bolzinger, A. (2007) *Histoire de la nostalgie*. Paris: Campagne Première.
Bougnoux, D. (2006) *La crise de la representation*. Paris: La Découverte.
Bourdon, J. (1996) 'Médias et mémoire'. *Le collège iconique de l'INA*, www.ina.fr/inatheque/activites/college/pdf/1996/college_12_06_1996.pdf (accessed 6 March 2013).
Boyer, R. (2013) 'Les crises financières comme conflit de temporalités'. *Vingtième siècle, revue d'histoire*, 117, pp. 69–88.
Boym, S. (2001) *The Future of Nostalgia*. New York: Basic Books.
Callender, C. (ed.) (2011) *The Oxford Handbook of Philosophy of Time*. New York: Oxford University Press.
Candau, J. (2005) *Anthropologie de la mémoire*. Paris: Armand Colin.
Carr, D. (2010) 'Y-a-t-il une expérience directe de l'histoire? La chute du mur de Berlin et le 11 Septembre'. *A Contrario*, 13, pp. 84–94.

Casalegno, F. (2001) 'Mémoire collective et existence poétique en réseaux. Éléments pour la compréhension des rapports entre nouvelles technologies, communautés et mémoire'. *MEI*, 15, pp. 153–167.

Cassin, B. (2013) *La nostalgie. Quand est-on chez soi? Ulysee, Enée, Arendt.* Paris: Autrement Editions.

Crivellari, F., Kirchmann, K., Sandl, M. and Schlögl, R. (2004) *Die Medien der Geschichte.* Konstanz: UVK Verlagsgesellschaft mbH.

Dames, N. (2010) 'Nostalgia and its Disciplines: A Reponse'. *Memory Studies*, 3(3), pp. 269–275.

Davis, F. (1977) 'Nostalgia, Identity and the Current Nostalgia Wave'. *Journal of Popular Culture*, 11(2), pp. 414–425.

Davies, J. (2010) 'Sustainable Nostalgia'. *Memory Studies*, 3(3), pp. 262–268.

Dayan, D. and Katz, E. (1996) *La télévision cérémonielle.* Paris: PUF.

Debray, R. (2000) *Introduction à la Médiologie.* Paris: PUF.

Deleuze, G. (1997) *Différence et repetition.* Paris: PUF.

Dika, V. (2003) *Recycled Culture in Contemporary Art and Film – the Uses of Nostalgia.* New York: Cambridge University Press.

Doane, J. and Hodges, D. (1987) *Nostalgia and Sexual Difference: The Resistance to Contemporary Feminism.* London: Methuen.

Duyvendak, J. W. (2011) *The Politics of Home – Belonging and Nostalgia in Western Europe and the United States.* London: Palgrave Macmillan.

Edgerton, G. R. (ed.) (2001) *Television Histories – Shaping Collective Memory in the Media Age.* Kentucky: The University Press of Kentucky.

Engelen, L. and Sterckx, M. (2011) 'Remembering Edith and Gabrielle Picture Postcards of Monuments as Portable lieux de mémoire', in B. Vandermeulen and D. Veys (eds) *Imaging History – Photography after the Fact.* Brussels: ASA Publishers.

Engell, L., Vogl, J., Pias, C., Fahle, O. and Neitzel, B. (1999) *Kursbuch Medienkultur – Die maßgeblichen Theorien von Brecht bis Baudrillard.* Stuttgart: DVA.

Garde-Hansen, J., Hoskins, A. and Reading, A. (eds) (2009) *Save as...Digital Memories.* Basingstoke: Palgrave Macmillan.

Gitlin, T. (1980) *The Whole World is Watching.* Berkeley, Los Angeles and London: University of California Press.

Gorin, V. and Niemeyer, K. (2009) 'Spectre du passé et enjeux géopolitiques du présent. La mémoire américaine du Vietnam dans la guerre d'Irak', in M. Michel and R. Latouche (eds) *Mémoire, histoire et medias.* Bruxelles: Bruylant, pp. 239–254.

Goulding, C. (2001) 'Romancing the Past: Heritage Visiting and the Nostalgic Consumer'. *Psychology & Marketing*, 18(6), pp. 565–592.

Grainge, P. (2002) *Monochrome Memories: Nostalgia and Style in Retro America.* Westport, CT: Praeger.

Greimas, A.-J. (2002) 'De la nostalgie: étude de sémantique lexicale', in A. Hénault (ed.) *Question de sémiotique.* Paris: Presses Universitaires de France, pp. 593–600.

Hartog, F. (2003) *Régimes d'historicité. Présentisme et expériences du temps.* Paris: Seuil.

Higson, A. (2003) *English Heritage, English Cinema: Costume Drama since 1980.* New York: Oxford University Press.

Hochmann, J. (2004) 'Nostalgie de l'éphémère'. *Adolescence*, Tome 22, numéro 4, Le Bouscat: L'esprit du temps, pp. 677–686.
Holbrook, M. B. (1993) 'Nostalgia and Consumption Preferences: Some Emerging Patterns of Consumer Tastes'. *Journal of Consumer Research*, 20, pp. 245–256.
Holdsworth, A. (2011) *Television, Memory and Nostalgia*. Basingstoke: Palgrave Macmillan.
Hoskins, A. (2001) 'New Memory: Mediating History'. *Historical Journal of Film, Radio and Television*, 21(4), pp. 333–346.
Huang, X. (2006) 'Performing Gender: Nostalgic Wedding Photography in Contemporary China'. *Ethnologies*, 28(2), pp. 81–111.
Hutcheon, L. (2000) 'Irony, Nostalgia, and the Postmodern'. *Methods for the Study of Literature as Cultural Memory, Studies in Comparative Literature*, 30, pp. 189–207.
Huyssen, A. (1995) *Twilight Memories. Marking Time in a Culture of Amnesia*. New York and London: Routledge.
Jameson, F. (1991) *Postmodernism, or, the Cultural Logic of Late Capitalism*. Durham: Duke University Press.
Jameson, F. (1998) *The Cultural Turn. Selected Writings on the Postmodern 1983–1999*. London: Verso, pp. 1–20.
Jankélévitch, V. (1974) *L'Irréversible et la Nostalgie*. Paris: Flammarion.
Keightley, E. (ed.) (2012) *Time, Media and Modernity*. Basingstoke: Palgrave Macmillan.
Keightley, E. and Pickering, M. (2006) 'The Modalities of Nostalgia'. *Current Sociology*, 54, pp. 919–941.
Kessous, A. and Roux, E. (2012) 'Nostalgie et management des marques: approche sémiotique'. *Management & Avenir*, 4(54), pp. 15–33.
Klein, K. L. (2000) 'On the Emergence of Memory in Historical Discourse'. *Representations*, 69, pp. 127–150.
Koselleck, R. (1979) *Vergangene Zukunft. Zur Semantik geschichtlicher Zeiten*. Frankfurt am Main: Suhrkamp.
Ladino, J. K. (2012) *Reclaiming Nostalgia: Longing for Nature in American Literature*. Charlottesville: University of Virginia Press.
Lasch, C. (1984) 'The Politics of Nostalgia'. *Harper's Magazine*, 269(1614), pp. 65–70.
Le Goff, J. (1988) *Histoire et mémoire*. Paris: Gallimard.
Loveland, K.-E., Smeesters, D. and Mandel, N. (2010) 'Still Preoccupied with 1995: The Need to Belong and Preference for Nostalgic Products'. *Journal of Consumer Research*, 37(3), pp. 393–408.
Lowenthal, D. (1985) *The Past is a Foreign Country*. Cambridge: Cambridge University Press.
Lowenthal, D. (2013) 'Nostalgic Dreams and Nightmares', *Change over Time*, 3(1), pp. 28–54.
Marcus, D. (2004) *Happy Days and Wonder Years: The Fifties and the Sixties in Contemporary Cultural Politics*. New Brunswick and London: Rutgers University Press.
Matt, S. J. (2011) *Homesickness: An American History*. Oxford: Oxford University Press.
Merzeau, L. and Weber, T. (eds) (2001) *Mémoire et Médias*. Paris: Avinus.

Milan, A. (2010) 'Modern Portrayals of Journalism in Film'. *The Elon Journal of Undergraduate Research in Communications*, 1(1), pp. 46–57.

Mitchell, C. and Weber, S. (1999) *Reinventing Ourselves as Teachers: Beyond Nostalgia*. London: Falmer Press.

Nash, J. E. (2012) 'Ringing the Chord, Sentimentality and Nostalgia among Male Singers'. *Journal of Contemporary Ethnography*, 41(5), pp. 581–606.

Niemeyer, K. (2011) *De la Chute du Mur de Berlin au 11 Septembre 2001. Le Journal Télévisé, les Mémoires Collectives et l'Ecriture de l'Histoire*. Lausanne: Antipodes.

Nora, P. (1972) 'L'événement monstre'. *Communications*, 18, Paris: Le Seuil, pp. 162–172.

Nora, P. (1997) *Les lieux de mémoire 1, La République*. Paris: Gallimard.

NYT. (2013) 'What is Nostalgia Good For?', *New York Times* online, 9 July 2013.

Panati, C. (1991) *Panati's Parade of Fads, Follies and Manias*. New York: Harper Perennial.

Reynolds, S. (2011) *Retromania, Pop Culture's Addiction to its Own Past*. London: Faber and Faber.

Richard, F. (2004) 'Temporalité, psychose et mélancolie'. *Adolescence*, tome 22, 4, Le Bouscat: L'esprit du temps, pp. 687–704.

Ricoeur, P. (1993) *Temps et récit. Le temps raconté*. Paris: Éditions du Seuil.

Ricoeur, P. (2000) *La mémoire, l'histoire, l'oubli*. Paris: Éditions du Seuil.

Robertson, J. (1997) 'Empire of Nostalgia: Rethinking "Internationalization" in Japan Today'. *Theory Culture Society*, 14, pp. 97–122.

Rosa, H. (2005) *Beschleunigung. Die Veränderung der Zeitstrukturen in der Moderne*. Frankfurt am Main: Suhrkamp.

Schnell, R. (ed.) (2006) *MedienRevolution – Beiträge zur Mediengeschichte der Wahrnehmung*. Bielefeld: Transcript Verlag.

Schwarz, O. (2012) 'Good Young Nostalgia – Camera Phones and Technologies of Self among Israeli Youths'. *Journal of Consumer Culture*, 9(3), pp. 348–376.

Spigel, L. (1995) 'From the Dark Ages to the Golden Age: Woman's Memories and Television Reruns'. *Screen*, 36(1), pp. 16–33.

Suominen, J. (2007), 'The Past as the Future? Nostalgia and Retrogaming in Digital Culture'. *Proceedings of perthDA2007. The 7th International Digital Arts and Cultures Conference. The Future of Digital Media Culture*, 15–18 September 2007, Perth, Australia.

Tannock, S. (1995) 'Nostalgia Critique'. *Cultural Studies*, 9(3), pp. 453–464.

Thorburn, D. and Jenkins, H. (eds) (2004) *Rethinking Media Change. The Aesthetics of Transition*. Cambridge, MA and London: MIT Press.

Viennet, D. (2009) *Il y a malêtre. Essai sur le temps et la constitution du soi contemporain*. Paris: l'Harmattan.

Virilio, P. (1989) *Esthétique de la disparition*. Paris: Galilée.

Volkmer, I. (ed.) (2006) *News in Public Memory – An International Study of Media Memories across Generations*. New York: Peter Lang.

Wilson, J. L. (2005) *Nostalgia: Sanctuary of Meaning*. Lewisburg, PA: Bucknell University Press.

Yerushalmi, Y. H. (1982) *Zakhor – Histoire juive et mémoire juive*. Gallimard: Paris.

Part I
Analogue Nostalgias

1
Analogue Nostalgia and the Aesthetics of Digital Remediation

Dominik Schrey

Obsolescence and retro-cultures

It has become a commonplace to describe the last decades as a period of unprecedented and ever-accelerating media technological transition and of increasingly mediated life environments. Our times have often been characterised as an era of planned obsolescence, turning yesterday's appraised new gadgets into today's decrepit devices and tomorrow's waste. Their disposability may even be 'one of the truly distinctive features of new media in our age', according to Jonathan Sterne (2007, p. 18). Moreover, even media formats with a strong tradition like the book (as a material object) or cinema (as a specific 'dispositif') are now perceived to be threatened by obsolescence and seem to be outpaced by their increasingly ephemeral digital successors. Referring to these correlating processes, science fiction writer Bruce Sterling proclaimed in 1995 that we live in 'the golden age of dead media' (2008, p. 80). It also seems to be a golden age of nostalgia for these allegedly 'dead media' that, in fact, continue to haunt a popular culture obsessed with its own past (Guffey, 2006; Reynolds, 2011). Jussi Parikka argues that retro-cultures 'seem to be as natural a part of the digital-culture landscape as high-definition screen technology and super-fast broadband' (2012, p. 3). This distinct sense of nostalgia that Western societies have developed has to be understood as an integral aspect of our culture of preserving and storing. As Hartmut Böhme notes, in everything that is preserved and remembered they emphasise that which is still lost and forgotten, and thus create a deliberate emptiness (2000, p. 25). With this in mind, it seems important to consider the 'mediality' of nostalgia itself.

Based on a brief overview of this culture of (un)dead media, I will discuss one of the most recent manifestations of this general trend of nostalgia: the longing for what is assumed to be lost in the continuing process of digitisation that accounts for contemporary media culture's widespread romanticising and fetishising of analogue media. Symptoms of this 'analogue nostalgia' in its broadest sense can be found in every area of culture and society. For example, in 2012, the Academy for Motion Picture Arts and Sciences awarded the most Oscars to *The Artist* (Michel Hazanavicius, 2011) and *Hugo* (Martin Scorsese, 2011). Both of these films celebrate not only the artistic qualities of early cinema but also the celluloid filmstrip as its material basis, and what David Bordwell calls the 'Steampunk flavor' (2012, p. 7) of analogue film projection. Similar trends can be observed in the context of avant-garde art. Many of the most successful contemporary installation artists display a deep affection for outdated analogue media, and 'today, no exhibition is complete without some form of bulky, obsolete technology', as Claire Bishop writes in her broadly discussed article 'The Digital Divide' (2012, p. 436). In general, these retrospective celebrations of the analogue range from defiant denunciations of digital production tools (as practised most famously by artists like Tacita Dean) to the fetishised commodification of the analogue object (like the ubiquity of the analogue audio cassette as an icon on t-shirts, tote-bags and smartphone covers). Most pivotal for this context, however, are those works that quote certain characteristics typically associated with analogue inscription *within* digital media in a more or less self-reflexive fashion. In 2000, Laura Marks described this digital remediation of analogue aesthetics as 'analog nostalgia', although today the term is applied to a broader range of phenomena.

This chapter will be less interested in the technical differences between 'the analogue' and 'the digital' than in the affective attributes of these respective fields. Specifically, I will examine why aspects that were once considered as disadvantages or problems of analogue media are now appreciated enthusiastically. To investigate what causes this retrospective revaluation of analogue media's malfunctions and the specific noises they create, I will draw upon Sterne's questioning of the 'metaphysics of recording' (2006) and the 'double logic of remediation' as put forward by J. D. Bolter and Richard Grusin (2000). Based on a brief analysis of a scene from the contemporary TV series *Californication* (Showtime, 2007–2012), I will argue in conclusion that the phenomenon of 'analog nostalgia' (in Marks's sense of the term) embodies a return to the seventeenth and eighteenth centuries' fascination with ruins and its fragmentary aesthetics, which eventually led to the construction of artificial ruins.

The mediality of nostalgia

Media can serve as a means of virtually accessing the past, and are thus an important resource for cultural memory. Consequently, they often establish the precondition for a nostalgic perspective on things past (and present). This nostalgia can be the content or style of media representation, and, beyond that, media themselves can become an object of nostalgia. In this case, the sentiment can be directed towards their specific medial constitution, their materiality, the aesthetics resulting from these factors, or all these combined: 'Our cultural memories are shaped not just by the production qualities of an era [...] but by subtle properties of the recording media themselves', as Reynolds (2011, p. 331) notes. This process, in turn, can then be reflected by media again, which is why nostalgia for outdated media technologies or their respective aesthetics can be regarded as a special case of self-reference in the media (Böhn, 2007).

Of course, the general phenomenon of nostalgia for outdated media is anything but new. According to Svetlana Boym, 'outbreaks of nostalgia often follow revolutions' (2001, p. xvi), which seems to be true not only in the context of politics she is referring to, but also in relation to mediahistorical periods of transition. In fact, nostalgia for seemingly obsolete modes of representation is a way of theorising changes in media with rich tradition and a surprisingly constant rhetoric. From the critique of writing in Plato's *Phaedrus* to the fears associated with the introduction of the printing press to the defensive reactions towards those new technologies of the nineteenth century that are now commonly referred to as 'analogue media' and the lamenting of the 'phantom world of television' (Anders, 1956), every media technological innovation can be, and has been, told as a nostalgic narrative of loss and decline (Serres, 2001). Evidently, the common denominator of these nostalgic narratives of media change is the fact that they assess the value of the new by the standards of the old, as Umberto Eco (1994) noted. While after almost 50 years Eco's analysis is still valid in many respects, it is important to stress the correlation between the flaws of apocalyptic media criticism he describes and the fact that new media always define themselves 'in relationship to earlier technologies of representation', as Bolter and Grusin assert (2000, p. 28). In their take on media history, '[w]hat is new about new media comes from the particular ways in which they refashion older media and the ways in which older media refashion themselves to answer the challenges of new media' (p. 15).

The metaphysics of recording

This is not the place to delve into the complex conceptual histories of the terms 'analogue' and 'digital'. However, it seems important to emphasise two of the most important prerequisites for the phenomenon of analogue nostalgia. First, a semantic vagueness characterises the distinction between analogue and digital; the common media-historical approach makes this distinction 'into a matter of new and old' (Rosen, 2001, p. 303), while Western societies have developed a 'wider cultural situation where vintage is considered better than the new' (Parikka, 2012, p. 3). Second, in order to understand media transition 'we must resist notions of media purity' and static definitions, as David Thorburn and Henry Jenkins (2004, p. 11) rightly point out. Yet, such pragmatic perspectives still seem scarce. Although often reduced to a simplistic dichotomy of mutually exclusive concepts, both terms, analogue and digital, have quite different implications and meanings in differing contexts. It is not only in their vernacular use that several overlapping semantic fields blur a precise understanding. The countless media-theoretical articles and books that have been written about the consequences of digitisation and the differences between analogue and digital representation in the last decades have fuelled the polysemy inherent in the terms and their distinction rather than offering clarification (Baudrillard, 2009). Film theorists of the 1990s and early 2000s, too, often described digitisation as a process of deprivation and disembodiment, a fundamental threat to film and photography as photochemical media (Sobchack, 1994). Based on idiosyncratic metaphors, like Roland Barthes's assertion that a 'sort of umbilical cord links the body of the photographed thing to my gaze' (2010, p. 81), the supposed continuous nature of analogue inscription and, especially, the direct connection between the representation and that which is represented were considered to be film's 'medium specificity' and were perceived as the very basis upon which film studies was built (Doane, 2007). In many accounts, the vaguely defined category of the analogue that gained contour mostly in contrast to its digital other was mistakenly identified completely with the indexical, as Tom Gunning (2007) and others have pointed out in recent years.

Most of the arguments put forward in this debate within film theory (and, to a certain degree, in media studies) had already been discussed in the context of audio recording and its question of 'fidelity' (Milner, 2010), yet these critical discourses have never intersected in a meaningful way. The forced displacement of analogue vinyl records and audio cassettes by the digital compact disc throughout the 1980s was one of the first moments when the scope of imminent media technological changes became evident to a broad public, creating an instant sense of nostalgia for the supplanted recording media. Many of the claims that the digital lacked something essential stem from this historical situation. As early as 1983, only a year after the official market introduction of the CD, an article entitled 'Digital Discontent' by David Lander was published in *Rolling Stone* magazine, stating: 'Maybe there's something in music that numbers and lasers can't translate' (1983, p. 88, cited in Chivers Yochim and Biddinger, 2008, p. 187).[1]

The concern behind this thought is obviously an epistemological one. In his trenchant article 'The Death and Life of Digital Audio' Sterne criticises this 'metaphysics of recording', specifically the idea that 'mediation is something that can be measured in terms of its distance from life' (Sterne, 2006, p. 338). According to Sterne, this notion originates in the age-old belief that a recording captures a certain amount of life and 'that as a recording traverses an ever larger number of technological steps, that quantity of life decreases, essentially moving it (and perhaps the listener) toward death' (p. 338). In their early days, those media now cherished as analogue were subject to the same criticism, as exemplified by Henri Bergson's *Creative Evolution*. Here, Bergson maintains that film, or 'cinematographic illusion', can never really capture the continuity of movement, as movement itself is always that which happens *between* the still images. Thus, in Bergson's perspective, movement essentially eludes recording, as it always 'slips through the interval' (1944, p. 334).

Sterne (2006) demonstrates that the same metaphysical argument is generally made regarding the discontinuity of digital inscription. Such arguments claim that the separate samples processed in binary code are merely 'simulations' of what they represent, hence missing the 'essence', the 'soul', the 'authenticity' or the 'aura' of the actual recorded sound. Sterne pleads for a re-evaluation of this question of 'life' in a recording as a 'social question, not an ontological or metaphysical one' (p. 339). Moreover, he proves that some analogue media, like the magnetic tape, are 'just as discontinuous as the 0s and 1s in digital storage' (p. 340f). Bolter and Grusin address the same desire for authenticity as part of a complex and seemingly contradictory double logic by assuming a discourse-analytical perspective. For them, one of the driving forces of media history is the desire for immediacy or the 'transparent presentation of the real' (2000, p. 21). This desire finds expression in media's attempt to erase all indicators of mediation[2] and present their representations as 'life itself' (or, at least, as a direct window onto it). At the same time, though, there is another tendency working in the opposite direction. The logic of hypermediacy enjoys the opacity of representation and highlights or even multiplies the signs of mediation. These two cultural logics of immediacy and hypermediacy do not only coexist; they are mutually dependent. Approached from a social or psychological perspective, it becomes evident that both logics share an 'appeal to authenticity of experience' (p. 71) that is socially constructed. In consequence, even the 'excess of media' (p. 53) can become an authentic experience; hypermediacy can thus become a strategy to achieve immediacy. This seemingly paradoxical relationship can be illustrated with a famous quotation from British radio pioneer John Peel: 'Somebody was trying to tell me that CDs are better than vinyl because they don't have any surface noise. I said, "Listen, mate, life has surface noise"' (Chassanoff, 2012). In this perspective, the specific signs of mediation that seem to distract from the immediacy of the recorded sound counter-intuitively create the authentic experience in the first place.

This reversal of the common logic of recording is characteristic of analogue nostalgia. In this context, Thomas Levin notes:

> In the age of digital recording and playback, the sound of error has changed significantly [...]: The moment of the scratch is no longer the signal of malfunction but is instead the almost nostalgic trace of a bygone era of mechanical reproducibility, one can say that it has become auratic, and as such it suddenly becomes available for aesthetic practices of all sorts.
>
> (1999, p. 162)

These aesthetic practices, however, can be remediated and appropriated in digital media to simulate or mimic this notion of an authentic or 'auratic' experience, as I intend to illustrate with the help of a scene from the recent TV series *Californication* in which the hitherto described discourses are neatly interwoven.

An analogue guy in a digital world

In an early episode of the series, the protagonist, troubled novelist and playboy Hank Moody, is shopping for groceries when he meets a woman who remains nameless throughout the episode and is only addressed as 'surfer girl' in the DVD's liner notes. As is typical of the series, they end up in Moody's apartment after a short and rather trivial conversation, sitting on the floor and smoking marijuana while listening to the writer's collection of old vinyl records. In this situation, the following dialogue unfolds:

Surfer Girl: 'I fucking love vinyl.'
Hank Moody: 'Yeah, it just sounds better. It's warmer, right? It's just human.'
Surfer Girl: 'You're just an analog guy in a digital world, aren't you?'

This highly clichéd scene encapsulates the basic concept of *Californication*. The series' appeal is based on the conflict between the 'old/authentic' and the 'new/superficial', situating its protagonist as an anachronistic 'last of his kind' character. Most of Hank Moody's key characteristics could be described as symptoms of a rather serious adaptive disorder, yet throughout the series he is depicted as irresistibly charming and as a stubborn and nostalgic romantic. Not only does he prefer his music to be played from vinyl records, but he also writes his books on an old typewriter instead of a computer. Of course, this affection for almost obsolescent media technology mirrors his equally obsessive clinging to outdated concepts and values like romantic love and artistic authenticity. He is tormented by the superficiality of Los Angeles and its entertainment industry, which turned his highbrow novel into a silly 'rom-com', and he is homesick for an idealised New York that apparently exists only in the past tense of fond memories, thus seeming ineffably remote. Hank Moody is the prime example of what Mark Desrosiers once called the 'R. Crumb Effect': 'when modernity gets you down, you can put yourself on the cutting edge by fetishizing ancient styles and technologies, and your antithetical influence will start making its mark on popular tastes' (2002).

To underline its nostalgia narrative, *Californication* relies heavily on the aesthetics of analogue film, which becomes particularly evident in the opening credits of the series. In a little less than a minute, the viewer is presented with the whole range of analogue artefacts (Flückiger, 2008, pp. 334–356), or typical flaws of decaying film stock. In the credit scene, the image looks dirty and gritty, laden with scratches and visible splices. A tattered grunge frame with rounded corners limits the picture as it would in an old 8 mm home movie. The film's grain is heavily visible, and, in some of the shots, the emulsion seems to be on the verge of dissolution. The perforation of the filmstrip, as well as the black intervals between frames, is repeatedly made visible. Additionally, numerous flash frames and lens flares emphasise the analogue nature of the footage. At first glance, the shots seem to represent Hank

Moody's memories of 'better' times, shot in a home video style to signify their 'pastness' (see also Chapter 2 in this volume). The shots are obviously set in LA, though, and the same style is repeated in the frequent interludes that serve the narrative purpose of connecting discontinuous scenes.

Surprisingly, *Californication* is shot completely with digital cameras; only the pilot was filmed in 35 mm, but this first episode did not yet feature the opening credit scene (Caranicas, 2011). All the described analogue artefacts were thus added digitally in the post-production process, proving Lev Manovich's assertion that the classic film look acquired 'a truly fetishist status' (1996, p. 58) in digital cinema. In fact, there are vendors like CineGrain.com who sell footage of raw analogue glitches for personal or professional use in collections ranging from $300 to $3000, advertising their products with phrases like the following: 'A film collection worn by time and too many projector changes. Here's the sought after looks for the messed up and scratched up, the tattered and dishevelled. Broken has never looked so beautiful.'

Analogue nostalgia and the aesthetics of virtual ruins

The term 'analog nostalgia' was originally coined to address aesthetic practices exactly like these. It appears for the first time in a chapter of Marks's book (2002); seven years later it reappears in Rombes's *Cinema in the Digital Age* (2009), though without an explicit reference to Marks. For Marks, analogue nostalgia expresses a 'desire for indexicality' and 'a retrospective fondness for the "problems" of decay and generational loss that analog video posed' (p. 152). Thus, in her perspective, the phenomenon is not about the refusal of digital technologies, but exclusively about the digital remediation of analogue aesthetics *within* the digital. To put it in terms of communication theory, analogue nostalgia is directed towards the noise, not the signal. In the broadest sense, it operates as a strategy of re-enchanting an object through aesthetic de-familiarisation as it is characterised by deliberate imperfection:

> In the high fidelity medium of digital video, where each generation can be as imperviously perfect as the one before, artists are importing images of electronic dropout and decay, 'TV snow' and the random colours of unrecorded tape, in a sort of longing for analog physicality. Interestingly, analog nostalgia seems especially prevalent among works by students who started learning video production when it was fully digital. (p. 152f)

Rombes does not explicitly link his only sketchily defined concept of analogue nostalgia to indexicality, but for him, too, there is 'a tendency in digital media [...] to reassert imperfection, flaws, an aura of human mistakes to counterbalance the logic of perfection that pervades the digital' (2009, p. 2). Sometimes, Rombes's text itself verges on a polemical and nostalgic manifesto, for example when he concludes his book with these sentences: 'In the end, it is the mistakes, the errors that we assert in the face of the code that keeps it from consuming us with its purity. Mistakes must be our answer to the machines of perfection that we ourselves have built' (2009, p. 156). In this regard, analogue nostalgia as an aesthetic practice is the paradoxical attempt to preserve decay and plan contingency.

'What is lost in the move to the digital is the imprint of time, the visible degradation of the image', writes Mary Anne Doane (2007, p. 117f), a claim that is intentionally or unintentionally reminiscent of Benjamin's famous description of the aura withering in the age of technological reproducibility (2008, p. 22). Assigning an almost organic quality to analogue media, David N. Rodowick notes that 'the material basis of film is a chemically encoded process of entropy' (2007, p. 20). From this perspective, analogue media do not merely contain a certain amount of life, as discussed in the context of the 'metaphysics of recording'; they even share certain essential qualities with it. In fact, analogue media age, and they show distinct signs of decay the older they get; each playing of a vinyl record or a celluloid film expedites its self-liquidation. This process leads to the traces of usage that typically appear exactly at those moments which were often replayed or rewound. This fact might be of great importance for a deeper understanding of analogue nostalgia.

In an article on cinephilia, Robnik writes that analogue 'rental videos confront you with traces, ruined images, left behind by someone else's fascination by a moment' (2005, p. 59). For him, the analogue's malfunctions constitute 'textual ruins' and are thus more than just indicators of age, as they can also be understood as traces of appreciation or pleasure.[3] When these traces of use are digitally simulated, we abolish the uncanny fact that in organic life – as well as in analogue media – the process of aging irretrievably leads to death or complete dysfunction, respectively. Analogue nostalgia simulates a process of aging that has not happened yet, and never will happen (at least, not in the form that is simulated). This condition is analogous to the artificial ruins of the seventeenth and eighteenth centuries, as it involves the artificial, or, rather, virtual, ruins of the digital age. However, these ruins are no longer 'signifiers of absence', as Böhme (1989) once defined the lure of ancient ruins. On the contrary, the purpose of this digitally simulated analogue decay seems to be the signification of presence: as it simulates exactly the life or 'soul' that the digital was always accused of lacking.

Notes

1. Certainly not by mere coincidence, the same year also saw the release of Herbie Hancock's *Rockit*, the first mainstream music title to feature scratching as an artistic practice. Speaking with Rosalind Krauss (1999), one could call this the 'redemptive role' of the threat of obsolescence that leads to an artistic reinvention of the medium and the ways in which it can be deployed.
2. In this context, it should be noted that a similar claim can be found in Walter Benjamin's famous *Artwork* essay and its description of the 'vision of immediate reality' as 'the Blue Flower in the land of technology' (2008, p. 35). The 'Blue Flower' as a pivotal symbol of German Romanticism is the idealisation of that which cannot be obtained, something that is always already lost and exists only in longing desire.
3. The best illustration for this assumption is Quentin Tarantino's 2007 film *Death Proof*, where he playfully suggests that the climactic moments of a lapdance scene might have been cut out of the film by the projectionist for his own collection, leaving the actual viewers of the film with a 'textual ruin' (Schrey, 2010, p. 189).

References

Anders, G. (1956) 'The Phantom World of TV'. *Dissent*, 3, pp. 14–24.
Barthes, R. (2010) *Camera Lucida. Reflections on Photography*. Translated by Richard Howard. New York: Hill and Wang.
Baudrillard, J. (2009) *Why Hasn't Everything Already Disappeared?* Translated by Chris Turner. London, New York: Seagull Books.
Benjamin, W. (2008) 'The Work of Art in the Age of its Technological Reproducibility' (second version), in M. W. Jennings, B. Doherty and T. Y. Levin (eds) *The Work of Art in the Age of its Technological Reproducibility, and Other Writings on Media*. Cambridge, MA; London: Belknap Press of Harvard University Press, pp. 19–55.
Bergson, H. (1944) *Creative Evolution*. Translated by Arthur Mitchell. New York, NY: Modern Library.
Bishop, C. (2012) 'Digital Divide'. *Artforum*, September 2012, pp. 435–441.
Böhme, H. (1989) 'Die Ästhetik der Ruinen', in D. Kamper and C. Wulf (eds) *Der Schein des Schönen*. Göttingen: Steidl, pp. 287–304.
Böhme, H. (2000) 'Der Wettstreit der Medien im Andenken der Toten', in H. Belting and D. Kamper (eds) *Der zweite Blick. Bildgeschichte und Bildreflexion*. München: Fink, pp. 23–43.
Böhn, A. (2007) 'Nostalgia of the Media/in the Media', in W. Nöth and N. Bishara (eds) *Self-Reference in the Media*. Berlin, New York: Mouton de Gruyter, pp. 143–153.
Bolter, J. D. and Grusin, R. (2000) *Remediation. Understanding New Media*. Cambridge, MA, London: MIT Press.

Bordwell, D. (2012) *Pandora's Digital Box. Film, Files, and the Future of Movies.* Madison, WI: Irvington Way Institute Press.
Boym, S. (2001) *The Future of Nostalgia.* New York: Basic Books.
Caranicas, P. (2011) ' "Californication" Leaves no Trail of Tape. Arri Alexa Allows Show to Shoot on Reusable Memory Cards'. http://www.variety.com/article/VR1118040091 (accessed 17 December 2012).
Chassanoff, A. (2012) 'Life has Surface Noise. (Further) Ruminations on the Record'. http://hastac.org/blogs/achass/2012/01/23/life-has-surface-noise-further-ruminations-record (accessed 24 June 2013).
Chivers Yochim, E. and Biddinger, M. (2008) ' "It kind of gives you that vintage feel". Vinyl Records and the Trope of Death'. *Media, Culture & Society,* 30(2), pp. 183–195.
Desrosiers, M. (2002) 'Maim that Tune. The Moldy Peaches and the Apotheosis of Lo-Fi'. http://www.popmatters.com/pm/column/desrosiers020306/ (accessed 17 December 2012).
Doane, M. A. (2007) 'The Indexical and the Concept of Medium Specificity'. *differences. A Journal of Feminist Cultural Studies,* 18(1), pp. 128–152.
Eco, U. (1994) *Apocalypse Postponed.* Translated by Robert Lumley. Bloomington and London: BFI.
Flückiger, B. (2008) *Visual Effects: Filmbilder aus dem Computer.* Marburg: Schüren.
Guffey, E. E. (2006) *Retro: The Culture of Revival.* London: Reaktion.
Gunning, T. (2007) 'Moving Away from the Index: Cinema and the Impression of Reality'. *differences. A Journal of Feminist Cultural Studies,* 18(1), pp. 29–52.
Krauss, R. E. (1999) 'Reinventing the Medium'. *Critical Inquiry,* 25(2), pp. 289–305.
Levin, T. Y. (1999) 'Indexicality Concrète: The Aesthetic Politics of Christian Marclay's Grammophonia'. *Parkett,* (56), pp. 162–169.
Manovich, L. (1996) 'The Paradoxes of Digital Photography', in H. von Amelunxen, S. Iglhaut and F. Rötzer (eds) *Photography After Photography. Memory and Representation in the Digital Age.* Dresden: GB Arts, pp. 57–65.
Marks, L. U. (2002) *Touch. Sensuous Theory and Multisensory Media.* Minneapolis, MN: University of Minnesota Press.
Milner, G. (2010) *Perfecting Sound Forever. The Story of Recorded Music.* London: Granta.
Parikka, J. (2012) *What Is Media Archaeology?* Cambridge UK, Malden, MA: Polity.
Reynolds, S. (2011) *Retromania. Pop Culture's Addiction to Its Own Past.* New York: Faber & Faber.
Robnik, D. (2005) 'Mass Memories of Movies. Cinephilia as Norm and Narrative in Blockbuster Culture', in M. de Valck and M. Hagener (eds) *Cinephilia. Movies, Love and Memory.* Amsterdam: Amsterdam University Press (Film Culture in Transition), pp. 55–64.
Rodowick, D. N. (2007) *The Virtual Life of Film.* Cambridge, MA and London: Harvard University Press.
Rombes, N. (2009) *Cinema in the Digital Age.* London, New York: Wallflower Press.
Rosen, P. (2001) *Change Mummified. Cinema, Historicity, Theory.* Minneapolis, MN: University of Minnesota Press.
Schrey, D. (2010) 'Mediennostalgie und Cinephilie im Grindhouse-Doublefeature', in A. Böhn and K. Möser (eds) *Techniknostalgie und Retrotechnologie.* Karlsruhe: KIT Scientific Publishing, pp. 183–195.

Serres, M. (2001) 'New Technologies'. *Mousaion*, 19(1), pp. 25–34.
Sobchack, V. (1994) 'The Scene of the Screen. Envisioning Cinematic and Electronic "Presence"', in H. U. Gumbrecht and K. Ludwig Pfeiffer (eds) *Materialities of Communication*. Stanford, CA: Stanford University Press, pp. 83–106.
Sterling, B. (2008) 'The Life and Death of Media', in P. D. Miller (ed.) *Sound Unbound. Sampling Digital Music and Culture*. Cambridge, MA and London: MIT Press, pp. 73–82.
Sterne, J. (2006) 'The Death and Life of Digital Audio'. *Interdisciplinary Science Reviews*, 31(4), pp. 338–348.
Sterne, J. (2007) 'Out with the Trash. On the Future of New Media', in C. R. Acland (ed.) *Residual Media*. Minneapolis: University of Minnesota Press, pp. 16–31.
Thorburn, D. and Jenkins, H. (2004) *Rethinking Media Change. The Aesthetics of Transition*. Cambridge, MA and London: MIT Press, pp. 1–18.

2
Homesick for Aged Home Movies: Why Do We Shoot Contemporary Family Videos in Old-Fashioned Ways?

Giuseppina Sapio

As the most important studies in the field have pointed out (see, for example, Bourdieu, 1965; Sontag, 1978; Chalfen, 1987; Odin, 1995; Zimmermann, 1995; Moran, 2002; Cati, 2009), the practice of home movie making has always been linked to technical and technological change. Indeed, the evolution of family video equipment, from Super 8 to digital, has allowed individuals to express themselves according to their social and cultural status. I reject the position that the symbolic effects of family images are connected consequentially to the technologies employed to realise them. However, I think that the material dimension of home movies cannot be neglected, because it is this that ultimately provides so much satisfaction to people wishing to pass on their memories.

This research concerns the evolution in France of home movie filming from the 1960s (Super 8 films) to the present (digital films) and the changes that have affected the family unit during this period. It brings together a theoretical dimension, the symbolic implications of the practice, and an empirical one, the findings emerging from an exploratory case study of nine French families shooting home movies. Based on the psychological, social and cultural study of these families, the multidisciplinary approach of this piece, combined with a qualitative methodology (in the form of several in-depth interviews with the members of those families), is meant to explore how family images and conversations help individuals to think about themselves and their roles within their groups. I narrowed down my choices of families to be interviewed by four criteria: geographical (I interviewed people living in Paris, or its suburbs, and in French provinces such as Nice, Orléans and Menton), social (I interviewed an industrialist, two housewives, two students, several shopkeepers, and so on), technical/technological (I interviewed families who shoot only Super 8 home movies and families who shoot only digital ones) and, last but not least, familial (I interviewed a nuclear family, some blended families, an adoptive family and a homoparental one). I conceived my field survey as a form of role-play in which the subjects were supposed to show me their home movies and talk about them: I interviewed family members separately (for instance, the parents together and then their children) about the same home movies in order to find out how people give several interpretations of the same representation of a family event.

I will argue that the making of home movies contributes to a family's sense of self-awareness by introducing a concept that we have named the *meta-family*. Nowadays, the capacity of groups to think about themselves through images arises when they decide, for example, to use video effects or vintage editing software to make their home movies look 'older'. Indeed, the return of an analogue aesthetic in digital family images is not only a matter of appearance. It is related to the history of home movies and to the awareness that individuals have of that history. This chapter thus proposes to consider nostalgia for analogue home movies as an expression both of the tendency people have to think about their family rituals and of their desire to evoke them.

Once upon a time there were Super 8 home movies

Before the introduction of digital cameras, the making of home movies (Super 8) was a hands-on activity that required the careful handling of the camera by the filmmaker, the use of scissors and glue during the editing process and the manipulation of the projector during the screening. Because of the high prices of these tools, home movies were generally shot by the father, and his main role in the practice was coherent with the establishment of the patriarchal nuclear family during the 1950s.

Patricia Zimmermann observed:

> The angle of the camera, its mobility, and its control over representation unfurl patriarchal prerogative. The woman and her children are immobilised by the camera, yet blissfully and almost self-reflectively

participate in its representation like a game of charades or a pantomime of *Parents Magazine* covers.

(1995, p. 112)

From this point of view, the anthropologist Chalfen showed that, in nearly all cases investigated for his study, 'the male head of the household used the camera most of the time. In a few cases, a teenage son (but not daughter) who was learning about cameras and filmmaking, took over this responsibility' (Chalfen, 1987, p. 60). He also noted that only one 'How To' guide considered the possibility of home movie filmmakers being someone other than the father. As Ganito and Ferreira (2011) have observed, home movies were generally shot by the father, but compiling a photo album was considered rather a feminine activity.

The most distinguishing feature of Super 8 home movies is their 'granularity'. The fragility of the analogue format is especially evident during screenings, when the footage is continually interrupted by the 'jumps' of the film in the projector and the movies are shown with all their imperfections: shaking grains and lightly jumping images. Odin (1995) argues that home movies are distinguishable from professional movies because they are 'badly done'. He considers that the family is more interested in the functionality of the home movie that preserves and passes on family memories than in its aesthetic quality. This reflection appears correct if one thinks in terms of the opposition between amateur and professional movies, but, if we are discussing the specificity of home movies, we have to reformulate Odin's reflections about their aesthetic status. In order to do that, the material changes that have affected home movies (and, thus, their aesthetic effects) have to be analysed. The aesthetic features of Super 8 home movies are related to several material conditions: a simple charger contains a film (15 metres long) allowing a movie to be shot that is three minutes and 20 seconds in length. Such time restrictions imply diegetic limits during the shooting, because filmmakers have to sum up in a few minutes the most important moments of family celebrations. Like shooting, editing is characterised by a strong handmade dimension: manipulation of the film is required, and the link between the filmmaker and the movie is direct and manual. That keeps out the other members of the group (children and wives) and makes the father the only author of the family tale. During screening, the father handles everything: the problems caused by the instability of the film running in the projector and the setting-up of the material in the living room (people have to turn off the lights or arrange the chairs around the screen) make this moment rarer and more emotionally involved than the screening of digital home movies.

Home movies in the age of VHS

In 1983, Sony released the Betamovie, the first Betamax camera, which allowed filming to last more than three hours: home movies in this format are better in terms of film quality than Super 8 ones. The drawbacks of the camera were the weight (2.5 kg), the noise made during shooting and the fact that previously recorded videos could not be watched. In the next few years, Sony and other companies marketed a new, smaller model using an 8 mm film called Video 8. Between 1987 and 1988, the Hi8 (an evolution of the 8 mm size) and the Super VHS (S-VHS) were exhibited. The robustness of the cameras and films is one of the most interesting features of these innovations, although their tapes are sensitive to dust, folding and grains. As for Super 8 home movies, amateurs' guides recommended a list of the best moments to shoot and taught filmmakers the technique of simultaneous shooting and editing, since it was impossible to watch immediately what had just been recorded. Thus, the 'family diegesis' was even simpler than that of the Super 8 home movies, but the division of labour among the members of the family was more flexible. Furthermore, the long duration of the videos meant a more relaxed attitude during shooting. The handling of more robust equipment also meant that family screenings became more frequent and emotional investment lessened. The father's authority in the making of home movies underwent a major change because the new cameras facilitated shooting and the VHS players made screenings easier. Indeed, the father's role was called into question by the VHS cameras' technique of direct editing that determined 'the end' of Super 8 manual editing. Digital technologies have emphasised these changes and at the same time have recorded several steps in the evolution of the family unit.

Then came digital home movies

During the 1990s many technical and technological innovations were commercialised. The first digital camera was marketed in 1995, and, three years later, the DVD player appeared in living rooms, succeeding the VHS player. Most digital cameras work with DV (Digital Video) tapes that are better than VHS tapes because of their high video and sound quality. As soon as digitisation began to occur, it started to affect the relationship between family images and family memory. As Halbwachs (1994) argues, family memory in the 1920s largely depended on material props such as knick-knacks, jewellery, photos and movies. But what happens when objects of memory become more permanent? What if, thanks to digitisation, family images do not 'age' anymore?

Sit, Hollan and Griswold (2005) point out that conversations about family photos are generally carried out in houses' communal spaces (for example, at the kitchen table or in the living room). In the days of analogue cameras, families did not watch their home movies as often as they would do nowadays because of the fragility of the film. Consequently, they invested emotionally in the screening of movies and saw the event as an important family celebration. Nowadays, we can watch our home movies on televisions, personal computers or mobile phones. We can make copies of them and share them on the web or by e-mail. These 'stronger' home movies grant us a more enjoyable screening experience. We are less worried by the fragility of the film and the screening is not continually interrupted by the 'jumps' of the film in the projector. We can observe here that emotional investment shifts to the quantitative dimension of the practice. We have a lot of photos and videos of our family, but we do not watch them in the way we used to. As Sit, Hollan and Griswold observe of family photographs, 'talk centred around online digital photos is infrequent, sparse and commonly unidirectional, lacking the richness and naturalness of conversational interactions around printed photos' (2005, p. 1). Today, there are two main ways in which families watch home movies. They do so either intimately, with family members watching films together, or privately, watching films alone on a personal computer or mobile phone. Another consequence of the introduction of digital technologies on home movies has been the dematerialisation of family images. In my exploratory case study, families do not develop their photos, preferring to store them on their computers. When they do decide to develop their photos, they choose only those they like. In the same way, in Ganito and Ferreira's study (2011) on photo albums, the interviewees said that they never printed their photos.

To return to the tactile dimension of cultural objects such as photos or home movies, Lisa Gye reminds us that 'sharing photographs, even when they are in albums, is often a tactile and sensual experience. Photographs are passed between participants who are invited to inspect them more closely' (2007, p. 283). With analogue cameras, people had to wait to see their images, and they could not throw away defective ones immediately; they could make their selection only after development. From this point of view, home movies have been dematerialised too: families do not have to handle the film, or edit it with scissors and glue, and they do not have to place it in the projector or make sure that it does not 'jump' from its sprocket holes.

Nostalgic home movies: Analogue aesthetic and digital strength

Home movies have lost their material appearance. VHS movies made a part of the family memory tangible. Before, they could be found in drawers or in boxes somewhere in the house; now, we rarely burn home movies onto DVDs and, even if we do, their thin, fragile appearance is a fitting embodiment of the loss of materiality on the part of family images. This kind of symbolic dematerialisation recalls what Walter Benjamin (2006) writes on the efforts of the bourgeoisie to compensate for what he calls 'loss of traces' in the city by using materials (velvet or plush covers) which preserved the impression of every touch. With regard to this, the new phenomenon of 'touch', enabled by touch-screen technologies, is of great interest (Paterson, 2006; Ratcliffe, 2008). As Puig de la Bellacasa (2009) argues, touching technologies imply an experience of sensorial immersion by imitating a connection to real objects. Thus, I support the idea that there is an important link between the dematerialisation of family images and attempts to find this lost 'sense of touch' again through the return of 'granularity' in family photos and videos. In my study, four families explain that they try to make their images 'warmer' by adding special effects or vintage filters. This effort to compensate for dematerialisation also takes place on other levels of society: in daily life, we often see the return of past values embodied in particular objects, for example in the clothing of those fashion phenomena known as 'hipsters'. There is an interesting website named 'Dads are the original hipsters' (Hipsters, 2013) that illustrates this desire on the part of young people to return to the times of their parents' generation and its perceived value of coolness, its music, its clothes and its accessories. Further to that, 'hipster' clothing marks a comeback for particular fabrics, just like the bourgeoisie and their plush and velvet covers. 'Hipsters' choose to wear their parents' clothes, or they look for similar items in second-hand clothes shops. They seem to look for 'worn-in' clothes. As DeLong, Heinemann and Reiley (2005) observe, searching for vintage items means searching for 'aura', the changes and imperfections that are the signs of use left by the passage of time. This return of the past can also be witnessed with vinyl collectors who prefer the warmer sound of records to the colder sound of digital. In Chivers and Biddinger's paper, a vinyl collector states that he likes 'the little fuzz that you get from a record. [...] It kind of gives you that vintage feel' (2008, p. 183). Plasketes (1992) argues that the use of vinyl suggests more than a technological preference. Listening to a record involves experiencing the feeling of an idealised connection with the past. A sense of touch is evoked even in fields where a tactile dimension is not directly implied. Accordingly, some companies offer their customers the ability to shoot their home movies in old formats. In the 'Frequently Asked Questions' section of the French company *Super 8 mon amour* (Super 8, 2013), we find an interesting answer to the question 'Why should you shoot your marriage film in Super 8?' The arguments given are the vibrant colours of the film, its grainy footage and its lightly jumping images. The company also writes that the film will not be cold or 'super-realistic' like DVs. This French company is an example of the comeback of analogue aesthetics. It offers a Super 8 movie on a DVD. In other words, we choose the Super 8 for its charming imperfections, not for its material disadvantages. In daily life, the return of analogue aesthetics can also be achieved through several kinds of video/photo effects (sepia, vintage and washed out) on photo-sharing programmes such as Instagram. Another interesting example is the editing software Ulead VideoStudio 6, the 'retro' interface of which is reminiscent of the old flatbed editor. According to my study, people use these video and photo effects in order for their images to have *granularity*. Digital technologies have dematerialised the images as objects, thus making family rituals (such as the group viewing of a home movie or the family album) weaker. Families seem to compensate for this loss by adding *grains* to images. The features of this are interesting for our analysis. First of all, the grain is not necessary. It was considered inevitable in analogue film, however, and its presence has established a 'home-movie style' that people try to reproduce in digital form.

Froger (2010) writes that the aesthetic of movies is not only a matter of art criticism. The 'badly done' style of home movies is necessary to make them 'good' home movies. The imperfections of this kind of amateur production are essential because they characterise the movies and their makers. The simple form of home movies makes it easier to identify family members in a film of a group celebration. Like Froger, I think that the aesthetic choices of amateurs are representative of their desires to forge and reinforce bonds. All the members of the families I interviewed confirm that the style of their home movies embodies their feelings of belonging, even if they were not directly involved in the shooting or editing. The simplicity of home movies is the result of the great importance attached to the practice as a genuine relational experience. Gestures and interactions during shooting and screening allow family members to renew their feelings of belonging to the group and of being part of family history. The grain of home footage confers a texture to it and thus allows people to consider their images as material traces of their memory. At the same time, the grain is neither a sign of deterioration of the film nor a mark of its fragility or, by extension, the fragility of the family memory. The grain reminds us of old family images. Adding it to 'new' (digital) footage gives people the feeling of belonging to a wider family group, inclusive of older generations. In other words, adding grains gives the idea of symbolic continuity to the reservoir of family images.

Conclusion

This chapter shows that family images have contributed to the symbolic evolution of families by allowing subjects to see themselves and, by checking their resemblances to other members of the family, to become more conscious of their belonging to the group. Nowadays, digital images are essential in shaping and sharing family memory. More than being objects, home movies are communicative interactions among individuals. The shooting of home movies is related to the cyclic dimension of family celebrations and emphasises the importance of moments such as birthdays, vacations and Christmas holidays. It aims at creating in all family members the euphoric feeling of belonging. When people shoot their home movies, they switch themselves to 'play mode'. They play together with the camera, and the rules of their play are comparable to those described by Goffman (1974) when he discusses play activities.

When home movies are edited, they gain an important function within the family by giving memories a material form. Indeed, individuals meet around their private screens, watch their home movies and talk about their memories. Just as I mentioned a 'play mode' in the shooting of home movies, I believe that, when families watch their home movies in private, they switch to 'taxonomic mode'. This concept has been introduced in order to define the behaviour of families when they are in front of their own home movies. They produce a series of actions such as describing everyone's qualities (for example, voice, pace, gesture and habits), naming those who appear in the movies and organising them into a hierarchy. Thus, they watch home movies to feel the pleasure of finding themselves. This is possible even when they are not in the movie, because everyone is able to recognise resemblances to other members of his or her family. As Chalfen observes, 'informants openly recalled the fun they enjoyed when they were *in* the movies rather than shooting the movies' (1987, p. 55). This 'taxonomic mode' is inspired by the concept of 'family resemblances' theorised by Wittgenstein (1984) when he talks about the features, relations and similarities of 'family games'. We are not able to define our family, but we can describe the network of features characterising it. In the history of painting, family portraits have an important function. They ensure the immediate recognition of a specific family. The painter is supposed to allow people observing the portrait to recognise both the painted subjects and their physical and social features, the latter showing that they belong to their specific family. According to Barthes (1988), photography presents an opportunity for people to view themselves differently from how they do in a mirror. This is particularly true since the practice has become popular within society. The role of these images in the accomplishment of family awareness is important; they can be considered as a kind of 'looking glass' for families, allowing them to understand their own structure and laws. As a part of this symbolic process, I suggest introducing this practice into the set of tasks that composes 'care-giving'. Family members carry out sets of actions in daily life in order to provide for each other. As a unit, they provide each other's care. The making and showing of home movies could be introduced into such a set of tasks. Family members care about the images (photos or movies) that will replace them in the future, when they will no longer be there. Thus, home movies can be considered as an example of symbolically taking care of the family. On the one hand, we take care of the family by keeping the movies at home, by passing them down from one generation to another and considering them important objects that support our family memories. On the other hand, we do so by repeating the interactions that we always perform together during the shooting, editing and screening of the movies. In other words, as objects, home movies embody our attempt to take care of family images in the present, as a promise of getting together in the future. As interactions, home movies embody the opportunity for the family to feel good by carrying out the same actions during family celebrations, by following a kind of 'family script'. This concept, introduced by Byng-Hall (1995), is interesting because it focuses on the double role of repetition within families: repetition helps maintain family stability and it gives families the incentive to change. To summarise, home movies show how media can operate on groups by verbalising their structures, laws and memories and thus help to understand them. Home movies involve an important verbalisation of family events. During their shooting, enunciation is mainly characterised by meta-communication, because the camera encourages people to present themselves and to speak about what they are doing. This kind of communication is apparently useless, because family members do not need to say what they are celebrating, why or where. They do so, however, and this meta-communication implicitly allows the family to think about itself. The second type of verbalisation takes place during the screening of home movies, when individuals switch to taxonomic mode and describe the features of their family, in particular by verbalising family resemblances. In furtherance of this, I introduced the concept of the *meta-family* to describe the role of home movies in the development of family awareness: the *meta-family* is the contribution of the images to individual awareness of the dynamics operating in their family. Thanks to the interactions in shooting home movies and the different types of verbalisation, the family is allowed to think about itself. The *meta-family* is not the real family, shooting or watching images, but represents the conscious and unconscious workings of the family members produced with, and through, the images. The evolution of the technical age and technologies in the practice of home movies has followed, recorded and sometimes predicted those conscious and unconscious changes within the family unit. From this point of view, it is extremely interesting to state how digital home movies have brought about such family changes. I think that the dematerialisation brought by digital technologies pushes families to find other ways to compensate for the loss of the material dimension of the practice. The dematerialisation is clear during the shooting, because of the smallness and lightness of the cameras, the components of which can be miniaturised thanks to the tiny size of Mini DV tapes. It is also clear during the screening, which no longer requires the installation of a projector and, thanks to personal computers and iPad/mobile phone screens, is generally easier.

    Home movies have physically disappeared from houses, and some families seem to find a kind of compensation in the digital texturing of images to possess the analogue aesthetics of Super 8 home movies. I do not believe that the nostalgic use of that medium is only a matter of appearance, but I suggest that (apparently insignificant) elements such as the grains on the images can provide a feeling of returning to past family values and nostalgia for 'aged' images. These elements seem to epitomise the attempt to compensate for not only the dematerialisation of images but also the dematerialisation of some models of family relationships. Furthermore, analogue home movies led to conversation and interactions around the screen, so some communal spaces in the house were emotionally invested in them (generally the living room). These nostalgic returns to the past as families' attempts to rebuild bonds can be understood as models and even spaces which are not simply romanticised or idealised, but reinvested in by individuals with their thoughts about family history. Concerning the concept of the *meta-family*, I think that the return of some nostalgic forms to the practice is an interesting demonstration of how home movies can push families to think about themselves by helping to lend a (perceived) formal continuity to their image.

References

Barthes, R. (1988) *Camera Lucida: Reflections on Photography*. New York: Noonday Press.
Benjamin, W. (2006) *The Writer of Modern Life: Essays on Charles Baudelaire*. Cambridge, MA and London: Harvard University Press.
Bourdieu, P. (1965) *Un art moyen: essai sur les usages sociaux de la photographie*. Paris: Editions de Minuit.
Byng-Hall, J. (1995) *Rewriting Family Scripts. Improvisation and Systems Change*. New York, London: Guilford Press.
Cati, A. (2009) *Pellicole di ricordi*. Milan: Vita e Pensiero.
Chalfen, R. (1987) *Snapshot Versions of Life*. Bowling Green: Bowling Green State University Popular Press.
Chivers, Y. C. and Biddinger, M. (2008) 'It Kind of Gives You That Vintage Feel: Vinyl Records and the Trope of Death'. *Media, Culture & Society*, 30(2), pp. 183–195.
De Singly, F. (1996) *Le soi, le couple et la famille*. Paris: Nathan.
DeLong, M., Heinemann, B. and Reiley, K. (2005) 'Hooked on Vintage!' *Fashion Theory*, 9(1), pp. 23–42.
Froger, M. (2010) *Le cinéma à l'épreuve de la communauté*. Montréal: Presses de l'Université de Montréal.
Ganito, C. and Ferreira, C. (2011) 'New Frames: How the Mobile Phone is Refashioning Family Photo Albums', Paper presented at the Annual Meeting of the International Communication Association, TBA, Boston, MA, http://citation.allacademic.com/meta/p488333_index.html (accessed 12 July 2013).
Goffman, E. (1974) *Frame Analysis: An Essay on the Organization of Experience*. Cambridge, MA: Harvard University Press.
Gye, L. (2007) 'Picture This: The Impact of Mobile Camera Phones on Personal Photographic Practices'. *Continuum Journal of Media and Cultural Studies*, 21(2), pp. 279–288.
Halbwachs, M. (1994) *Les cadres sociaux de la mémoire*. Paris: Albin Michel.
Hipsters (2013) 'Dads are the Original Hipsters'. http://dadsaretheoriginalhipster.tumblr.com/ (accessed 17 July 2013).

Moran, J. M. (2002) *There's No Place Like Home Video*. Minneapolis, London: University of Minnesota Press.
Odin, R. (ed.) (1995) *Le film de famille: usage privé, usage public*. Paris: Méridiens Klincksieck.
Paterson, M. (2006) 'Feel the Presence: Technologies of Touch and Distance'. *Environment and Planning D: Society and Space*, 24(5), pp. 691–708.
Plasketes, G. (1992) 'Romancing the Record: The Vinyl De-evolution and Subcultural Evolution'. *Journal of Popular Culture*, 25, pp. 109–122.
Puig de la Bellacasa, M. (2009) 'Touching Technologies, Touching Visions. The Reclaiming of Sensorial Experience and the Politics of Speculative Thinking'. *Subjectivity*, 28(1), 297–315.
Ratcliffe, M. (2008) 'Touch and Situatedness'. *International Journal of Philosophical Studies*, 16(3), pp. 299–322.
Sit, R. Y., Hollan, J. D. and Griswold, W. G. (2005) ' "Digital Photos as Conversational Anchors", Digital Documents and Media Track'. *System Sciences, HICSS'05: 38th Annual Hawaii International Conference*, pp. 1–10.
Sontag, S. (1978) *On Photography*. New York: Farrar Straus and Giroux.
Super 8 (2013) 'Super 8 mon amour'. http://super8monamour.com/ (accessed 17 July 2013).
Wittgenstein, L. (1984) *Philosophical Investigations*. Oxford: B. Blackwell.
Zimmermann, P. R. (1995) *Reel Families: A Social History of Amateur Film*. Bloomington: Indiana University Press.

3
The Instant Past: Nostalgia and Digital Retro Photography

Gil Bartholeyns

> Tempora non vacant.
> Augustine of Hippo

Once upon a time in the wonderful world of images, a few brave engineers discovered how to turn light into digital signals. But they were unaware that their invention would eventually lead to the pixellation of our entire visual world and that this new technology would soon create upheaval in the longstanding pairing of image and time.

When digital becomes analogue

Over the course of a decade, digital cameras became so highly automated and so effective that the images they produced began to be described as cold and disembodied in comparison to traditional pictures. Analogue photography was expensive and its results were uncertain, yet they had the advantage of being 'alive'. There was greater nostalgia for the warmth of these renderings than for the people and things they depicted, and it was this that caused the birth of the lo-fi photography movement. In the vanguard was Lomographische AG, a company that marketed cheap cameras with unpredictable photo outcomes and, in doing so, brought to light hundreds of thousands of 'lomographers' around the world. Digital technology, however, was not about to stop just when things were going so well. Having achieved optical perfection, it could now simulate photographic imperfection. And so, in 2009 and 2010, a series of mobile phone applications began offering to simulate the square-format photos of the old Brownie, the warm colours of the Polaroid and all the delightful imperfections of family photography in the 1960s–1980s, such as vignetting and over-exposure. The pretence went as far as reflecting the physical nature of prints, reproducing the ravages of time, such as desaturation and scratching (Figure 3.1).[1] Indeed, to take up the slogan of Hipstamatic, one of the key apps on the market, 'digital photography never looked so analogue'.

In 2013, there are several dozen photographic apps (as well as video apps, imitating Super 8 film and the silent movie era) which enable the analogue images of another age to be digitally produced and the photographs themselves to be presented as older than they are. There are hundreds of millions of people more or less actively engaged in what fans and manufacturers alike call iPhonography, following the success of the iPhone and the pioneering apps available on it. There are currently several billion retro images in circulation via social networks apps and image-sharing websites.[2]

No one among the prophets of media use could have foreseen that Western visual retromania at the start of the twenty-first century would be led by mobile phone photography. No culture maven could have envisaged that the images of advertising, music, photojournalism (Lavoie, 2012), the arts and even cinema would all fall prey to the charms of a vintage aesthetic that is both crude and kind, with mobile apps necessarily acknowledged as blazing the historical trail (Bartholeyns, 2012). Outmoded images fit perfectly into the contemporary culture of remakes, patinas and reuse, which has taken the luxury goods and design world just as much by storm as it has average consumers (Miller, 2009), the culture industry (Reynolds, 2011), supporters of economic de-growth and lovers of second-hand objects (Gregson and Crewe, 2003). The 'structure of feeling' (Williams, 1977) and those who lamented the passing of analogue and toy cameras (Meredith, 2010) gave an indication of how successful these images might be if extensively taken up by digital technology.

The rise of a mimetic technology

An explanation given in terms of 'the spirit of the age' is never a satisfactory one. First, it is wrong to see passion for visual vintage as a generational effect. If it were, the fans of revisiting the past would be people who had lived through the relevant periods. That said, this is part of it: a new chapter to be added to the sequence of generational nostalgias that have often been described. However, when objects or trends come back into favour it is not always down to those who grew up with them and for whom they act as generational identity markers

Figure 3.1 The apps replicate the look produced by old technical processes. They reveal the materiality of photographs and how images age[3]

(Davis, 1979; Wilson, 2005). The last analogue generation may drive the market and cultivate the myth, but it is evident that most users are, in fact, digital natives. Heritage anthropology (Berliner, 2012), medievalism and dinosaurs are striking examples that prove people can feel nostalgia for situations that they have not lived through. There is a wealth of this exogenous nostalgia in today's cinema (Beumers, 2005; Cook, 2005). It is entirely possible to fantasise about 'the halcyon days' before you were born and to feel the mythologising effect of intentionally aged images. These images act in the same way for everyone because they exist in the present but bear the hallmarks of authenticity that suggest they also existed in the past: 'the tense of the mythological object is the perfect: it is that which occurs in the present as having occurred in a former time, hence that which is founded upon itself, that which is "authentic"' (Baudrillard, 1996, p. 75).

In the early 2000s, we were at a socio-technical bottleneck. Traditional digital cameras already offered black-and-white and sepia photos in the 1990s. Creative retouching software had long provided a wide choice of filters and effects. Neither of these two options, however, enabled vintage style to become widespread in amateur photography. Four events then occurred at almost the same time. First, cameras were added to the telephones people carried everywhere. This convergence altered the very status of photography. Already a part of family life and the amateur sphere, photographs became more opportunistic and even more routine: slices of life and intimate scenes, commemorative in nature and potentially nostalgic, could now be enhanced by historicising filters. Second, photography software for mobile devices was developed. Unlike computerised retouching, which takes time and skill, image processing now happens as the picture is taken, while processing at a later stage is extremely simple. Third, built-in cameras improved: their move from five million to eight million pixels in 2010 was a deciding factor in the extent to which technology would become mimetic. Finally, apps were linked to specialist and general social networks (Instagram, for example, was embedded in Facebook), leading to an unprecedented insertion of photography into the vernacular system of communication.

The triumph of the aesthetics of the imperfect is certainly due to the aspects of the prevailing atmosphere that I have pointed out above (Bartholeyns, 2012, 2013b), but it was innovations, such as the camera phone, mobile apps, high-quality digital technology and then 'sharing', that really enabled them to take off. Although technology rarely determines culture, it is quite clear that improvements in mobile phone cameras (rather than the desire to computerise old prints) were the precondition for an illusionist technology that would ultimately produce simulations of analogue photographs, which would be able to evoke the same emotional associations as the originals. Since it is deliberate and immediate, the metamorphosis of present into past has given rise to a new kind of nostalgia.

Nostalgia isn't what it used to be

Before now, nostalgia was a feeling experienced only when revisiting where we came from, looking through family photo albums or going over escapades from the past with our friends. Time always came between us and the subject of our nostalgia. Waiting was required. Time had to do its work. It was necessary to forget and then to be reminded by a search or conversation or by seeing a photograph again. Nostalgia, like nightfall, took us by surprise. This Proustian emotion would suddenly bring us close to tears, its sweetness flooding through us as we thought back to moments so distant that they seemed to have been experienced by someone else. In short, nostalgia could not be ordered on demand. Now, however, we can conjure it up and, even as we experience it at the sight of something on the street, at home or on a journey, we have the means to display it and be moved by it (Figure 3.2).

I am going to call the feeling of nostalgia deliberately brought about by a specific action 'self-induced nostalgia'. The ways in which we do this – by writing poems, going up into the attic or taking meditative walks – could be regarded as Foucauldian 'techniques of the self', or methods we use to bring aesthetic value to our lives. In this respect, photo apping is a brand new way of practising nostalgia. Davis (1979) has suggested that we talk about the 'aesthetic modalities' of nostalgia. There is an art to evoking nostalgia in music, dance or painting, to finding 'aesthetic equivalents of this form of consciousness'. Depending on the period, each artist decides on the forms and themes most likely to trigger an experience of nostalgia. The use of filters in photography is one of these aesthetic modalities. It differs from the rest, however, in that it is practised by millions of ordinary people rather than by professional artists. The current modality is far more widely shared than that of a painting or a performance. Lastly, the distinction Davis (1979, pp. 122–124) made between 'private' nostalgia and 'collective' nostalgia is even more problematic than he stated himself. This is because photographs are both personal and widely distributed. It is possible here to talk about 'biographical nostalgia'. Photos are not where collective nostalgia is located. However, the individual experience to

Figure 3.2 Little Tripping Nostalgia by Vlad Lunin, 27 December 2010[4]

which they bear witness is massively shared. An extensive investigation based on global image-storing and sharing sites Flickr.com, Picasa.com and Photobucket.com, which host a mixture of professional and candid photography, does indeed show that pictures produced by the apps we have referred to are deliberately associated with nostalgia. Certain photos are composed with the aim of conveying that feeling to the photographer or an outside observer. The connection to nostalgia is made by the users themselves when they identify pictures by titles, tags and comments, which they do to a greater extent than for traditional photos. This is confirmed by an analysis of the relatively manageable material on WeHeartIt.com (Figure 3.3), a site that allows its members to bring together media found elsewhere (on Facebook, Tumblr, or Blogspot blogs).

Of the first 2,000 images with the 'nostalgia' tag (3 May 2013), 43 percent involved the use of photo apps,[5] despite there being a more heterogeneous range of images (moments from television, old pictures, quotations) than on the larger sites already mentioned, which bring together photos taken by their members. On Flickr (a search returned 286,925 'nostalgia' tagged photos on 13 May 2013), for instance, there

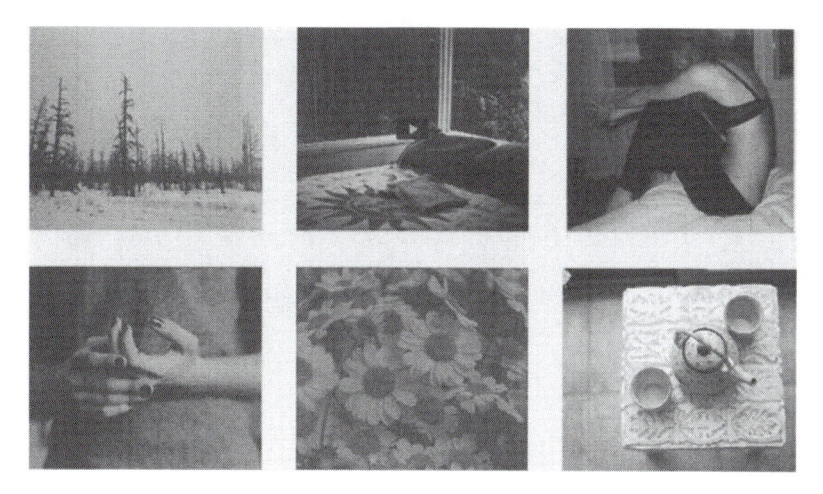

Figure 3.3 Screenshot of the list of WeHeartIt.com, 3 May 2013

are entire series with the title Nostalgia,[6] and any visitor may add nostalgia tags or leave comments. The nostalgic component of these images is usually obvious: two girls taking a photograph of themselves in a shared moment, an old tractor overgrown by weeds, someone sitting alone on the beach. Sometimes, the aesthetic component is all it takes for seemingly neutral subjects, such as an empty swing, a dish served in a restaurant, or a country cottage, to be 'nostalgised'. Their description alone may induce a feeling of nostalgia. All that is needed is a period look or an instruction on how to interpret the image. This is what I refer to as the 'nostalgiability' of the world. What normally happens first is as follows: an analogue rendering is imposed on scenes or objects with the immediate effect of making them seem older than they are, as in this 1980s-style view of Charlotte, North Carolina, taken in July 2011,[7] or this halo-effect, black-and-white view of a New York street, taken in November 2012 and entitled Leone Tribute.[8] Over and above the various practices, two major trends stand out. Either the subject matter itself prompts the use of vintage filters or the apps encourage shots of older subject matter. Let us look at both of these.

Emotion: The accelerating factor

Personal subject matter with an emotional charge linked to the passage of time or to days gone by is conducive to the use of backward-looking aesthetics. It includes holidays, visits abroad, homecomings and, a subject that is always changing, children. A sentimental snapshot of a flower on flickr.com, burnished and in close-up, triggers an autobiographical story and aptly uses and illustrates the Collins English Dictionary's definition of nostalgia:

> Nostalgia – a wistful desire to return in thought or in fact to a former time in one's life, to one's home or homeland or to one's family and friends; a sentimental yearning for the happiness of a former place or time. Because when the old people visit, I get very nostalgic for a time when we lived two miles apart. Wordy wednesday #27
> Amber Estrella, 186/365 – nostalgia, 6 July 2011[9]

The intensity of certain moments, the reason they are photographed in the first place, calls out to be conveyed in graphic form, something no traditional photo could do. Outward appearance relays the inward perception of the moment. This sensitive layer intensifies both the photographed subject and the lived moment. One person offers the following story to go with their picture of the Ala Moana Centre (Honolulu, Hawaii) taken using Instagram:

> Taken this morning on my way to work. This building was always so distinctive to me as a kid because of the spaceship-looking restaurant that sat at the top. I still remember once my mom and I ordered a soda, and sat in there until it did one full revolution. My current primary care physician has an office in here. I also got drug tested for my first post-college job in this building. I feel nostalgic looking at it.
> allysonnona, 180/i365: Ala Moana Building, 29 June 2011[10]

This type of association does not appear in classic snapshots. Old photos may also be photographed and then 'retro-ised' (Figure 3.4). A digital image can be processed, as the caption to a photo of two children playing in a garden explains: 'Cousins. Original photo taken with a Canon p & s, photo imported into iPhone 3GS and modified with the app Lo-Mob'.[11]

A boy, his satchel on his back, walks away down a street. The image is orange and highly vignetted. A mother has just taken a photo of her son going to school. It's his first day at secondary school. She looks at the photo and writes:

> Our eldest son started secondary school today. It's one of those moments when you reflect on human mortality, the much too fleeting nature of time, pride, love, loss, happiness, sadness, nostalgia... a

Figure 3.4 Covers and analogue simulations of old digital photos. Top and bottom: *Gak, halfway up Mt McKay circa the early 1980's*, 18 February 2011, by Gary A. K.; *Cousins*, 26 April 2010, by Anne H.[12]

Toy Story 3 moment...;). I would've cried proud, happy, sad, nostalgic tears had the 3 years old not decided to have a screaming tantrum at the moment No1 son left the house! Although, writing this and looking at this photo of him stepping out alone, too long trousers, baggy jumper, dwarfed by his mahooosive backpack...there is a lumpy throat and a damp eye.

Sas & Marty Taylor, Breaking free..., 10 September 2010[13]

This mum, who has seen her son setting off for school, has just photographically manufactured a memory and a moment. The aesthetic of the photo is complicit in her emotion, as is the choice of ambience. Her impression and her comments would have been different if the picture had not had the appearance of times gone by. There is, therefore, the question of what goes on when real time comes between vintage photos and the person who took them. A quick survey reveals that, after two or three years, these images give the impression that 'more' time has elapsed. It is precisely this sense of time passing, this feeling of distance, that lies at the heart of our visual nostalgia. Svetlana Boym (2001, pp. 41–55) distinguishes between 'restorative nostalgia' and 'reflective nostalgia'. Our subject here is certainly not the former, since restorative nostalgia seeks to recreate what has been lost or to return to a former situation. Nor, however, is it entirely the latter, since reflective nostalgia relates to the individual or collective feeling of a bygone age that may now be enjoyed by remembering it and appreciating its material culture. The nostalgia here is staged but it has no referent. It is not based on anything that came before. Rather, it is generated in a bid to render the present more poignant. This is achieved through the added emotional value provided by a temporal distance that is made visible by a dated aesthetic and by passing off photographs as older than they are. The mother experiences nostalgia not at seeing her son go off to school but at seeing the photo of her son going off to school. This really is a self-induced nostalgia and even, to some extent, a tautological one.

Time regained and the nostalgia market

Pin-up posters, old cars, obsolete instruments. Apps encourage photographs of the out-of-date objects and old-fashioned decors that people have at home or encounter in the outside world (Figure 3.5).

The WeHeartIt.com sample discussed above reveals that old or old-fashioned things constitute the subject matter of half the vintage images

Figure 3.5 To photograph ancient artefacts and environments, to disclose their historicity. Top and bottom: *Coastal drive*, 10 October 2012; *The Allure. Vintage photo booth vendor at the San Bernardino County Fair*, 5 May 2011[14]

with a 'nostalgia' tag: a train, a typewriter, a tea set, a clock, etc. These objects, such as a Volkswagen Van or a little cottage in the woods, conjure up an alternative, premodern or bohemian lifestyle. There are two prime reasons why people hang on to things. The first is design, which is a major time marker because it often changes so rapidly. The second – judging by the impressive amount of old-style telephones, record players, rolls of film, old photos and even silver-process cameras displayed together in photographs – is technology. The still life with a predilection for *mise-en-abyme* is making a surprise comeback.

When enveloped in a dated aesthetic, objects and settings appear to have been reinstated to their respective periods. These periods are usually a generic 'past time', although it does seem that there are attempts to give subjects the 'colour' appropriate to their periods (Figure 3.6). The car and even the moped photographed on 5 January 2011 (second picture of Figure 3.6) are emblematic of a given period and have the texture the image would now have acquired had it been taken at that time.

More than anything else, the aim is to bring back the atmosphere created by the thing seen. The flash of nostalgia may be caused by the object itself, and, indeed, this is often what triggers the reflex to take a vintage photo, but what the vintage visual achieves is the expansion of a given object's nostalgic range with the image as its focal point. Apps are marketed on the basis of three selling points, in addition to the existence of the picture-sharing community. These are nostalgia, personalisation and their status as analogue artefacts. This can be seen in the way these apps are described: 'Instant Nostalgia now free' (Retro Camera), 'Find out how your photos would look like if you took them decades ago' (Old Photo Pro), 'The Hipstamatic brings back the look, feel, unpredictable beauty [...] of cameras of the past'. This latter web publisher is a good example. Its promotional website, wiki.hipstamatic.com, presents cases, films and flashes as if they had physical existence, and their names (Ina's 35 or 69, etc.) speak volumes. The parent company, Synthetic, hooked up with Nike to offer a 'hipstapak' with the slogan 'Past meets present meets you' (Figure 3.7).

This publisher has also provided a story of the product's origins. The story is told by Richard, older brother to the two main characters, on the history.hipstamatic.com blog. In 1980s Wisconsin, the Dorbowski brothers, inspired by a Russian plastic camera, had put their own version into production when they were killed by a drunk driver. The app was created as a tribute to them. Symbol creators, to use David Hesmondhalgh's term, leave nothing to chance. The triangle

Figure 3.6 Restoring the visual aesthetics of their time to things. Top and bottom: *Got the deck hooked up*, 10 July 2011, by John Common; *Nostalgia in Snow*, 5 January 2011, by Tanja Taube[15]

64 *Analogue Nostalgias*

Figure 3.7 The virtual materiality of cameras and films. 'Past meets present meets you'[16]

of engagement – reason, appeal, spirituality – is an equilateral one. In actual fact, the marketing strategy merely dramatises our normal relationship with photography in general. Indeed, all these apps reiterate the 'nature' of what is photographed. From its inception, photography has been experienced and used as a melancholy medium, preserving what is in the process of disappearing. 'The photographer', Susan Sontag wrote (1979, p. 67), 'is not simply the person who records the past but the one who invents it.' Every photo transforms its current subject into a touching antiquity. Sontag's remarks about classic photography in the chapter 'Melancholy Objects' (1979) are still very much pertinent today, and apply even more here: 'in addition to romanticism (extreme or not) about the past, photography offers instant romanticism about the present'.

Expressivism, pictorialisation, and the past as an aesthetic experience

Whether applied to old objects or to scenes of daily life, the goal of imposing a backward-looking aesthetic is to provide a visual sensation of the atmosphere attached to the photographed object or moment. From iPhonographers' blogs and forums, it is clear that apps enable a certain something about the moment to be expressed, its resonance conveyed: the 'weeping' street of heartbreak, the 'pastel' landscape of melancholy. The general function of photo apps for phones is to reproduce the context that has been felt. Pic Grunger, for example, offers a wide range of patinas (e.g. aged, cracked, creased, scuffed), while the official site, Saspring.com/picGrunger, shows 'war-torn' photos of concerts and parties. This expressivism brings photo apping closer to the pictorialism of the end of the nineteenth century, the romanticism and anti-modernism of which have been stressed on many occasions. Photographers set about using all the arts of retouching to simulate that certain something, that aura, which photographs lost with the arrival of high-quality lenses (Benjamin, 1999, p. 517).

Representation is imbued with a degree of iconicity. The transparent representation of things becomes an image (Bartholeyns, 2013b). Photography is no longer a medium intended to record the real. The image is no longer secondary to reality. The subject matter can no longer be detached from its image. We no longer pass through the image; we see it; it is present. Contemporary artists have similarly put image before representation, working on and with time (Bartholeyns, 2012) – damaging their photographs (Deborah Turbeville), rescuing neglected old prints and negatives (Joachim Schmid, Figure 3.8) and using techniques from the past (McDermott and McGough).

The emotion no longer comes primarily from immediate access to the 'that-has-been', the classic, Barthesian modality for the photographic emotion. It stems, instead, from the visual contamination of the subject photographed. Nostalgia used to depend on the denial of access to the subject, on its unreachable presence. Now, there is an effective formula to encourage nostalgia. The cult of the referent is being replaced by the cult of the reference, reference to an iconography that, in its form, is typical of memory. The indexical nature of photography is giving way to the power of fantasy (Bartholeyns, 2013b).

What is it that we are doing, exactly, when we take a picture of a scene as if it were not here and now but, rather, some time ago? The answer could be that we are making the present – or the moment that has

66 *Analogue Nostalgias*

Figure 3.8 Between the subject matter and ourselves: the 'image'. Arcana 1996/2008, Cambridge, March 1992 by Joachim Schmid[17]

just gone by – omnipresent, thus presenting further proof for Hartog's theory of 'presentism' (Hartog, 2003). This would be wrong, however (Bartholeyns, 2012). First, a liking for artificial patinas is nothing new (see, for example, Charpy, 2012), even though today's relationship with the past is very different from what it was (Bartholeyns, 2013c). Indeed, from the point of view of experience, it is quite the opposite: it is no longer the past that is injected into the present but the present that is projected back into the past. The contemporary is being destroyed for the sake of a more intimate, less impersonal perception. Similarly, when an outmoded object is photographed with an aesthetic from a time when it was not out of date, the historicity of things is revealed and anachronism created in the present (Bartholeyns, 2013a, pp. 125–130). Nostalgia is a time-induced melancholy. Logically, it 'operates' through the signs of the times. It also teaches the reverse, that the past is an aesthetic category in its own right, far removed from history (Bartholeyns, 2010).

What nostalgia does to the present

Although there are problems in seeing nostalgic imagery as a way of immediately enjoying the memory of something that has only just happened, we might nevertheless wonder (without entering into a societal analysis) what anxiety this imagery is a symptom of, or, to put it less clinically, what the effect might be of this kind of photography on temporality. It makes it possible to appropriate present time, to be the contemporary of our own emotions. This fact, which practitioners discuss among themselves, chimes with thinking about the modern experience of time (Flaherty, 2010). On the basis of research into the subjective perception of time, Hartmut Rosa (2010) explains that a time rich in experiences goes very quickly but gives the impression of having been incredibly long, whereas successive and passive activities have the opposite qualities. Indeed, it is this latter type of activity that is characteristic of life today: our daily routine consists mainly of isolated activities – working, shopping, looking after children, watching television – which leave few 'memory traces' because they are isolated, de-contextualised, not connected to one another in any significant way. This is the opposite of times full of 'lived experiences' (the *Erfahrungen* Walter Benjamin contrasted with *Erlebnissen*, episodes of experience).

The backward-looking aesthetic appears to be a way of cordoning off the time we find so hard to inhabit, of playing with how it is ordered and perceived and of mounting a defence against the feeling that time passes quickly, leaving no trace. The outcome, the feeling of nostalgia, connects the present to the past. Above all, it puts the present at the forefront of existential depth. There is a paradox in wanting to isolate the present by making it pass more quickly, but such is the law: everything that is transformed into the past and rendered tangible as such will be saved from the void.

Notes

1. To gain an understanding of this new photography, the reader is asked to visit the following websites: www.ippawards.com, www.iphoneographie.

com, or individuals' photostreams, for example www.flickr.com/photos/32368901@N02/page2/ or www.flickr.com/photos/bluemoonrabbit/
2. For convenience, I do not follow the useful distinction Reynolds (2011) makes between 'vintage' (real objects from the past) and 'retro' (which simulates a past style).
3. Top and bottom: *Memories of San Clemente Pier – Hipstamatic & Pic Grunger*, 29 March 2010; *Dragonfly – AE TTV Desaturated*, 21 March 2010; *Window Rock, Arizona – News Emulsion*, using Lo-Mob, 21 March 2010, by Jeffery Turner (CC = Creatives Commons).
4. Screenshot of flickr.com/photos/vrevolution/5298548170/ (Courtesy of the Author).
5. A small margin of error must be taken into account because some images are ambiguous. With some exceptions, I have not retained these. All Internet links quoted were checked in May 2013.
6. Most of our examples are from Flickr because the URLs are relatively short.
7. flickr.com/photos/danielstaten/5898880409/
8. flickr.com/photos/vinzo/5149324192/
9. flickr.com/photos/westars3/5983832356
10. flickr.com/photos/ahinpgh/4554977604/in/photostream/
11. flickr.com/photos/ahinpgh/4554977604/in/photostream/
12. flickr.com/photos/gak/5496550888/in/photosof-gak/ and flickr.com/photos/ahinpgh/4554977604/in/photostream/ (CC BY-NC-SA 2.0).
13. flickr.com/photos/dacheeses/4977847410/in/set-72157624879220569
14. Images by Notorious JES (CC BY-NC-ND 2.0).
15. With courtesy of the authors, photos taken in 2011.
16. Screenshot of 30 June 2011 editorial at www.nike.com/be/en_gb/
17. On paper, 35×39 cm, print was made from found negative, http://schmid.wordpress.com/works/1996-arcana/ (Courtesy of the Author).

References

Bartholeyns, G. (2010) 'Le passé sans l'histoire. Vers une anthropologie culturelle du temps'. *Itinéraires. Littérature, textes, cultures*, 3, pp. 47–60.
Bartholeyns, G. (2012) 'L'iPhonographie: la machine à fabriquer le temps'. *Culture Visuelle*, http://culturevisuelle.org/blog/10514 (accessed 9 July 2013).
Bartholeyns, G. (2013a) 'Voir le passé: histoire et cultures visuelles', in C. Granger (ed.) *A quoi pensent les historiens? Faire de l'histoire au XXIe siècle*. Paris: Autrement, pp. 118–134.
Bartholeyns, G. (2013b) 'Le retour de l'image: iPhonographie et esthétique du passé', in D. Dubuisson and S. Raux (eds) *A perte de vue. Les nouveaux paradigmes du visual*. Dijon: Les Presses du réel, forthcoming.
Bartholeyns, G. (2013c) 'Loin de l'Histoire'. *Le Débat*, 177(5), pp. 117–125.
Baudrillard, J. (1996 [1968]) *The System of Objects*. London and New York: Verso.
Benjamin, W. (1999 [1931]) *Little History of Photography*. Selected Writings vol. 2. Cambridge: Harvard University Press.
Berliner, D. (2012) 'Multiple nostalgias: The fabric of heritage in Luang Prabang (Lao PDR)'. *JRAI*, 18(4), pp. 769–786.
Beumers, B. (2005) *Nikita Mikhalkov. Between Nostalgia and Nationalism*. London-New York: I.B. Tauris.

Boym, S. (2001) *The Future of Nostalgia*. New York: Basic Books.

Charpy, M. (2012) 'Patina and the Bourgeoisie: The Appearance of the Past in Nineteenth-Century Paris', in V. Kelley and G. Adamson (eds) *Surface Tensions. Surface, Finish and the Meanings of Objects*. Manchester: Manchester University Press, pp. 49–59.

Cook, P. (2005) *Screening the Past. Memory and Nostalgia in Cinema*. London-New York: Routledge.

Davis, F. (1979) *Yearning for Yesterday: A Sociology of Nostalgia*. New York: The Free Press.

Flaherty, M. G. (2010) *The Textures of Time: Agency and Temporal Experience*. Philadelphia: Temple University Press.

Gregson, N. and Crewe, L. (2003) *Second-Hand Cultures*. Oxford: Berg.

Hartog, F. (2003) *Régimes d'historicité. Présentisme et expériences du temps*. Paris: Seuil.

Lavoie, V. (2012) 'War and the iPhone: New Fronts for Photojournalism'. *Etudes Photographiques*, 29, pp. 204–241.

Meredith, K. (2010) 'Toy Cameras, Creative Photos: High-end Results from 40 Plastic Cameras, Rotovision'. http://lomokev.com/books/toy-cameras-fantastic-plastic-cameras/ (accessed 2 July 2013).

Miller, D. (2009) 'Buying Time', in E. Shove, F. Trentmann and R. Wilk (eds) *Time, Consumption and Everyday Life: Practice, Materiality and Culture*. Oxford: Berg, pp. 157–169.

Reynolds, S. (2011) *Retromania: Pop Culture's Addiction to Its Own Past*. London-New York: Faber & Faber.

Rosa, H. (2010) *Alienation and Acceleration: Towards a Critical Theory of Late-Modern Temporality*. Malmo: NSU Press.

Sontag, S. (1979) *On Photography*. London: Penguin Books.

Williams, R. (1977) *Marxism and Literature*. Oxford: Oxford University Press.

Wilson, J. L. (2005) *Nostalgia: Sanctuary of Meaning*. Lewisburg, PA: Bucknell University Press.

4
Retromania: Crisis of the Progressive Ideal and Pop Music Spectrality

Maël Guesdon and Philippe Le Guern

Whether in music production (through the widespread use of sampling, mashup and cut-up techniques, through vintage sounds and instruments or the lo-fi design), in listening habits, in institutional frameworks established for pop culture (commemorative events, its integration into museums, etc), in behaviours and fashion styles (the increasing number of 'retro' movements), in visual as well as symbolic spheres, pop always refers to its history and increasingly relies on it. With a past being reinvented, remixed, idealised or made ever 'kitscher', bygone days have become the raw material for novelty. Sound ghosts – whose presence simultaneously follows an aesthetic, existential, social and commercial logic – increasingly invade the present and make their mark across styles in the way of a memory kaleidoscope whose spectres, like samples of samples, keep multiplying exponentially.

Several factors immediately come to mind to explain this trend. From a historical point of view, first, today's pop has to deal with its own heritage, which is, by definition, becoming more and more significant. From an aesthetic point of view, past references relating to the glory of bygone eras provide plenty of material which can be made easily available and can potentially reach an already familiarised audience. From a technological point of view, the growing number of hardware or software solutions allowing the capture and remastering of sound fragments, as well as audio filters digitally recreating the sound of instruments or old amps, facilitates the reproduction of a sound marker calling to mind a specific era or style.

However, the stakes are especially high from a commercial point of view: how can we recover and make profit out of an inherent nostalgic trend within pop which, as we shall see later, parodies itself in a meta-discursive mode? While avoiding the anxiety-inducing consequence much dreaded by the capitalist mass media, how can one reinvest the emotion experienced when listening or replaying some music that accompanies our own recollection and makes it nostalgic; an emotion that progressively meddles with the affects that we carry and that make us who we are? How can we use, in essence, the psychological effect created by repetition, which, by bringing back a sensitive marker of the past each time, makes it possible to experience again always in a new way a specific emotional state and to simultaneously understand the temporal belonging, the distance and the modulations of such a state?

The 'capital-intensive motive' turns the nostalgic spiral into a selling point and develops on an industrial level the trend described by Simon Reynolds (2011) as 'retromaniac' by inventing and spreading the idea of an irreparably lost 'golden age of pop', evident today only through its echoes. Being constantly adapted, the fragmented availability of a staged lack gives the listener, through fundamental dissatisfaction, a renewed delight when experiencing backward-looking occurrences (from retro sound to remixed compilation albums, numerous reunions or even holograms bringing back to the stage the bodies and voices of missing stars). This is, therefore, the constant objective for rethinking ways of promoting pop culture and streamlining tastes related to it: to stage authenticity in order to guarantee for the consumer that he will retain a glimmer of what time cannot give him.

Hits, obsession, recollection

Pop culture can be defined as the art of making hits, which means being able to worm one's way into the listener's mind in the way of what Peter Szendy, quoting James Kellaris, describes as 'earworms' (2008, p. 11). As a musical tune or fragment which can insidiously and obsessively impose itself, like a foreign body, into the listener, the 'earworm' acts as a virus clinging to the memories of its host. This common tune instantly connects to the intimate past and invokes haunting memories, perceptions and thoughts. It leaves a trivial yet singular mark – different for each listener – on our most intimate affects as well as a generic element, from one replay to another, and a specific way for this element to live in our minds without belonging to us.

From this perspective, notwithstanding that several publications have attempted to chart the rational dimensions of song reception and the production of hits (Hennion, 1981; Boyd, 2008), the way this contaminating power works never ceases to amaze. On the one hand, the hit is always 'already known' and yet produces something new by mixing triviality and singularity; an original *déjà vu* (or *déjà entendu*, already-heard) entity. On the other hand, we surprise ourselves by liking hits, notwithstanding any aesthetic judgement, following the logic of 'bad music' described by Proust in *Les plaisirs et les jours* as 'the one which does not require any artistic legitimacy to come and remain inside us' (1971, pp. 121–122). As emphasised by 'the obsessive or rather haunting melody' phenomenon addressed by Peter Szendy (2008, p. 44), following psychoanalyst Reik (1960), the hit in itself has a particular relation to the past. Having been recently promoted as an object of research (Szendy, 2008; Poncet, 2012), it highlights the socio-historical or socio-economic conditions of the machinery for generating success, and, more importantly, it is an attempt to understand, in an approach similar to the phenomenological, what is at the heart of pop lovers' experience in which nostalgia has a central or even determinant place. This feature is based on several phenomena. As Simon Reynolds points out, following Fred Davis, the mass-media culture has progressively replaced the big political events that used to be the chain and framework for generational memory (Reynolds, 2011). Based on the power of media dissemination, hits also use the (musical as much as commercial) efficiency of nostalgia by drawing on the load of archived documents made increasingly abundant and easily accessible via the Internet. The record and the radio have sharply transformed our experience of listening to music by integrating it into the intimate sphere and implying a potentially infinite reiteration in our relation to artists' oeuvres. Moreover, as ethno-psychiatrist Tobie Nathan (2012) argues, the human brain is the opposite of a video camera or a tape recorder. It does not see; it imagines. It does not listen; it remembers. Machines record the present; our brain projects itself into the future or dwells on the past. Our hit experience fits into this particular temporality. Listening always takes place in a certain context. As part of a network of personal and collective events, the hit is at the same time broadcast via mass media and perceived on an intimate level through imaginary projections and reflective cycles. As a promise of something original and known, the hit, therefore, implies the return of a bygone age which, as a new sound, fitted into its present as the future and represents the past for the future (our present). The spectral trait of the hit is the echo of such a phantasmal promise, its soon-to-be-lost contemporaneousness.

The emotion related to listening to a hit, listening in the sensitised state and through inner repetition, is composed of affects linked to occurrences of perception. Following the first listening and the replay, an inner melody is created and changes according to successive encounters of the song; it is marked by experienced events while keeping track of the very first listening occurrence. By encompassing both the memory of the discovery and the variations (depending on contexts, emotions) created by each repetition, the hit has a specific power of recollection. For each of these occurrences, it creates an echo of a past sensitive state while emphasising the growing distance of this state. In such a nostalgic tension, our emotional variations then become perceivable, and, in our relation to hits, 'haunting melodies', 'earworms' or any other case of *spectrality* or *obsession* become a faint experience of the hungry past self. In this regard, Svetlana Boym speaks, as quoted by Reynolds, about 'nostalgia of a pre-nostalgic state' (2011, p. 27), which explains why, for so many hits, the songs relate, in a meta-discursive mode, to their own relation to nostalgia.

From an aesthetic and anthropological perspective, the hit and our backward-looking relation to it can be seen as the symptom of a broader phenomenon. The relation of pop culture to its own past (quoted, staged, parodied) leads to a new question regarding the generalisation of retro culture as the prevailing modality of our contemporary relation to culture and music. It raises the question of whether pop culture, through its nostalgic nature driving itself to always use more of its own references, has progressively become an aesthetic movement doomed to depletion. This was underlined in *Retromania* by Reynolds, who, by highlighting the numerous phenomena of nostalgic self-celebrations, condemns pop cannibalisation by pop culture itself and emphatically criticises this nostalgic trend. While every decade used to be defined by a prevailing sound or musical genre, Reynolds considers that the most recent age is one of homage and quote, which is more dominated by a logic of cultural industry than by one of creativity or innovation. From Amy Winehouse and her suggestive album title 'Back to Black' to Oasis mimicking the Beatles, numerous groups or artists borrow the sound signature of earlier eras. The omnipresent retromaniac position would, therefore, be expressed in a symptomatic way through various backward-looking forms: vintage aesthetics and the authenticity requirement, the coming back of vinyls, the fetish-worship of the object and of the ideal sound, old bands reunited or new successful tribute bands (for example, Abba Mania, The Australian Pink Floyd), the coming of posthumous albums to the market, the creation of new critical (retro-futurism, hauntology) or aesthetic categories (hypnagogic movement).

From lost authenticity to the commercialisation of nostalgia, a critical history of pop culture

The epistemology of rock history has led to a number of critical readings targeting the trend to subsume the explanatory factors – economic and social factors, which are well portrayed by Richard A. Peterson, for example – into interpretations which place a major emphasis on exceptional creators (Elvis Presley or Chuck Berry). These critics call into question the trend to idealise rock through a simplistic ontological reading which would turn it, in essence, into a power disintegrating social conservatisms and consequently into a vector encouraging the renewal of democratic aspirations. On the contrary, they maintain that rock has been presented for a long time as a mythologised narrative only, which is economically rationalised and carefully sustained by 'original' values related to authenticity, purity and independence, where the use of nostalgia, linked to the idea of a now lost 'fundamental purity', makes its mark as an inevitable component of delight for the listener-consumer. As Simon Frith recalls, the industry cynically exploits the use of anti-commercial pictures to guarantee 'the authenticity' of products they help sell, such as the use of the Beatles's Revolution song for an advert. Sooner or later we have to face the question of why 'we actually believe that rock was a real movement in the past, [why] our desires could then be unequivocal' (Frith, 1991). Should we, therefore, deduce that rock's ideal was stillborn while the knell of recycling was ringing, and any progressive perspective is an illusion? In his analysis of 'popular' music, particularly addressing the case of 'progressive rock', Frith first points out that the very idea of progress, as regards pop culture, is problematic. Indeed, if pop culture (as an art of appearance holding depth in the apparent absence of depth) envisages the concept of creation as one free from the authenticity myth, it provides few direct arguments for any progressive-like discourse. Moreover, Frith takes a greater interest in the various outlines of pop representation in their historical dimension. In this regard, he depicts five conceptions for this history. The first one (*business model*) grants a central place to technologies as means of achieving progress. Each new recording technique is sold and generally considered as better than the previous one, and to pretend otherwise (to like records better than CDs or mp3s, in my case) seems eccentric (Frith, 2001). Yet, no matter what the reasons are (a marketing campaign targeting former generations wanting to revive their vinyl-populated past or young people looking for historical references and fundamentals), the record and the nostalgia created by the object in a context of dematerialisation and disappearance of physical artefacts seem to actually imply a sound ideal against mp3 and compression for some music lovers nowadays. The second (musicological) conception sees the genre at the centre of the analysis. It seems here that, although genres go through unavoidable development cycles, the self-parodist entropy announcing the end of their lifetime, one cannot easily speak of progress when a genre subsumes another one. Likewise, it seems difficult to consider the 'musicological' paradigm as described by Frith as an 'achievement'. Indeed, musical emotion is often associated with the sense of a bygone past, but a past which is seen as better. The 'historical' paradigm actually goes in the same direction. It underlines the tendency to consider that creative talent and the artist's ability to innovate (Dylan, the Rolling Stones) do not improve with time but, if anything, deteriorate. Finally, the 'art history' paradigm indicates that the 'tradition/innovation' dialectic regarding pop culture is highly asymmetrical. According to Frith, new bands are generally praised more for their ability to go back to the essence of rock 'n' roll than for their aptitude to break free and introduce radically innovative styles.

Thus, following Frith, the question is not whether an original track played on an old acoustic guitar and recorded in a studio in Mississippi is worse or better than its electro-remixed modern version. What matters is to understand the various examples of limited cases one encounters when trying to link the idea of progress to rock. As an example, the fact that CDs or mp3s did not manage to definitely dethrone records, and the fact that the latter are even being used again, are symptoms of our fetishist relation to artefacts. For a large number of users, this relation expresses a technique ideal related to the representation of an era or sound. On a marketing level, the 'vintage' label works today as an efficient sign of authenticity. From the serial production of guitars with finish scratches to artificial rusty mikes, the search for real-life experience artificially marks instruments themselves. By staging the authenticity sustaining the illusion of a historical depth, this industrial manufacturing of peculiarity here again sounds like a call to the past in which the *guitar-hero* myth was symbolised by the blood, sweat and tears carved into the wood of the instrument itself.

Sampling, or its impossible coming back

As Richard Shusterman rightly suggested, one of the most remarkable impacts of digital technology is the possibility to create original sound manipulations. The sampler in particular, by allowing the sampling of fragments extracted from songs and inserted into original compositions, made it possible to create new aesthetics. While pop artists asserted themselves through hit art and rock artists placed more emphasis on mastering their electro-amplified instruments and their sonic potential, sample users or electro artists display their knowledge as real music archivists working more on meta-text than on text itself. In this sense, the sampler can be defined as a time-travelling machine scratching the layers of sound sediments. While the sampling technique is based on the capacity to excavate the past, it also exposes our way of telling stories and producing sound narratives and shows our relation to time. The culture of the mix and sampling confuse art history as a normative structure based on the accumulation of progress. As a self-referencing art, the sampler disassembles the subject–artist unity (embodied in pop music by the star) as well as the linearity ideal which belongs to a strictly chronological conception of evolution. The constant quest for new music references to quote certainly implies an acute sense of archiving and indexing. In this way, the sampler asserts itself as the modern form of a sophisticated sound archival science where one can easily encounter Mahler and Robert Johnson in one and the same hybrid form. However, with musical fragments not necessarily following a chronological order, connection being established through sound textures, rhythm interweaving or genre confrontation, the sample culture can legitimately be described as 'hauntological', following Fisher's and Reynolds's formula, which is a type of spectral anthology using the past within the present. Combined with the Internet, it seems to produce a post-historical and post-geographical register that arouses curiosity about the way technology redetermines our sense of time and space. It then leads to what Kirby calls 'digimodernism' (2009): a combination of post-modern hybridism based on collages and reconfigured space–time. This combination is such that the very idea of context sometimes disappears in the flow (the referent of the dated album, for example) and one ends up confused as to which direction Radiohead's evolution took, for instance (did it go from a grunge-influenced pop rock in the first albums to an Intelligence Dance Music-like electro pop in the second part of their work, or the opposite?), or as to who was first and inspired the other, Oasis or the Beatles.

An example of nostalgic aesthetics: The case of the hypnagogic trend

The hypnagogic trend, represented by artists like James Ferraro and Spencer Clarke (The Skaters) or Ariel Pink, belongs to the growing propensity to retro-futurism in contemporary pop. The Skaters described such aesthetics as the 'after-image' of subliminal influences inspired by the soundtrack of their early youth (credits of 1980s TV programmes, for example), heard from one's bed in a deadened and distorted way, half asleep, through the partition wall separating the bedroom from the living room. Used and conceptualised by David Keenan in August 2009 in *The Wire*, the term 'hypnagogic' can be seen as one avatar of post-modernism. It reactivates, almost ironically, cultural references from the past, including from TV or radio culture. As regards aesthetic theory, the hypnagogic trend's originality does not lie in its capacity to identically reproduce past references, as is the case with revival music, but in its ability to graft together scraps of a bygone popular culture to turn it into a hybrid type which is both modernist and backward-looking. Keenan (2009), then, defines the hypnagogic trend as pop music refracted in the memory of one's memory: a movement whose visual aesthetics (blurred black-and-white photocopies of photocopies, colour photos recalling the kitsch style of the 1980s) most certainly intensify the sound claim underlined. We can describe hypnagogic aesthetics as revisionist nostalgia, not in the sense that 'everything used to be better' but because it rewrites collective memory with a view to being more faithful to an idea or to the memory of an original than to the original itself. Some songs created by the Skaters sound suspiciously like soundtracks of typical films from the 1980s which, nonetheless, never existed. These tracks create new entities, hybrid memorial beings that are larger than nature.

Nevertheless, Keenan's conceptualisation of hypnagogia triggered a number of questions, precisely challenging the status of nostalgia in avant-gardist pop. As an example, an enlightened fan, who is convinced that Ferraro's music gives the past a more hallucinatory look than a truly nostalgic one, indicates that Ferraro himself challenged Keenan's interpretation (Wordpress, 2013). This review shows that the idea of nostalgia has become a convenient topic to refer to any attempt at revisiting the past through music, although the emotional load of nostalgia often does not correspond to the spirit of such repertoires. From an analysis of the way an aesthetic theory is produced to a complex description of formal elements giving shape to Ferraro's protean work, the review starts with the observation that the 'Memory Theater' song, for example, is based on a simplistic harmonic resolution. Its cadence is interrupted at regular intervals to play the initial C chord (hence the construction is regular in its irregularity). This seemingly elementary music progressively produces sound fragments which add up and juxtapose against each other, but, since their frequencies are poor, it is difficult to distinguish one from another. As the commenter argues, the song is 'holographic' (as used by Brian Eno) insofar as it is aimed at the subconscious rather than at an analytical level. To these formal descriptions could be added a whole series of complementary observations regarding the technology and techniques used which associate this music genre with the Low-Fi trend and value what are generally considered as crippling defects, such as background noise, crackling, radio static, and so on. With its hypnotic repetitive effects and its strong taste for obsolete technology, the hypnagogic movement can be seen as an aesthetic response to the growing feeling that time is speeding up: a feeling that often proves to be one of the fundamental components of advanced modernity. While digital technology gives rise to a paradoxical view of the preservation of repertoires and their obsolescence and deeply modifies our sense of history in this perspective, the hauntological movement maintains that the cultural content should not be trivialised. Far from simply gathering interchangeable signs in the manner of postmodern pastiche aesthetics, it gathers carefully selected and recontextualised objects for their emotional power.

Founded on repetition (the intrinsic repetition of the concept of song, the characteristic repetition of mass-media means of conveyance and the cyclical processes of inner reflection), pop music releases a nostalgia linked to our intimate relation to time which shapes us and escapes us at the same time. In pop's evanescence as art of appearance, in the *obsession* of tunes, but also in the technical recording system (which, as shown by Jacques Derrida, immediately doubles up the presence of the speaker, who becomes a potential spectator of himself) the progression of time, its recollection and omission raise awareness of the tension existing between 'vanishing' and 'return' as a definition of nostalgia. It also opens the possibility of dramatising the presence – the insistence – in ourselves of an emotional past being replenished with new projections.

This relation to spectrality characteristic of the recording system, residing, as Derrida argues, in the 'track which marks in advance the present with its absence' (Derrida and Stiegler, 1997, p. 131) currently follows various continuations. While it musically translates into hauntological technologies such as sampling and cut-up techniques, for instance, this relation is also at the heart of original forms of staging when we look at holograms: a form staging the coming back of a missing track related to the body and voice of a star. Holograms double up the effect of spectrality peculiar to visual and sound capture, since they reconstruct in three dimensions a picture of the absent referent. The holographic picture itself can then be captured as well, thus showing the trend of the spectrality to reproduce itself. At the heart of pop culture, this doubling up, be it memorial, technological, generational or stylistic, which comes from the same tension, ends up in one of two opposing tendencies. The first tends to turn the interference effect caused by the absence of a referent and the vanishing of the origin into a backward-looking renewal of a lost ideal (which finds its strength precisely in the fact that it is not accessible). The second, however, uses the characteristic ambiguity of the musical, social, historical and technological presence of pop as a powerful inventive tool, turning nostalgia into a creative material. Between the logic of the rock icon, in which a mythology of historicity operates for commercial purposes, and the logic of creativity, which looks for potential in the openness created by the gaps of repetition and vanishing of the original, two antagonistic approaches are developed; they carry the same component, and are both conceptions that reflect the ambivalence of nostalgia itself.

Translated from French into English by Sandie Zanolin.

References

Boyd, J. (2008) *White Bicycles: Making Music in the 1960s*. London: Serpent's Tail.
Derrida, J. (1995) *Mal d'archive*. Paris: Galilée.
Derrida, J. and Stiegler, B. (1997) *Échographies de la télévision: entretiens filmés*. Paris: Galilée.
Frith, S. (1991) 'Souvenirs, Souvenirs...', in P. Mignon and A. Hennion (eds) *Rock, de l'histoire au mythe*. Paris: Anthropos, Coll. Vibrations, pp. 247–262.
Frith, S. (2001) 'Pop Music', in S. Frith, W. Straw and J. Street (eds) *The Cambridge Companion to Pop and Rock*. Cambridge: Cambridge University Press, pp. 94–108.
Hennion, A. (1981) *Les professionnels du disque. Une sociologie des varietes*. Paris: Métailié.
Keenan, D. (2009) 'Hypnagogic Pop'. *The Wire*, vol. 306, pp. 26–31.
Kirby, A. (2009) *Digimodernism: How New Technologies Dismantle the Postmodern and Reconfigure Our Culture*. New York: Continuum.
Nathan, T. (2012) *Les tubes, ces diables de musiques*. http://tobienathan.wordpress.com/2012/06/13/les-tubes-ces-diables-de-musiques/ (accessed 17 June 2013).
Poncet, E. (2012) *Éloge des tubes, de Maurice Ravel à David Guetta*. Paris: Nil.
Proust, M. (1971) *Jean Santeuil*. Paris: Gallimard.

Reik, T. (1960) *The Haunting Melody. Psychoanalytic Experiences in Life and Music.* New York: Grove Press.

Reynolds, S. (2011) *Retromania. Pop Culture's Addiction to Its Own Past.* London: Faber and Faber.

Szendy, P. (2008) *Tubes. La philosophie dans le juke-box.* Paris: les Éditions de Minuit.

Wordpress. (2013) http://decemberembers.wordpress.com/2012/03/18/liminal-reinventions-hypnagogia-in-the-music-of-james-ferraro-and-grouper/ (accessed 5 May 2013).

Part II
Exploited Nostalgias

5
Retrotyping and the Marketing of Nostalgia

Michael Pickering and Emily Keightley

Nostalgia is a multifarious phenomenon. Although it is always in some manner a response to social and cultural change, and particularly to the increasing divergence between experience and expectation that has developed in the modern and late-modern periods, it becomes manifest in a wide range of forms, with the feelings, meanings and values associated with it being dependent on specific social and historical contexts. We have sketched out the general scope of these different kinds of nostalgia elsewhere, stressing the importance of distinguishing between them and showing how nostalgia may develop and be deployed as a source of creative renewal or critique of changed conditions within the present (Keightley and Pickering, 2012, chapters 4 and 5). In this chapter we want to move in an alternative direction to the reflexive applications of nostalgia and discuss what is involved in its commercial exploitation. While this is part of a broader commodification of the past, which any extended treatment would have to account for, we shall take just one specific example of it here in order to show, in close detail, precisely how nostalgic feelings and values can be manipulated for quite different ends and under quite different conditions from those which give rise to them in the first place. In identifying and understanding the precise mechanisms by which nostalgia is commercially exploited, we hope that this will help us, within the field of memory studies, to refine our use of nostalgia as a conceptual and analytical category.

The example is directly aligned with Britain's favourite television advert. Known as the 'Boy on Bike' advert, this was made by Ridley Scott in the early 1970s before he became famous as a film director. Although the most famous, it is one element in a long series of advertising campaigns conducted over the past 40 years or so by Hovis, the bread manufacturer owned by Premier Foods, one of Britain's largest food manufacturers and owner of various household brands. The adverts

84 *Exploited Nostalgias*

used in these campaigns share a number of characteristic features, which all contribute in one way or another to the regressive nostalgia in which and by which they trade. By 'regressive nostalgia' we are referring to those forms of nostalgia which, through a limited set of idealised images of the past, appeal only to the component of backwards longing in nostalgia, and conceal or deny the loss and painful sense of lack which elsewhere are its other two components. In this way it inhibits, and maybe even prevents, effective cross-temporal movement and the active use of the past in a progressive manner within the present.[1] We shall identify these features of regressive nostalgia in the particular advert we focus on in the chapter. It derives from 1993, and shows a family gathered around their dining table for Sunday tea (Figure 5.1).

Figure 5.1 Hovis print ad from 1993: 'Sunday Best'

The advert was accompanied by the following script:

> I've a theory. The older we get, the more we relive childhood. Myself, I love to recall those old memories...

Walking back from church, with the smell of fresh
   baked bread to guide us home.
Father switching on ITMA on the wireless, mother
   fussing out her best teapot.
Toasting bread over the coals on a long fork – that was my job.
There was a real art to getting it evenly brown.
Old memories, stirred up by the taste of a country
   white loaf from Hovis.
A sturdy white slice that tastes like real bread used to.
Anyway, that's why I'm here with my old toasting fork
   crouched over a fire in a grate that hasn't been
   lit for twenty years.
As good today as it's always been.

Everything in this print advert revolves around the process of remembering – stirring up 'those old memories', but remembering in a quite distinctive way. The speaker in the script is the boy in the ad, looking back to his childhood from late middle age and demonstrating his belief that as we grow older we increasingly relive our childhood. This is a common expression, although, of course, the past can never be relived, only reconstructed in various ways. The way it is reconstructed here centres on the special day in the week when his family were with each other more than on other days, and around a time on a Sunday when this togetherness was celebrated by a simple meal of toast and tea. The period is the Second World War, a time before television, teabags, toasters and other such gadgets. The only item of modern technology on display is the wireless, now in retrospect looking decidedly dated in its wooden casing; it is also tucked away in the corner of the room and peripheral to the family meal. It is this meal, as it is set out on the table, that is the centre of visual attention. The food shortages of the time are forgotten because the food being fondly recalled was simple and straightforward, centred around 'a country white loaf from Hovis', slices of which were skilfully toasted with an extendable fork on an open coal fire. Such food would perhaps seem spartan by post-war standards, in a period of supermarket abundance, but that, of course, was part of the ad's appeal, harking back to a time when toast and jam would happily suffice as the basis for a family meal, and when much was made of little.

This simple family meal acts as the central metaphor for a past working-class idyll whose cosiness is built around such items as the fireplace and the wireless on which the father has tuned into the BBC comedy programme *ITMA*, the initials of which stood for *It's That Man Again*, a reference to Hitler that was adopted by the programme from a *Daily Express* headline of 2 May 1939.[2] Inclusion of this programme brings period humour into the idyll alongside all the other idealised features of nuclear family life, humour which followed in the wake of dutiful attendance at church and Sunday School and imparted a light-hearted ambience to the activities of mashing the tea and toasting the bread. This was the boy's job, and assignment of this task increases the sense of belonging which underpins the advert. It is this sense which is glorified at virtually every point in its visual and 'spoken' components. It emanates from the working-class family as this is symbolised by hearth and home, connects via the 'Sunday best' associations with belonging to the Church of England and a religious nexus that brings all social classes together in worship and devotion, and imagines a community of the nation as this is hailed by the BBC reaching out across the land to listeners united by their attention to such comic characters as Colonel Chinstrap, Mrs Mopp and Mona Lott. This weekly family gathering involves both face-to-face interaction and para-social interaction, with an emphasis on the familiar and relaxed encounters and exchanges of both forms of interaction (Horton and Wohl, 1956). Beyond that, the choice of this particular radio programme, rather than solely offering a reference to broadcasting more generally, is quite deliberate, for *ITMA* was said to be central to upholding national morale on the Home Front during the wartime period in which the ad is set. Family, community, nation: these are conjoined as the first becomes a positively reassuring synecdoche for the other two categories of association, with bread, the staff of life, bringing symbolic unity, compatibility and harmony to these various spheres of belonging.

We are identifying the family as working-class because of the plainness of the meal, the homemade tea-cosy and the paraphernalia on the mantelpiece, though quite where this family stand in terms of social class is rendered somewhat vague and ambivalent by their wearing Sunday clothes, as, for example, the mother's best print dress with lace around the neckline. Their class status is, in any case, not assigned as much importance in the advert as their ordinariness and the visual references to a stable set of social norms and conventions, designed to have a broad-based appeal. It is the 'Everyman' associations that count rather than any specific class attribution. Within such associations, what is being celebrated is a sense of social coordination and integration, manifest in everyday life and extending from the nuclear family to the broader society. It does this by being visually drenched in what the Dutch call *gezellig*, an almost untranslatable word but one that generally carries the connotative senses of relaxing surroundings, convivial atmosphere, time spent with loved ones and social togetherness. Seeking out and savouring these life-affirming qualities in particular settings and intimate relationships is something most of us do, since it is vital to maintaining our personal identities, our relationships with others and our sense of belonging. What we cherish in this sense is the feeling of being at ease with ourselves, with others and with the contexts in which we live. Desire for this feeling is 'a powerful, fundamental, and extremely pervasive motivation' (Baumeister and Leary, 1995, p. 497). Here this desire and its satisfaction are located in the family living room, a place deeply endowed with value, affection and longing, and paradigmatic of the transformation of space into place. This involves a thoroughgoing and ongoing sense of familiarity which is associated with the home's ordinary, intimately known objects, objects which become 'almost a part of ourselves' in their at-homeness (Tuan, 1977, pp. 73, 144). It is with these senses, feelings and values that the advert seeks to align itself, but it does so in a highly sentimentalist manner which operates by eradicating sources of tension and conflict in social life and by generalising intimate and uncomplicated belonging as the overriding nature of social habitation and interaction in a previous historical period. This is central to the ideological work being undertaken in this advert. It delivers a romanticised interpretation of the past and an essentialised conception of everyday life built around unquestioned gender roles and relations.

The stereotypicality of such roles and relations is solidly implicit in the mock-photo because they are seen as indubitable, a condition that is integral to the construction of a sense of stable familial organisation despite the social tensions created through women entering the workplace during this period, and the restructuring of the nuclear family brought about by other events and processes of change of the period, including the Second World War. The construction of the visual dimension of the advert as a mock-photo is crucial to the optical illusion it creates of a real family and real scene, as it once existed, a moment caught on camera and serving not only as a reminder of 'old memories' but, more significantly, as a validation of them, for, as the popular saying has it, 'the camera never lies'. The fact that it is a monochrome photo adds to its apparent documentary status, while at the same time it is spoken to in the script as a personal photograph, one that could have been placed within a family album, contributing there to a shared narrative of experiences of place and time. If this scene had been represented in a painting, that would only have highlighted the idealisation that is involved. Photographic realism, instead, makes claim to the authenticity of what is depicted. In this way, as well, the advert's ideological function slips quietly into concealment.

The advert is a classic example of regressive nostalgia, operating through a process we call *retrotyping*. This is a distinctive manner of remembering which depends on a purposive selectiveness of recall that celebrates certain aspects of a past period and discards others that would compromise the celebratory process and, of course, in this case undermine its commercial intent. In demonstrating how the concept of retrotyping can be analytically applied to just one media item, the general approach we are taking in doing this is in some respects aptly summarised by Patrick Hutton (2011, p. 98) in his observation that,

> mesmerised by the insatiable needs of a consumer society, we have neither the time nor the motivation to consult the past for guidance. Rather, our excursions into that realm are too often a search for idealised images that may serve as aesthetic gloss for advertising calculated to incite the desire for more consumption.

To extrapolate from this, underlying the late-modern syndrome it identifies is a lack of sufficient time or purpose for engaging with and drawing on the past, caused by the hectic pace of contemporary social and cultural change, leaving us prey to reiterative cycles of consumption which mimic the incessant patterns of wider social change and further dislocate us from the past, our only compensation for this being the aesthetic idealisation of highly selective aspects or features of the past that are exploited in the advertising and promotion of commodity goods and services. Such an analytical view is compatible with what we want to say here about retrotyping and the regressive form of nostalgia it helps to sustain. It cannot simply be taken on its own, without extension or qualification, for clearly this would render it too sweeping and generalised, but it nevertheless helps us identify both what underlies and what arises as a consequence of the consumerist uses of nostalgia in meretricious advertising where the past is closed off in its own longed-for, but now unreachable, landscape – the landscape of church spires, relatively car-free streets and smoke curling lazily skywards from cottage chimneys that is evoked in this particular example of the promoter's art.

In focusing on such uses of nostalgia, our concern is particularly with the ways in which popular memory is exploited to enhance the market appeal of commodities. Such exploitation not only involves the selective adaptation and opportunist representation of popular memory. It also reveals quite clearly one of the centrally defining features of commodities. This inheres in the way they bring use-value and exchange-value into combination, using the former in the interests of the latter. Reference to use-value acknowledges a potential buyer's want or need of particular goods and services; this may be realised prior to purchase but is only satisfied after purchase has taken place. Within the act of purchase, exchange-value predominates. The commodification of goods and services is predicated on transforming their use-value to the buyer into their exchange-value for the producer or provider, and, apart from maintaining good customer relations, there is little, if any, interest for the exchange-value in the post-sales use of the commodity. This is particularly the case with commodities produced and marketed on an industrial scale. What is unique to a commodity is that these different values are brought together by it and, therefore, within it. The ensuing combination always exists in a contradictory relation. It is that contradictory relation which defines a commodity within the marketplace, and within it exchange-value always predominates, even though it appears to be subservient to a good's use-value and aesthetic-value, putting appeal before what can be derived from that appeal in exchange for the good that is on offer. Promotion and advertising serve the interests of exchange-value by transforming the use-value of a product into an object that will be desired and sought after, and they do so by hiding the interests they are serving behind the sophistry of this transformation and the promise of personal fulfilment which purchase of the commodity will bring. Their purpose is to aid the movement from use-value to exchange-value, and that is where the development of what W. F. Haug (1986) calls commodity aesthetics comes crucially into play. Such aesthetics dwell upon all that, it is anticipated, will enhance the promise of satisfaction in the purchase of a commodity. Don Slater sums up the process well:

> The production of the appearance of use-value has become a specialist technology within advanced capitalism, an alienated one in that it develops its commodity aesthetics, the commodity's 'second skin', independently of the commodity's material body. The commodity aesthetic is, moreover, rigorously subordinated to 'the valorisation standpoint' in that every aspect of the commodity's appearance is calculated in relation to increasing sales.
>
> (1997, p. 113, and see Haug, 1986)

It is in light of this standpoint that, if the past has consumer appeal and can be used as a form of aesthetic enhancement in selling a particular set of goods or services, the past will be subsumed to this purpose. Here is where retrotyping steps in, for retrotyping then forms the commodity's second skin and, though it operates to facilitate sales, seems to exist outside that, in a different source of interest. The element of marketing sophistry in this lies in establishing the illusion that creating or appealing to that alternative source of interest, and not the calculation of increased sales, is its primary intention. When deployed in the service of marketing, retrotyping is conducive to the establishment of this illusion because of the intrinsic appeal it seeks to achieve in its references back to a previous period in time. Retrotyping always constructs a bespoke past. It develops a uniform impression of a past time or scenario, and does so by simplifying, screening out what is undesirable in promoting a product, amplifying what will render it more alluring in one way or another and, overall, creating an artificial sense of social harmony and unity in partnership with the product that is being sold. In this respect, retrotypically oriented consumerism exploits a generalised sense of pastness rather than a sense of particular pasts.

This is clearly apparent in the Hovis ad. Although it is set in a period of war, this period in Britain subsequently became a source of nostalgia for a time when the whole nation pulled together in the interests of the war effort and strived to ensure that everyone stood a fair chance of emerging successfully through a time of struggle and privation. The ad draws on and appeals to this wartime nostalgia through its emphasis on 'old memories' – indeed, on the general oldness of what is remembered – and does so without bringing into view, or reviewing, what has led to the memories becoming 'old' – the changes and departures, the shifts and transformations that are as much part of the historical process as any continuities or recurrences. Its construction of oldness and pastness conceals the loss that is involved in historical change. Neglecting the pain of loss that is inherent in other forms of nostalgia is always a consequence of retrotyping, and this, of course, aids and abets the commercial exploitation of any nostalgic impulses or longings. Longing for the past is the sole focus of seductive arousal in the ad, because it is through connection with the wholesome nature of this past that the wholesome nature of the commodity is assured. Regardless of the goods or services involved, that is the aim of commodity retrotyping: transmogrifying longing for a falsely enchanted past into satisfaction through consumption of the product in the present. Retrotyping operates not only by glossing over what has happened subsequently in the movement from 'new' memories to 'old' memories, but also by creating the pretence that the past it evokes is the past that once was, not so much in its entirety but rather in its essential qualities, as these are presented. In this case, as we have noted, retrotyping plays up the unity and stability of nuclear family life, and plays down the strife and conflict that it also involves. In addition, aside from the reference to *ITMA*, the war itself is virtually absent, since the fireside and tea-table scene is intended to create almost a timeless quality, a quality that renders more substantial its retrotypical reconstruction of a past that was allegedly more stable and straightforward, when the pace of life was more gentle and assured, when people were not mesmerised by insatiable consumer needs. The retrotypical illusion here is that this was a past that was itself more solidly rooted in its own past, and could turn more readily to that past for guidance.

The ad exploits this illusion, for the bread whose values are centrally extolled is closely entwined with the notion of such beneficent guidance from the past, being 'as good today as it's always been', so ensuring dependability and continuity across time even in periods of disruption or calamity. There is the sense of embedding the commodity in tradition through the reference to religious observance; through the reference to a geography of the past and a feeling of belonging to a landscape of national heritage in walking back home from the church; through the reference to wartime comedy and how linking up to the nexus of national radio broadcasting united the family (with family entertainment) as much as it did the nation (with light-hearted diversion from the toils of war). The emphasis is on continuity, for the link that is being forged here in the speaker's strong connection with 'old memories' is what guarantees the dependability of the commodity's quality. The man in the script holds his old toasting fork, and this connects him to the sturdy quality of his childhood past in direct association with the sturdy quality of the white slice he used to brown evenly over the fire. Hovis locates itself as embedded in a simpler national past and in social stabilities, for what they underwrite is the quality of always being 'as good today as it's ever been'. It is in the interests of this claim to immutability of product quality that the advert operates as a vehicle for retrotypical cultural memories and the idealisation of a wartime past. In connection with this claim, there is even an implied reference to the sensory qualities of memory, the ways in which sudden evocations of the past can be triggered by a particular smell or taste. The feeling that this may create, of historical distance collapsing and historical difference becoming insignificant, is a further element of memory which retrotyping may exploit, but always through an acritical, unreflexive quality of non-contemporaneous contemporaneity.

This is all of a piece with the emphasis on continuity through enchanted temporal connection. The only reference to the passage of time, and to growing up and growing old, is that there hasn't been a fire lit in the same grate for over 20 years, yet, even though central heating may have replaced the old open fire, he is still in the same house, and the fireplace is still there, with all 'those old memories' centred around it. Indeed, with the sentimental burden of the advert being on intimate belonging, in both time and place, there is little sense that this involves change as well as continuity, that belonging is not static and fixed but is transfigured over time as we change and develop. Retrotyping always acts to inoculate us against this sense of historical movement and change. In constructing either idealised images of past moments or a generalised sense of pastness, it obstructs any conception of how past, present and future are dynamically interconnected. In this way it stunts the mnemonic imagination.[3]

The effect of retrotyping and the regressive nostalgia which it fosters is to make it more difficult to reconnect with the past or to use the past to think critically about all that has changed and is changing. There is a desire, perhaps even a yearning, to return – as we kneel in front of an unlit grate holding an old toasting fork – but this can only be satisfied by the consumption of this particular product, for it is only this, in today's rapidly changing world, which remains 'as good as it's always been'. Through consumption of this product we can recapture or redeem a lost past stability. The ideological functionality of retrotyping, as it operates through this example, should now be clear. What it involves is a consumerist packaging of the past, made, in the first instance, in order to achieve wide sales of a household commodity, but, in the second, creating a version of the past that is highly conducive to this purpose. In some ways it strives to be quite exact, as, for example, with the homemade cushion on the settee, the old-fashioned wind-up clock on the mantelpiece, flanked at either end by the china cocker spaniels – in themselves symbolic of trustworthiness and evocative of Englishness. There is also the framed family photograph of a loved and still-mourned former member of the family, which again creates a sense of strong links back to the past being forged across the generations. But the links don't work: they fail to act as telling detail in making this remembered domestic scene specific and distinctive. These particular objects-that-become-us are almost stereotypical in the detail they provide, and in this way they conform with and contribute to the sentimentalist association and the vague, diffuse sense of pastness in which retrotyping traffics. The acuity of a particular past moment is anathema to what retrotyping seeks to achieve. The insistence, instead, is on the construction of 'surfaces of meaning through the manipulation of association and evocation' (Chaney, 1996, p. 106). Through such manipulated surfaces, as second skins, the power of retrotyping lies in its ability to mimic, as in a distinct echo, the recollection of lived experience and, with this, a shared social memory. Here is a boy 'reliving' his childhood, a childhood set in a wartime period which has also been fondly burnished in national collective memory, making childhood nostalgia and wartime nostalgia blend seamlessly together. Its power in this respect is at one with its limitations as a selective and static view of the past. For that reason, with our example in this chapter so many of the visual details in the picture – the clothes, the household ornaments, the furniture – appear stereotypical because retrotyping works precisely by stereotyping the past, dealing in readymade short-cuts, clichéd signs of generality, homogenised historical experiences and surface historical associations. Retrotyping is confined to stock images and reliant on a constricted historical repertoire because it needs the past it constructs to be not only benign but also widely embraceable. That is why it specialises in stylised views of past periods or stylised iconic moments, not moments that leap out of the memory and pierce us to the heart in their sudden unexpectedness and the anguish of loss they entail. Retrotyping works ideologically by remaining relentlessly presentist, offering a one-way projection backwards from an exclusively contemporary perspective and acting only in the interests of what a past in its selective, idealised parts can give to the present and the pursuit of profit for merchandise that is being sold now. Through retrotyping we only ever see the past in its Sunday best.

Notes

1. For more on this and on our general conceptualisation of nostalgia, see Keightley and Pickering, 2012, chapters 4 and 5. Katharina Niemeyer also deals with the issue of regressive nostalgia in the introduction to this book.
2. The reference was transferred to the lynchpin of this radio programme, Tommy Handley. The programme ran from 1939 to 1949, with the scripts being written by Ted Kavanagh. For most of the wartime period, during which it was the BBC's most popular comedy show, it was broadcast from Bangor in north Wales. See Kavanagh (1949), Calder (1971, pp. 75–76, pp. 416–418); Snagge and Barsley (1972, pp. 133–143), Wilmut (1985, pp. 152–153).

3. On the concept of the mnemonic imagination and the manifold theoretical considerations it entails, see Keightley and Pickering (2012).

References

Baumeister, R. F. and Leary, M. R. (1995) 'The Need to Belong: Desire for Interpersonal Attachments as a Fundamental Human Motivation'. *Psychological Bulletin*, 2(2), pp. 497–529.
Calder, A. (1971) *The People's War*. London: Panther.
Chaney, D. (1996) *Lifestyles*. London and New York: Routledge.
Haug, W. F. (1986) *Critique of Commodity Aesthetics*. Cambridge: Polity.
Horton, D. and Wohl, R. R. (1956) 'Mass Communication and Para-social Interaction'. *Psychiatry*, 19, pp. 215–229.
Hutton, P. (2011) 'How the Old Left has Found a New Place in the Memory Game'. *History and Theory*, 50, February, pp. 98–111.
Kavanagh, T. (1949) *Tommy Handley*. London: Hodder & Stoughton.
Keightley, E. and Pickering, M. (2012) *The Mnemonic Imagination: Remembering as Creative Practice*. Basingstoke and New York: Palgrave Macmillan.
Slater, D. (1997) *Consumer Culture and Modernity*. Cambridge: Polity.
Snagge, J. and Barsley, M. (1972) *Those Vintage Years of Radio*. London: Pitman Publishing.
Tuan, Y.-F. (1977) *Space and Place: The Perspective of Experience*. Minneapolis: University of Minnesota Press.
Wilmut, R. (1985) *Kindly Leave the Stage! The Story of Variety 1919–60*. London: Methuen.

6
Anti-nostalgia in Citroën's Advertising Campaign

Emmanuelle Fantin

According to Vladimir Jankélévitch, nostalgia is triggered by the regret of a subjective event, place or time. The fact that time is intrinsically both semelfactive[1] and irreversible would cause our melancholic longing for the fugitive past. Thus, he explains: 'It is not what is to be regretted that is regretted (because maybe there is nothing to regret), it is the arbitrary, unreasonable and even irrational fact of the pastness in itself' (1974, p. 353). What he calls the pastness, the fact of being past, would be the ineffable cause of nostalgia. From this perspective, every object of the past, even the most useless, would have the ability to evoke an entire epoch. Day-to-day life objects such as clothes, furniture or cultural items serve as triggering factors for nostalgia, maintaining a link to the lost past that continuously perpetuates its relevance. They give the illusion of touching it again through a kind of materiality.

In this context, one can argue that cars have always been perfect embodiments of the past. A few, like the famous Citroën DS, have become true legends. The car was destined to be mythical as soon as it was conceived and named. 'DS' is a pun for French-speaking persons; it is the perfect homonym of the word *déesse*, which means 'goddess'. The name seems to have been prophetic, as the car had a legendary destiny. It became the official car of President Général De Gaulle, and his DS19 helped him escape an attempted assassination in 1962. It was said that in this 'attentat du Petit Clamart' the car, riddled with bullet holes, miraculously saved the President's life. The myth of the car was also enhanced by its numerous appearances in the popular films of the 1960s and 1970s. With its very specific aerodynamic design, the DS progressively grew into a perfect symbol of the golden age, the 'glorious thirties'. In 2009, the automotive group launched a new version of the model from the 1950s. However, the new model, named the 'DS3', bears no resemblance to the original design that served as the source of inspiration and drove its conception. The brand strongly hints at the past with the name of the new car, which implies direct relation to the legendary DS, but none of its original features survived. At first glance the two models really seem to have nothing in common. So, in order to tell a convincing story, the brand developed around this product a communication platform never used before: they continuously referred to the past by using the name of the original car and archived pictures of iconic idols of the 1950s and 1960s to embody the campaign – while simultaneously rejecting the past as a model, as described in the tag line 'Anti-retro' (YouTube, 2013a, 2013b).

Two TV advertising campaigns were broadcast, built on a strict parallelism. The first ad is a video of John Lennon in black and white, as he looked towards the end of the 1960s. The camera focuses on his face in what seems to be an interview context. His voice seems genuine and was kept in the original French version that used French subtitles to translate what he is telling us. He says: 'Once a thing's been done, it's been done. Why this nostalgia? Looking backwards for inspiration, copying the past? How's that rock and roll? Do something on your own, start something new, you know. Live your life now, you know what I mean?' Then the tag line 'anti-retro' appears in capital letters, written in white on a black background, with unidentified dynamic and vintage-sounding rock music piped throughout. This image is followed by several views of the moving car on the same black background, and the ad ends with an image of the brand logo. The second ad starts with Marilyn Monroe in the exact same context as John Lennon. Her words mirror Lennon's: 'I don't know why so many people live in the past. It wasn't better to be young then. You should create your own idols and way of life, because nostalgia isn't glamorous. If I had one thing to say it would be: live your life now.' The dichotomy of the product positioning lies between the continuous references to the past and urging consumers not to use nostalgia as a crutch to recreate and relive the past. Thus, Citroën introduces a disruption in the nostalgia trend by trying to reconcile past, present and future at the same time. How can those contradictory messages conveyed by Citroën, when put together, become consistent?

Citroën's ad campaign expresses nostalgia through the filter of what we could call 'baroque aesthetics'. If the analogy with Baroque seems at first glance anachronistic to describe a contemporary ad, we argue that this notion enlightens the symbolic depth and the core meaning of this campaign. Baroque comes from a Portuguese word *barroco*, which was initially used to describe pearls that were not perfectly shaped. This etymological idea of irregularity led the term 'baroque' both to signify by the end of the nineteenth century a 'striking oddity' (Littré, 2000) and to circumvent *a posteriori* an artistic and literary movement of the end of the sixteenth century and the beginning of the seventeenth century. In art and literature, Baroque is defined by its inclination to illusions, contrasts and antithesis, representing the place where borders between opposite concepts vanish, where everything seems to be reconcilable: death and life, dream and reality, and, of course, past and present. Baroque was also defined in opposition to Classicism, whose main features are harmony, unity and coherence. These ideas of strangeness, transmogrifications or evasive representations are typical manifestations of this aesthetic category that seem relevant to explore in this campaign. The contrasts and illusions that visually and semantically structure this ad reveal a precarious, though audacious, balance between a world rooted in memory and one striving for progress.

In essence, the message of the brand, through these ads, relies on antithesis as a tool. We know that rhetoric usually defines antithesis as the connection between two opposite ideas or words. Here, the antithesis is more accurately used as a semiotic device, as the brand creates a link between two signs that appear naturally opposed. We observe a plurality of the level of antithesis with the constant presence of pressure between expressions of nostalgia and denial of nostalgia. For example, there is an opposition between what we could call, in a Barthesian meaning (1964), the denoted images of Lennon and Monroe (archived images of people who, it appears, are being interviewed) and the linguistic and narrative content of their speeches ('I don't know why so many people live in the past', 'You should create your own idols and way of life', 'So why this nostalgia?' etc.). In the same vein, the connoted images of Lennon and Monroe (pop and film stars of the 1960s and the 1950s) are also opposed to the narrative content of their speech and to the linguistic message of the brand and the ad: 'Anti-retro'. Another antithesis can be seen between the entirety of the visual, musical and iconic components of the ad and the product that refers to the past (stars, name of the car, music, design) and the linguistic message of the brand and the ad: 'Anti-retro'.

This idea of a contradictory message at the very core of the advertising is scattered among several semiotic components of the ad, but gathered into the tagline that appears to be the climax of the advertising narrative. Consequently, we understand that the tagline 'Anti-retro' condenses in a specific way the treatment of nostalgia by the brand.

This network of antithesis conveys a distorted and indirect vision of nostalgia: idealisation of the past is claimed to be both approved and disapproved at the same time. Nevertheless, the tagline lies like an understatement because nostalgia remains the main topic of the video, the referent that helps to define every sign of the advert. By using hugely influential and greatly admired figures of the past like Lennon, Monroe, and above all the DS, the alleged denial of nostalgic feelings is instantly tarnished. By claiming the opposite, the brand emphasises the density of the past and reinforces its will to trigger nostalgia in the audience. Ultimately, the word chosen by the brand, 'retro', is no coincidence and helps to highlight its nostalgia. The word in itself is currently fashionable and enhanced, and one should consider that the final result of the advert would have been different if the word chosen had been a French equivalent of the words 'fusty', 'creaky' or 'old-fashioned'. The understatement lies also in the choice of the central appealing word. Moreover, Deleuze's analysis of Baroque's relationship with illusion illustrates one of the core mechanisms of the campaign: 'The main characteristic of Baroque is not to fall into illusion, nor to eliminate it; it is to achieve something in illusion itself' (1988, p. 170). As a baroque campaign, the adverts dissolve the barriers between real life and fiction, especially with the *presence* of Monroe and Lennon in *trompe-l'oeil* in order to reinforce the blurring that can lead to nostalgia. The various temporal illusions and referential overlapping that Citroën maintains throughout these adverts are an example of that. First, we observe that the two films are divided into two non-homogeneous parts: the archived images of the two idols, out of context, are followed by more 'classic' representations of the product, expected in any advertising. By introducing the adverts with archived material, the brand creates the illusion of a documentary or a historical TV show, and in doing so introduces a phatic process: a documentary would be interrupting the commercial break. Thus, the commercial purpose of the communication is minimised by the 'historical' value of these images. This approach helps to create nostalgic feelings in the audience, as archived images are prone to activate our connection with the past more than a simple commercial.

An illusion is created by the pseudo-context of interview of the two idols: a misconception maintained by the idea that they would actually have uttered these exact sentences, suggesting that they expressed their own feelings about rejection of nostalgia. Their tone of voice sounds authentic, but it becomes clear that their words are not genuine. They are both saying almost the same thing, and there is a strict parallelism between their discourses, adapted to their personality: Lennon refers to rock and roll, Monroe to glamour. The absence of synchronisation between sound and image reveals prosopopoeia, which allows the brand to mix several temporalities into the narrative, and abolish chronological barriers. Here, doubts around the historical truth of these images of interview blur time levels and help to create a referential illusion to link the past of the idols and present time. The archival element of the advert involves aspects of temporal superimposition, meaning that archive is not motionless; it is a dynamic process, a social production constantly reshaped and restructured. The treatment of archived images in this campaign echoes what Niemeyer defines as a 'lieu-de-mémoire-in-motion' (2011). This concept, built as an extension of Nora's, considers media as a process that can reactivate and actualise memory.

Additionally, this interviewing context creates an emotional relationship between the audience and the two stars. Lennon and Monroe are engaging with someone in the distance, not included in the frame of the shot: the camera is performing close-up shots that only show their faces. According to Deleuze (1983), a close-up shot constructs 'affection-image', as opposed to 'perception-image' and 'action-image'. The notion 'affection-image' is employed by extracting the character of all its spatial and temporal coordinates; by cutting Monroe's and Lennon's faces out of space and time referential with close-ups, their faces are turned into pure 'entities' or 'wholes'. The 'affection-image' is used in these adverts to bring more powerful representations of the lost idols – thus, of the vanished past. The two interdependent characteristics of 'affection-image' echo back the nostalgic mechanism: the primacy of the affection over action and reflexion, and abstraction of space and time. More accurately, this 'whole' status conveyed by the framing reinforces the value of the prosopopoeia. Finally, we could analyse the link between Citroën's advert and nostalgia as a chiasmus that strengthens the nostalgic strategy: not only does the brand strongly convey nostalgia in these adverts, but it uses specific and inherent elements of nostalgia to build its own message.

Advertising discourse is a privileged way to access contemporary social imaginary. The nostalgia trend has been increasingly used as a source of inspiration by brands; references to memorable events, mimics of vintage design or revival of old ideologies have become standard resources of marketing. Consumers have become accustomed to these anachronisms of the 1950s and 1960s, this 'consumerist packaging of the past' (Chapter 5) being used to trigger vivid memories of the idealised 'good old times'. According to Harmut Rosa (2010), temporal structures have a social nature. He proposes that, today, society is increasingly tense because we are guided by the cult of innovation and progress; we suffer from the significant pressure of rapid social, technical and cultural advancement. For that reason we would, almost mechanically, counterbalance modernity by yearning for a golden age. He considers that, after every thrust of acceleration, we experience both an acceleration and a deceleration discourse, longing for a 'slow world' where retrospective vision prevails over high-speed rhythms. Some historians go further in their reflection about modernity, such as Jacques Le Goff (1988), who emphasises the core ambiguity of every form of modernity. Therefore, modernity would paradoxically have a tendency to deny itself. Modernism at the edge of the present would retreat to the past to such a point that 'modernity and retro go by pair' (pp. 101–103). Boym points in the same direction: 'Somehow progress didn't cure nostalgia but exacerbated it' (2001, p. xiv).

In this context, why is Citroën's appeal for nostalgia so striking? The brand pretends to stand for resistance to this nostalgic trend of marketing, as we have already seen. But, in reality, Citroën is just introducing a new and, maybe, stronger relationship with nostalgia. The brand gives Monroe and Lennon the roles of real gurus. First, from a grammatical point of view, we notice that the chosen tense, the imperative, has a fundamental directive value and expresses an injunction. Then, the lapidary form of the peremptory motto 'Live your life now' conveys a pseudo-iconoclastic idea in the global nostalgic marketing trend. This expression represents a messianic appeal to Horace's *carpe diem*, paradoxically uttered by symbolic figures that encourage us to focus on the past. Moreover, the visual display of the tagline reflects this antagonism: the words 'anti' and 'retro' appear on different sides of the screen. Then the two words reverse and cross each other to form the tagline 'Anti-Retro', standing for the crossroads of past, present and future.

But, when they declare 'Live your life now', which 'now' are the two idols talking about? Is it the present of the alleged enunciation, which would be the past for us? Or is it the present of the advertising enunciation? This core ambiguity has a paradoxical effect: while the contrast between past and present is emphasised by several semiotic indications that are highlighted (black and white, archived images, name of the car, etc.), this sentence erases the distinction between the epoch of Monroe and Lennon and our own. Time barriers are, if not abolished, at least entirely blurred. Thus, their discourses introduce porosity between present, past and future, reinforced by the enigmatic tagline 'Anti-retro'. In the end, nostalgia is rejected but sacred at the same time, as if it is not possible to escape from it. Another way to analyse Citroën's positioning in this campaign is to consider Jean-Marie Floch's semiotic square of the automotive sector adverts (2002, p. 131). He defined this visual mapping to determine an axiology of consumption, and identified four different valuation types underpinned by several cars' representations. First, he draws the line between 'use values' and 'basic value', illustrated by the fundamental opposition between *using* a car that can fulfil our needs, and *enjoying* a car that can fulfil our desires. Based on this initial contradiction, he distinguishes four positionings of valuation types. First, he defines the practical valuation, which refers to utilitarian values of the car (comfort, robustness, etc.). Then, the utopian valuation reflects existential values (identity, adventure, life). As for playful valuation, it refers to the negation of utilitarian values (luxury, sophistication or uselessness, etc.). Finally, the critical valuation illustrates the negation of existential values (price–quality ratio, cost, etc.). According to Floch's semiotic square of the automotive sector, this campaign for the DS3 would be located between playful and utopian valuation. This assumption is supported by the lack of references made to either technology and options or to its price or robustness, basic consumption assets. The brand message is completely focused on symbolic assets of the car, while all crucial details about the car (mechanical and financial) are strictly omitted. The advert communicates several messages, but nothing about the car. The brand, through its muses, declares a generic position about 'existential values' such as life or the past. Moreover, the utopian valuation appears especially relevant; it echoes the nostalgic process in itself. Nostalgia joins utopia in several ways: it struggles against time's irreversibility, but, at the same time, it tries to reach an intangible and blurred time. Nostalgia strives for timeless time, untied from the historical continuum. This 'timeless time' refers to the 'unrealistic place' of utopia. Furthermore, etymology brings utopia and nostalgia closer. The place (*topos*) that does not exist in *u-topia* echoes the journey to our home place (*nostos*) that makes us suffer in *nost-algia*. Utopia and nostalgia both have a compensatory function: to break away from present time or melt away with the unreality of an inaccessible world.

Could this utopian value be applied to all cars in themselves? Indeed, a car provides a real enclosed place that can embody the past. It represents time discontinuity, and allows a time elision, with the merging of past, present and future. As Baudrillard states,

> A car opens an absolute parenthesis to everyday nature of all other objects. The material that it transforms, time and space, is beyond compare. [...] The movement in itself is constituent of a certain

happiness, but mechanical euphoria of speed is different: in our imaginary it is built on the miraculous idea of moving.

(1968, p. 94)

From this perspective, it is no surprise that a car is such a perfect embodiment of the past. Even though the past is not present at all in the design of the DS3, the object in itself helps us move into space and, consequently, into time. It can be argued that the DS3 stands for real heterotopia. The philosophical concept of heterotopia was developed by Foucault (2001). He builds the definition of heterotopia as a mirror of utopia: as utopia is a place without place, heterotopia is a fulfilled utopia in a real place, a place out of every other place, even though it is possible to localise it. In other words, a heterotopia is a located utopia. Foucault states several features of heterotopias, which he also calls 'counter-spaces'. He first assumes that heterotopias exist in every culture and social group. Then, he announces that a heterotopia has the ability to have different functions, depending on the time period. This is very interesting for the DS3 studied here: heterotopias can gather several incompatible places into one real place. Foucault illustrates this feature with the example of the stage of a theatre, which stands both for the stage in itself and the place of the action in a play. Heterotopias would also be mostly linked to what he symmetrically calls 'heterochronias', defined as dissolution of real traditional time. This principle is illustrated by examples of museums or libraries that collect and save many temporal and historical levels though books or art works. Heterotopias would also have an opening and closing system that makes them both isolated and penetrable. Finally, and most importantly, a heterotopia would have a determined function compared with other spaces: to create a place of illusion or a compensatory place. The parallelism between Foucault's concept and the DS3 appears heuristic; each feature of heterotopia is illustrated in Citroën's car. As a heterotopia, the DS3 is, at the same time, the original car of the 1950s and the new one. As a heterotopia, the DS3 is linked to dissolution of time and it is a concrete place that can host dreams and imagination. Thus, the concept of heterotopias invites us to question the relationship between spatial matters and living matters. It invites us to consider the relation with the other, especially the other self that we have been or could have been. In the end, heterotopias represent an interaction between presence and absence, between present and past, and that is why the car promoted by Citroën is so nostalgic. More than the presence of Lennon and Monroe in the campaign, it is the materiality of the object that introduces a temporal discontinuity and overlapping. The DS3 becomes an anachronistic object, erasing historical time and being both real and unreal: Citroën leads us to transform our perception and give profound meaning to the car. In the end, what could be considered as the most trivial object of our day-to-day life is also the most phantasmal and powerful.

Nostalgia condenses spaces, times, characters that seem to represent a sheltered past to reach. Jankélévitch considers the nostalgic person to be both here and there, present and absent, omnipresent and, thus, nowhere (1974, p. 346). If this act of duplicity is the major sign of a nostalgic state, Citroën seems to have transposed it perfectly in its commercial communication. Paradoxically, temporal superimpositions and historical references give the product an ahistorical value: the DS3 is never quite the same, nor quite another. The truth of the car lies in this interstice. Citroën seems to answer Gérard de Nerval's imperative: 'In the end, to invent is to remember again' (1994, p. 73). The tension between the appeal for nostalgia and its rejection though the central word 'anti' is annihilated because there is only one era that is coveted. The brand imagines future and innovation by reshaping the past, and the car stands for a palimpsest of time. Floch, while analysing Citroën's advertising in the 1990s, observed: 'Citroën's capital is its myth – if we consider that a myth is a narration that is constructed in a way that reconciliation of the opposite such as nature and culture, life and death or identity and alterity is possible' (2002, p. 143). With this campaign, Citroën stays grounded in its traditional culture; the past and present are reconciled by the myth of the brand. The car allows a fantasy projection through the process of consumption. We can consume the past again through the nostalgia embodied in this object. The car is a pretext for the nostalgic consumer to reach the past and struggle against time's irreversibility. The advert illustrates how media and consumption can reshape our conception of time, indicating a reiterative and cyclic time. It also highlights the strength of today's commodities and goods and their ability to turn our memories into an illusory enchanted past, a 'generalised sense of pastness', as studied by Pickering and Keightley in this volume. The nostalgia trend in advertising and consumption in general symbolises the quest for the unreachable. The past has a something, a 'je-ne-sais-quoi' that causes an unrepeatable emotion. Jankélévitch answers the question posed by Citroën, with the help of John Lennon's 'So why this nostalgia?', because, perhaps, nostalgia's cause is equally to be found in the present:

> We cannot explain why the present is not charming: the present does not need that we come back; it is already here, within easy reach; it

is the surrounding air, the world of serious praxis, it is the day-to-day news and ordinariness. Maybe we would not say the same about the present that is full of memories. But the present is surely the world of tasteless and painless prose.

(Jankélévitch, 1974, p. 372)

Note

1. This notion initially defines an aspectual class of verb, but was used by Jankélévitch to define a core time feature: 'Each moment of our life is semelfactive; in other words, it happens just once during the whole eternity and would never be again' (1974, p. 368).

References

Barthes, R. (1964) 'Rhétorique de l'image'. *Communications*, 4, pp. 40–51.
Baudrillard, J. (1968) *Le système des objets*. Paris: Gallimard.
Boym, S. (2001) *The Future of Nostalgia*. New York: Basic Books.
Deleuze, G. (1983) *L'image-mouvement*. Paris: Les Editions de Minuit.
Deleuze, G. (1988) *Le pli – Leibniz et le baroque*. Paris: Les Editions de Minuit.
Floch, J.-M. (2002) *Sémiotique, marketing et communication, sous les signes les strategies*. Paris: PUF.
Foucault, M. (2001) 'Des espaces autres', in *Dits et écrits*, edited by Defert, D. and Ewald, F., tome 2, pp. 1571–1581. Paris: Gallimard.
Jankélévitch, V. (1974) *L'irréversible et la nostalgie*. Paris: Flammarion.
Le Goff, J. (1988) *Histoire et mémoire*. Paris: Gallimard.
Le Littré. (2000) *Dictionnaire de la langue française*. Paris: Hachette.
Nerval de, G. (1994) *Les filles du feu*. Paris: Flammarion.
Niemeyer, K. (2011) *De la chute du mur de Berlin au 11 septembre 2001*. Lausanne: Antipodes.
Rosa, H. (2010) *Accélération – Pour une critique sociale du temps*. Paris: La Découverte.
YouTube (2013a) http://www.youtube.com/watch?v=4KEWbrnS_Rs (accessed 7 July 2013).
YouTube (2013b) http://www.youtube.com/watch?v=2w1aAN8h484 (accessed 7 July 2013).

7
Networks as Media for Nostalgia in an Organisational Context

Thibaut Bardon, Emmanuel Josserand and Florence Villesèche

Nostalgia is popularly associated with the idea of the difficulty of letting go of a past when life was somehow 'better' (Gabriel, 1993). Such a perspective is reflected in the organisational literature, for example through the work of Strangleman (1999), Brown and Humphreys (2002) or McCabe (2004), who show how nostalgia can be present in an organisational setting. These works also highlight that nostalgia is a social emotion that is shared and co-constructed; it follows that nostalgia is to be experienced not only individually, but also with others, and thus through a variety of media. This idea that nostalgia is a social emotion has notably been leveraged in marketing, and is discussed in the related literature (see, for example, Cutcher, 2008; Kessous and Roux, 2008), but there is no discussion of the media aspect. Thus, these literatures fail to inform us about how nostalgia is mediated in organisational contexts. Given the general lack of scholarship about the functional relationship between media and nostalgia (see volume Introduction by Niemeyer), this is hardly surprising.

This overall paucity of literature linking media and nostalgia thus opens up rich possibilities, but also necessitates identifying and conducting research on types of media that are relevant in a given context. In an organisational setting, we do know that networks are key carriers of norms, values, standards and practices (Burns and Wholey, 1993; Owen-Smith and Powell, 2008). Taking an interest in networks thus appears to be a reasonable way to provide a first exploration of media for nostalgia in an organisational setting. In this chapter, we therefore propose an exploration of how nostalgia is mediated within organisational settings, and thus contribute to the development of research about the mediation of nostalgia.

As an empirical setting, we present the case of the alumni network of MultiCorp, a US-based multinational corporation producing consumer goods. Analysis of the interviews of 21 alumni in the US and in Europe allowed us to uncover four interpretive repertoires through which alumni justify their membership in the network: Business case, Best in class, Family and Giving back. These repertoires – several of which can be combined by a single individual – show that, although alumni can justify their participation in network activities for business reasons, motives for becoming active members of networks such as a corporate alumni network also pertain to nostalgia. Our study thus shows how networks can be a medium for nostalgia in an organisational setting, opens rich perspectives for researchers interested in media and nostalgia, and should encourage them to take more interest in the life in and around work organisations.

Nostalgia in organisational settings

In organisation studies, a small number of contributions have taken an interest in nostalgia, following the call from Gabriel (1993) to acknowledge the importance of emotions such as nostalgia in an organisational setting. The work of Brown and Humphreys (2002), for example, show that employees who have difficulties in embracing an organisational change express nostalgia about the past organisational situation. In that perspective, nostalgia is perceived negatively by the organisation, as it means that employees are not embracing the new state of the organisation, and long for what they remember as a better situation.

Nevertheless, works in organisational theory also show how nostalgia may be beneficial for organisational participants. Indeed, Brown and Humphreys (2002) show how nostalgia can help maintain social and historic continuity and prevent anxiety among groups of employees confronted with an organisational change initiative. Such research echoes studies in the field of psychology that have already highlighted the functioning of nostalgia as a positive emotion, since the nostalgic experience can lead to a state of happiness, and thus uncovered the existential functions of nostalgia (see, for example, Sedikides et al. 2008, Wildschut and Baden, 2004).

The organisational literature also shows how management can try to reverse the nostalgic sentiment. One way is to diffuse organisational discourses that promise a 'golden future' to employees in order to replace nostalgia with postalgia among organisational participants (Ybema, 2004). Another approach is, after organisational change has occurred, to highlight how the present is 'a land of milk and honey' compared with the previous situation (McCabe, 2004). Also, nostalgia might be replaced with nostophobia, that is, the selective reconstruction of the organisational past in a negative light, in order to win acceptance of an organisational change project (Strangleman, 1999). Overall, this stream of research thus shows that nostalgia can be present in an organisational setting, and also highlights that nostalgia is a social emotion, which can create cohesion, but also confrontation between distinct groups that value the past, present and future in dissimilar ways.

Networks as media

In this chapter, we consider nostalgia in an organisational setting, and, rather than simply accounting for nostalgia or for its causes and consequences, we seek to explore how organisational nostalgia is mediated. In organisation studies, among the most studied media are networks, since they have been identified as key carriers of norms, values, standards and practices in corporate contexts that are commonly labelled 'network organisations' (Baker, 1993; Josserand, 2004). This means that networks (such as alliances, knowledge-sharing networks, etc.) will be the media through which ideas, but also management practices, will be diffused from one organisation to the next. Burns and Wholey (1993), for example, show that the propensity of an organisation to adopt a matrix management structure depends on its position in local networks. Similarly, Davis (1991) suggests that business organisations tightly connected with firms using 'poison pills' – a governance mechanism put in place to prevent hostile takeovers – are more likely to implement this mechanism than firms that are less connected with such companies.

Numerous other studies have shown how networks contribute to the diffusion of practices in various settings (see Fligstein, 1985; Mizruchi, 1992; Westphal and Zajac, 1997). In this view, networks are treated as channels that constitute the circulatory systems through which practices are disseminated (Owen-Smith and Powell, 2008). This also means that networks are a specific type of media that can lead to the emergence of a 'collective rationality' within social groups, meaning that media also constitute channels through which actors make sense of themselves and others (Meyer and Lampel, 2008). The network literature thus converges in an account of the role of networks as media that foster the emergence of categories that further support the development of social structures.

The properties of networks as media depend on their structural configuration. For instance, the number of boundary spanners is a key factor in understanding the formation of groups (Oh, Labianca and Myung-Ho, 2006). The degree of closure of the network, meaning the degree of interconnectedness of all members of the network, is also an important element that will impact its properties. Indeed, networks characterised by redundant ties – these are networks where several paths exist between two actors – facilitate cognitive and normative convergence (Coleman, 1988; Adler and Kwon, 2002). Relatedly, the maturity of a network (i.e. its length of existence) as well as the strength of ties developed over time between members of the network (i.e. the frequency of contact, level of trust, etc.) – increase the capacity of networks to relay complex (Hansen, 1999) or privileged information (Bouty, 2000). With time, networks can thus become rich media that convey complex information among and through members connected by strong ties.

Methods

Our goal, to explore networks as media for nostalgia in an organisational context, leads us to consider the case of corporate alumni networks. Corporate alumni networks regroup former employees of a focal organisation. In the academic literature, the rationale for the existence of such corporate alumni networks includes the reduction of rehiring costs (Sertoglu and Berkowitch, 2002) and the improvement of knowledge retention (Koc-Menard, 2009), but also effects on corporate image, brand and lobbying, as well as access to intellectual capital and financial resources (Sertoglu and Berkowitch, 2002). In the accounting literature, there have also been a few contributions showing the importance of corporate alumni networks in audit firms, as they have an influence on the attribution of audit contracts (Lennox and Park, 2007) as well as the level of audit fees (Basioudis, 2007).

Given this relation to a past professional setting, corporate alumni networks appear as a rich setting in which to explore the idea of networks as media for nostalgia in an organisational context. In the empirical part of this chapter, through a case study (Yin, 2009) we will attempt to understand how alumni concretely justify their participation in such networks, and see whether in this way we can find indications that alumni express nostalgia and that nostalgia is mediated through the corporate alumni network.

Case presentation

The MultiCorp alumni network was created and is managed by alumni, and the firm has supported the network-related efforts only since 2002.

Currently the network has more than 20,000 members worldwide. The data collected for the case study consist of 21 semi-structured interviews of alumni. The interviews lasted between 45 minutes and two and a half hours, and a better understanding of the network was also gained thanks to access being granted to the full contents of its website.

Data analysis

Individual interviews were coded using Nvivo9®. Regarding our particular interest in the way former employees of MultiCorp justify their participation in the alumni network, the objective of the coding was to construct relationships between the use of simile, metaphor and specific vocabulary inside and across individual discourse in order to construct what are called interpretive repertoires. Originating in social psychology, the notion of interpretive repertoires was chiefly developed by Potter and Wetherell (Potter and Wetherell, 1984; Wetherell and Potter, 1988; Potter, 1996). Interpretive repertoires can be considered as the building blocks that individuals use to talk about themselves and others. The combination of repertoires can give a rough image of how individuals construct the way they give value to their environment and to themselves.

Results

The analysis of the data allowed us to outline four interpretive repertoires. These repertoires have been regrouped in two categories. The first contains a repertoire of instrumental justification for spending time in such a network: the business case repertoire. Then, in contrast, three further repertoires were highlighted during analysis, and are linked to emotions: the Best in class, Family and Giving back repertoires. These repertoires allow us to show and later discuss the mediation of nostalgia through the alumni network, and the wider implications regarding the study of media for nostalgia in an organisational setting. Individual respondents can combine a number of repertoires when explaining their reasons for being active participants in the alumni network of MultiCorp; we, however, present them separately to highlight each repertoire's singularity as well as the differences between the repertoires.

Instrumental repertoire

We find a single repertoire that is instrumental, namely, the Business Case repertoire. This repertoire is one that can reasonably be expected from a professional network: in order to make an efficient use of their time, individuals seek to be part of a network in which they can develop ties with relevant and reputable contacts for their own professional development.

Business case

Compared with other existing networks, being an active member of the MultiCorp alumni network is considered to be the right choice. Because they worked for the same firm, the proximity between members makes contacts easier; in the words of one of our interviewees, 'people are very nice when you tell them that you also worked for MultiCorp and they try to be helpful'. Also, it is a place where one is sure to find similarly minded people who will be of business interest: 'Today, what I find great with the alumni network, is that we kept a common way of thinking, but it is a mix since people have also gathered experience outside [...] so we are twice as rich!'

Being a member thus constitutes a business case, which is a rational justification for joining the network. We can thus say that this interpretive repertoire provides an instrumental justification for participation; however, this instrumentality itself is based on a strong belief that the past professional setting is something to long for. Indeed, as we see from the second quote, previous colleagues are seen as sharing the same mindset, and half their worth comes from actually having been an 'insider' at MultiCorp in the past. With the three subsequent repertoires, we will see how emotions are also mediated by the corporate alumni network, which adds to the more expected instrumental, business justification for their membership in the MultiCorp alumni network.

Emotional repertoires

As well as the instrumental interpretive repertoire of the 'business case', alumni we interviewed also justify their participation in the alumni network through the use of three emotional repertoires. To start with, they feel proud to be in the same network as others whom they think of as brilliant former colleagues. Also, their relationship with their former workplace and colleagues appears to span across the public–private or work–life divide when they use the interpretive repertoire of Family. Finally, their motivation to be members is also justified by non-instrumental benefits, such as the satisfaction of Giving back, or the individual feeling of being a good person who continues to live under the same strong values.

Best in class

The higher quality of business connections that can be made in the network of their past employer is a strong instrumental motive to look to the past again, as we have seen in the business case repertoire. However, this resonates with a more emotional longing for a unique environment in which they find themselves surrounded by the best people possible, and feel a part of this elite again. Indeed, MultiCorp prides itself in almost exclusively hiring the best graduates of the best universities, and this elitist logic is kept in the internal training (strong corporate culture of winning) and promotion system (up or out); having worked there thus singles alumni out as part of the 'best in class'.

Membership in the network is thus an expression of their higher status, as only people like them can be part of it:

> When you are at those meetings, it 'flies high' like we say [...] They don't say MultiCorp is good for no reason, I mean, the level they ask for! [...] When I got in I didn't have an MBA, but the people who worked with me were all from Yale, Stanford, Harvard, that's it.

Participation in a network they are proud to be part of thus brings up emotions; as nostalgia is a social emotion, this justifies their participation in order to be able to share it with others: 'When you have had that environment [...] that's what you expect to get again when you go to these alumni reunions' (MultiCorp alumni). Their pride in being part of this group of best in class is mediated through participation in the alumni network, thanks to which they can relive the emotions of the past.

Family

In this repertoire, the vocabulary of family ties is heavily used. Being an active alumnus is as valuable as attending family reunions. Former colleagues are considered as family members, given the trust ties developed during long working hours: 'when you work for a corporation, you spend so much time working with a group of people and they kind of become another family for you' (MultiCorp alumni). Going to the meetings is thus an occasion to meet them again, and to express that they are still part of the family: 'the alumni network is strong, and it is an outgrowth of that loyalty and the fact that you feel a real kinship with the company, even after you've left'. It is a broad family, which includes former colleagues, but also the former employer.

Indeed, the firm itself is considered as a parent that teaches them values they will stick to long after having left the firm, as can be seen when an interviewee told us that:

> Your parents instill certain things in you throughout your life; that good parenting means those core values are strong and they work with you; MultiCorp does that along the lines of business: ethical strategies, not so much morality, but I don't know. [...] Stuff that you would learn at Girl Scouts or from your mum at the kitchen table, MultiCorp teaches you in a business setting.

Nostalgia is here expressed regarding the personal, emotional relationships developed at and with MultiCorp. These feelings and values are mediated through participation in network activities:

> It's great to see people sharing values and camaraderie; that's enjoyable. I think we can do great things and doing great things is worth it by itself. [...] It's just a labour of love. There may be business that comes out of it, but that's not the reason I do it.

Participation in the alumni network thus clearly goes beyond the business, instrumental aspect: the network mediates emotions that are very strong, leading alumni to describe other alumni as their family, with which they long to be reunited. This nostalgic sentiment towards other alumni is shared with others through participation in the alumni network.

Giving back

Tied to this idea of 'doing good' with members of their (former) 'family', the notion of giving back is central for many alumni of MultiCorp. They value what they see as the generosity of the company to the point of feeling the urge to redistribute their own wealth, in knowledge and philanthropic activity. This common urge brings them together and encourages them to maintain this behaviour throughout their lives:

> Most of the people, and this is something I really feel strongly about, most of the people in MultiCorp are lucky. [...] Of course, people make their own luck and they work hard and so on, but they are also lucky and it's only normal that they share or give back to society some of what they earned. You know, MultiCorp has a book called 'Statement of Purpose' and included in there is being good citizens of

the countries and the communities in which we live and really doing good and helping the world.

Nostalgia is expressed here regarding the values and goals of MultiCorp. The network is where the shared values between themselves, their colleagues and the firm can be witnessed, notably through the extensive philanthropic activity the alumni network is known for:

> At some point, I think we have to give back what we have learned; it's the mission of the alumni network. I accepted to get in for that, not for business, but for charity. At this point in my career I was ready to give time and discover causes in which my knowledge could be invested.

Nostalgia is thus mediated by the network, and through specific practices developed in, for instance, philanthropic projects, in which alumni can jointly project their nostalgia for MultiCorp's charitable values.

Discussion and concluding comments

Our results show that in three out of the four identified repertoires (Best in Class, Family and Giving back) alumni express nostalgia to justify their belonging to the alumni network. In these three emotional repertoires, alumni express not just a 'business' want, but also a nostalgic sentiment that makes them want to stay connected to the past, to their former 'family', to which they want to 'give back' and with which they want to share not only business but also moral values, and feel part once again of this small, elitist club of the 'best in class'. The corporate alumni network is, in turn, the medium through which nostalgia is mediated. This chapter thus constitutes a first exploration of media for nostalgia in an organisational context. This brings us to further discuss our results and propose research avenues with regard to the importance of paying more attention to organisational nostalgia and to the media through which nostalgia is diffused in an organisational context. The particular case of alumni networks that we presented here also appears to be potentially fruitful for researchers in media as well as in organisation studies, and we propose specific research avenues in that direction.

With our case study, we thus contribute to media and memory studies, and to the emerging and cross-disciplinary 'nostalgia studies', by showing that networks are media through which organisational nostalgia is expressed. Our interviewees justify their participation in the MultiCorp alumni network by underlining that they want to give back, and that they share moral values with what they consider as a family of best in class individuals: their active participation in the MultiCorp alumni network thus testifies to their nostalgia for their past professional experience at MultiCorp. Quite obviously, we encourage future research to identify and explore the other media through which nostalgia is diffused in organisational settings. In particular, organisational artefacts (Schein, 1985; Cook and Yanow, 1993) such as corporate history-making, everyday conversations and use of culturally specific language, or firm museums, could be considered as media for nostalgia. Such research would help us understand how firms leverage media to develop and strengthen a nostalgic feeling both among their current employees and among their stakeholders, the different groups of individuals who are not formal organisational members but who have an interest tied to the firm (former employees, but also clients, suppliers, local communities, etc.). Such contributions will notably extend existing scholarly work interested in how nostalgia can be instrumentally used by management teams for facilitating change initiatives (Ybema, 2004), as well as the stream of research looking into how nostalgia can be used for business development and marketing purposes (Cutcher, 2008; Kessous and Roux, 2008).

We also strongly encourage future studies to explore the relationship that exists between the choice of medium used by people to express their nostalgia and their degree of emotional attachment to the past. Indeed, although we cannot measure the strength of nostalgic feeling among alumni, we can underline that these people express an enduring emotional attachment to the past. This expression of nostalgia in an organisational context shows that it may be particularly difficult for some individuals to let go of a professional past time when life in that past era was considered as somehow 'better' (Gabriel, 1993). Alumni networks are, thus, a medium through which people express their nostalgia and make it visible in the world. Nostalgia is, thus, not only an individual and possibly fantasised experience, but also a repeated collective experience that can take concrete forms, such as the many social activities organised within the network. In this respect, we may hypothesise that people participating in such alumni networks experience a stronger attachment to the past than those who only express nostalgia through less engaging channels, such as more informal conversations or encounters with small groups of friends and former colleagues. Indeed, being a member of a corporate alumni network means having a formal, official affiliation with your past employer and your past colleagues, and it also means dedicating time, efforts and even financial resources (membership fees or event fees, travel to go to meetings, sponsoring events, donating to philanthropic projects, etc.). This appears to testify to a particularly proactive engagement with the past. We thus strongly encourage future research to document the relationship that exists between the media used by organisational participants to express their nostalgia and the strength of their emotional attachment to the past.

References

Adler, P. S. and Kwon, S.-W. (2002) 'Social Capital: Prospects for a New Concept'. *Academy of Management Review*, 27(1), pp. 17–40.
Baker, W. E. (1993) 'The Network Organization in Theory and Practice', in N. Nohria and R. G. Eccles (eds) *Networks and Organizations*. Boston, MA: Harvard Business School Press, pp. 397–429.
Basioudis, I. G. (2007) 'Auditor's Engagement Risk and Audit Fees: The Role of Audit Firm Alumni'. *Journal of Business Finance & Accounting*, 34(9/10), pp. 1393–1422.
Bouty, I. (2000) 'Interpersonal and Interaction Influences on Informal Resource Exchanges between R&D Researchers across Organisational Boundaries'. *Academy of Management Journal*, 43(1), pp. 50–65.
Brown, A. D. and Humphreys, M. (2002) 'Nostalgia and the Narrativization of Identity: A Turkish Case Study'. *British Journal of Management*, 13(2), pp. 141–159.
Burns, L. D. and Wholey, D. R. (1993) 'Adoption and Abandonment of Matrix Management Programs'. *Academy of Management Journal*, 36(1), pp. 106–138.
Coleman, J. S. (1988) 'Social Capital in the Creation of Human Capital'. *American Journal of Sociology*, 94(1), pp. 95–120.
Cook, S. D. and Yanow, D. (1993) 'Culture and Organizational Learning', in J. M. Shafritz and J. S. Ott (eds) *Classics of Organizational Theory*. Belmont, CA: Thomson Learning, pp. 400–413).
Cutcher, L. (2008) 'Creating Something Using Nostalgia to Build a Branch Network'. *Journal of Consumer Culture*, 8(3), pp. 369–387.
Davis, G. F. (1991) 'Agents without Principles? The Spread of the Poison Pill through the Intercorporate Network'. *Administrative Science Quarterly*, 36(4), pp. 583–590.
Denison, D. and Mishra, A. (1995) 'Toward a Theory of Organizational Culture and Effectiveness'. *Organization Science*, 6(2), pp. 204–223.
Fligstein, N. (1985) 'The Spread of the Multidivisional Form among Large Firms, 1919–1979'. *American Sociological Review*, 50(3), pp. 377–391.
Gabriel, Y. (1993) 'Organizational Nostalgia – Reflection on the "Golden Age"', in S. Fineman (ed.) *Emotion in Organizations*. London: Sage, pp. 118–141.

Hansen, M. T. (1999) 'The Search-Transfer Problem: The Role of Weak Ties in Sharing Knowledge across Organization Subunits'. *Administrative Science Quarterly*, 44(1), pp. 82–111.

Josserand, E. (2004) *The Network Organization: The Experience of Leading French Multinationals*. Cheltenham, UK: E. Elgar.

Kessous, A. and Roux, E. (2008) 'A Semiotic Analysis of Nostalgia as a Connection to the Past'. *Qualitative Market Research: An International Journal*, 11(2), pp. 192–212.

Koc-Menard, S. (2009) 'Knowledge Transfer after Retirement: The Role of Corporate Alumni Networks'. *Development and Learning in Organizations*, 23(2), pp. 9–11.

Lennox, C. S. and Park, C. W. (2007) 'Audit Firm Appointments, Audit Firm Alumni, and Audit Committee Independence'. *Contemporary Accounting Research*, 24(1), pp. 235–258.

McCabe, D. (2004) ' "A Land of Milk and Honey"? Reengineering the "Past" and "Present" in a Call Centre'. *Journal of Management Studies*, 41(5), pp. 827–856.

Meyer, A. D. and Lampel, J. (2008) 'Guest Editors' Introduction: Field-Configuring Events as Structuring Mechanisms: How Conferences, Ceremonies, and Trade Shows Constitute New Technologies, Industries, and Markets'. *Journal of Management Studies*, 45(6), pp. 1025–1035.

Mizruchi, M. S. (1992) *The Structure of Corporate Political Action: Interfirm Relations and their Consequences*. Cambridge, MA: Harvard University Press.

Oh, H., Labianca, G. and Myung-Ho, C. (2006) 'A Multilevel Model of Group Social Capital'. *Academy of Management Review*, 31(3), pp. 569–582.

Owen-Smith, J. and Powell, W. W. (2008) 'Networks and Institutions', in R. Greenwood, C. Oliver, K. Sahlin and R. Suddaby (eds) *The SAGE Handbook of Organizational Institutionalism*. Thousand Oaks, CA: Sage Publications, pp. 594–621.

Potter, J. (1996) *Representing Reality: Discourse, Rhetoric and Social Construction*. Thousand Oaks, CA: Sage.

Potter, J. and Wetherell, M. (1984) *Discourse and Social Psychology: Beyond Attitudes and Behaviour*. Thousand Oaks, CA: Sage Publications.

Schein, E. H. (1985) *Organizational Culture and Leadership*. San Francisco, CA: Jossey-Bass.

Sedikides, C., Wildschut, T. and Baden, D. (2004) 'Nostalgia: Conceptual Issues and Existential Functions', in J. Greenberg, S. Koole and T. Pyszczynski (eds) *Handbook of Experimental Existential Psychology*. New York: Guilford Press, pp. 200–214.

Sedikides, C., Wildschut, T., Gaertner, L., Routledge, C. and Arndt, J. (2008) 'Nostalgia as Enabler of Self-continuity', in F. Sani (ed.) *Self-Continuity: Individual and Collective Perspectives*. New York: Psychology Press, pp. 227–239.

Sertoglu, C. and Berkowitch, A. (2002) 'Cultivating Ex-Employees'. *Harvard Business Review*, 80(6), pp. 20–21.

Strangleman, T. (1999) 'The Nostalgia of Organisations and the Organisation of Nostalgia: Past and Present in the Contemporary Railway Industry'. *Sociology*, 33(4), pp. 725–746.

Wells, D. (2005) 'Wined and Dined by Wall Street', *Financial Times Online* 28 June.

Westphal, J. D. and Zajac, E. J. (1997) 'Defections from the Inner Circle: Social Exchange, Reciprocity, and the Diffusion of Board Independence in U.S. Corporations'. *Administrative Science Quarterly*, 42, pp. 161–183.

Wetherell, M. and Potter, J. (1988) 'Discourse Analysis and the Identification of Interpretive Repertoires', in C. Antaki (ed.) *Analysing Everyday Explanation: A Casebook of Methods*. Newbury Park, CA: Sage, pp. 168–183.

Ybema, S. (2004) 'Managerial Postalgia: Projecting a Golden Future'. *Journal of Managerial Psychology*, 19(8), pp. 825–841.

Yin, R. K. (2009) *Case Study Research: Design and Methods*. London: Sage.

8
Media and the Closure of the Memory Boom

Andrew Hoskins

The memory boom

The start of the contemporary memory boom (Huyssen, 2003; Winter, 2006; Hoskins and O'Loughlin, 2010) is marked for many by the mass affordability and the availability of the video cassette recorder, the premiere screening of the Holocaust television miniseries on NBC in 1978 (Shandler, 1999) and the 1980 publication of the English translation of the Godfather of collective memory: Maurice Halbwachs' *On Collective Memory*. Since then: boom, boom, boom! By whatever measure, celebrated and derided, the turn to and on the past has been relentless. The contemporary memory boom's centrifugal force is the anchoring and atomising debate around the nature, form and status of the remembering of conflict, the 'globalising of Holocaust discourses' (Huyssen, 2003), the trauma of everything, and the 'right to remember'. Its driving factors include the increasing obsession with the commemoration and memorialisation of the traumas and triumphs of, particularly, twentieth-century conflicts and catastrophes (Winter, 1995; Sturken, 1997; Simpson, 2006).

And there is no doubt that commemoration is a defining public mode of the memory boom. In recent years there has been a stacking up of the markings of events from the catastrophic and nodal through to the most banal, which are churned through commemorative cycles that seem to spin ever closer to the present, a point I develop in a moment. We can also see the emergence of digital television channels as archives in themselves, and in the past few years in Britain the channels 'Yesterday' and 'Blighty' have been launched, which mix a kind of popular TV nostalgia with what Paul Gilroy (2006) would call part of a 'postcolonial melancholia' (which I return to below).

It is not difficult to take any one unremarkable day and to browse through its news coverage to find the stacking up of a series of events made newsworthy again principally by virtue of their commemorative marking: for example, in 2009 the 70th anniversary of the sailing of the little boats across the channel to rescue the stranded troops at Dunkirk, 30 years since the success of Pink Floyd's *The Wall* album, and a year since the death of Michael Jackson all jostle for news time and space, affording them an equivalence of sorts in an almighty collapse of memory. The single archive makes commemoration one of the lowest common denominators of a public past: there is little that is resistant to this kind of blanket reductionism and revisionism. The juxtapositionism defining all news formats is not new, but 'post-scarcity culture' (Hoskins, 2011) has facilitated the appropriation of commemoration by news as an unbounded and unbridled genre that leaches value from memory even as it spectacularly promotes it.

And it is the satirists who have a good grasp of the devaluation contained in the commemoration of everything. For example, in 2007 the BBC's *Broken News* satire on the flux of frenetic 'prediction, speculation and recap' that today passes as news ran a spoof commemoration of 'Half Way There Day', notably 'the day that marked the half way point between each end of the Second World War'.

However, news media also drive this twentieth-century memorial arc, imposing the instant reassurances of the certainties of past survival on their intensive coverage of emergent conflicts and catastrophes. So, in this chapter I ask: What is the essential engine of extension of today's memory boom? Is the persistent churning of twentieth-century and earlier conflict particularly functional in rendering our current exposures to visceral uncertainties more intelligible? Or is it the processes of 'mediatisation' that define our new memory regime embedded in the everyday present through the immediacy, pervasiveness and volume of digital media? By 'mediatisation' I mean the process of shifting interconnected individual, social and cultural dependency onto media for maintenance, survival and growth (Hoskins, 2014).

I begin by exploring an example of the enduring memorial arc of twentieth-century war in the developing news reporting of the story of London 'under attack' in July 2005, the London Bombings, in which four suicide bombers killed 52 people and injured more than 770 in coordinated attacks in central London. Then I move on to argue that today mediatisation facilitates a 'new structure of memorialisation' that fuses the immediacy of the compulsion to commemorate with post-scarcity's plundering of past conflicts.

The 2005 London Bombings

The dominant 'media template' (Kitzinger, 2000; Hoskins, 2004; Brown and Hoskins, 2010) imposed across all news genres on '7/7' was 'the Blitz'. The Blitz was the intense and continuous German bombing of London (and other major UK cities) from September 1940 to May 1941, and the 'Blitz spirit' is invoked as the capacity to carry on with a degree of the normality of daily life in the face of the uncertainty and devastation of daily bombing attacks. Media templates are the frames, images and, more broadly, discourses (presumed by news editors and producers to have resonance with their audiences) that are routinely employed as often instantaneous prisms through which current and unfolding events are described, presented and contextualised.

Within hours of the first explosions on 7 July 2005, UK news reports were running still images and film footage of the Blitz, interleaving live coverage of the emergent terrorist attacks with interviews with Second World War survivors, as the story of the bombings unfolded. Templates are particularly effective as visual schemas in multiple windows on screen media or as chronological spreads in print. For example, on 8 July 2005, *The Sun*[1] (the UK's best-selling national tabloid newspaper of the day) offered a sequence of templates across two pages, headed: 'Worst Since Blitz'. This placed 7/7 in a series of visual stills and photographs, beginning with the 1940 Blitz, and including other bombings of the capital: the Old Bailey in 1973, Harrods in 1974, Hyde Park in 1982, and Canary Wharf in 1996. And the news feature was centred with a cropped, inverted image of Herbert Mason's famous photograph of St Paul's Cathedral standing defiantly above the smoke and flames of the London Blitz in December 1940.

To complete the media template, the Blitz comparison was authenticated with one of the most compulsive of news devices, witness testimony. The living memory of a survivor of the Blitz was set out in a column next to the St Paul's image in the form of an interview with 71-year-old Daphne Brundish, with photographs of her then and now: 'The Germans couldn't destroy us. Neither will these terrorists.'

Media templates, then, can be seen to be part of the stock functioning of news in 'containing' the catastrophic. For example, Silverstone (2002) writes of the terrorist attacks on the US on 11 September 2001:

> The shocking and the threatening has to be made into sense. Despite the singularly catastrophic moments of September 11 the media have a stock of images, frames and narratives available in their conscious

and unconscious archive which will hold as well as explain. This is the container of the familiar, the familiar which is claimed, sooner or later, to soften the blow. There is safety in the cliché. There is comfort in the tale.

However, news discourses operate paradoxically in that they shift or 'modulate' between the amplification and the containment of terror and terror threats (Hoskins and O'Loughlin, 2007, p. 14). News is naturally drawn to the catastrophic as something intrinsically newsworthy, but then has to render it intelligible and manageable for its audience. So, even early on 7 July 2005, Sky News was already running a highly speculative (as the motives of the perpetrators was not at all established at the time) visual series of al-Qaeda-linked terrorism templates of the attacks of 11 September 2001, Bali 2002, Istanbul 2003, and Madrid 2004.

The attempt to frame the 7/7 experience and resilience of Londoners as a new instance of 'Blitz spirit', however, is not at all straightforward. The use of the Blitz templates is striking in that they downplay the massive loss of life in London during this period, around 40,000 people, in favour of a discourse of 'business as usual' (Brown and Hoskins, 2010). And Charles Glass also challenges the comparative legitimacy of the Blitz template:

> The near-empty bus dropped me in the West End, where notices in windows apologised that restaurants were still closed. Employees, they said, could not get to work. George Rodger noted that in 1940 'it was a matter of pride that no shop ever remained closed unless it had been completely destroyed.' Two days before Christmas 1940, the *Daily Telegraph's* Frederick Salfeld wrote, 'Every morning, no matter how many bombs have been dropped in the night, London's transport runs, letters are delivered, milk and bread come to one's door, confectioners get their supplies, and the fruiterers' windows are filled.' I found one open restaurant called Automat on Dover Street that was owned by an Argentinean and staffed by Poles. A month later, Transport for London announced that use of the tube was down 10 to 15 percent during the week and 30 percent on weekends.
>
> (2005, p. 48)

So, Brown and Hoskins (2010) argue that the media template of the response to 7/7 as 'Blitz spirit' implies that the historical distance between the two events and the huge social and political differences at stake can be covered over by inscribing both events in a collective memory of Londoners. But the Blitz spirit's sustenance in media memory can also be attributed to a different kind of history, notably a working-through of the legacy of the decline of British Empire. In this way, Paul Gilroy sees the multicultural prospects of Britain as 'frustrated by a social, cultural and psychological blockage' that he calls 'postcolonial melancholia' (2006, p. 27). Gilroy draws on Freud in defining 'melancholia' as 'a state of pathological sadness interspersed with manic elation, guilty self hatred and disgust' (2006, p. 39). He asks, regarding the British struggle against Nazi Germany: 'Why do all of Britain's subsequent conflicts acquire irrefutable legitimacy if they can be presented as its analogues or extensions?' (2006, p. 30).

So, the Blitz spirit template is an odd amalgam: a kind of warped nostalgia or melancholia, which the catastrophic media, whose databases are primed for the next disaster, rapidly reaffirm. And it is the velocity and pervasiveness of this mediatisation that suppress alternative or counter-interpretations.

The new structure of memorialisation

However, the difference with twenty-first-century emergent events (compared with the memorial evolution of earlier ones) is that they are subject to a more intense set of media-memorial logics. The turning point of what I am calling a 'new structure of memorialisation' is the intensity and immediacy and sense of mediatised connectedness to contemporary events that are seen to be *in need of* remembrance, and 'the current overflowing of memory' (Le Goff, 1992, p. 54) is intimately connected. The arcs of twentieth-century wars and catastrophes are characterised by initial, relatively lengthy periods of limited and mostly private recollection, denial, unspoken trauma and non-memory, and then a much later entry into the fevered cycles of commemoration and memorialisation of the contemporary memory boom. However, many of the emergent events in this environment are always already mediatised and instead collapsed immediately into post-scarcity culture.

Consequently, the potential time available for individuals and societies to work through the meaning and to assimilate and manage the catastrophic is shrunk to nothing. The mediatisation of memory founded on post-scarcity culture facilitates both a memorialisation of the digital present and a more intense plundering of the past to contain the incoming uncertainties. 'Memorialise now!' seems to be the mantra of the political and news-driven response to seismic terror events. So we have what Erika Doss (2010) calls 'memorial mania', and David Blight

(2012) argues that the haste and nature of debate over the form and content of the public marking of September 11 is indicative of a new 'rage for memorialisation'.

Blight, for example, as a historian of the American Civil War, was asked to be a member of the 9/11 memorial advisory group within a few days of the catastrophe itself. This seems a somewhat hasty exploration of how this day should be remembered, given that at the time there was only an emergent and highly partial accounting for the attacks and the number of victims and missing amid the shock of the aftermath. Thus, as Blight explains,

> We immediately look back for some kind of hook, some kind of marker, some kind of place in the past that will help us understand what is happening to us. After all, without that, we're lost, we're lost in time, we're lost with only the present and the future which is very very frightening. And hence at that moment [...] the constant analogies in the immediate aftermath of 9/11, not only to Pearl Harbor, but to Antietam – the bloodiest single day of the Civil War.[2]

However, this does not necessarily mean that the imposition of templates to this end is successful. Indeed, US television news networks initially struggled to establish a template of sufficient scale and impact that would hold as a point of comparison on the unfolding coverage of 9/11. Even Pearl Harbor and the Vietnam War, with their defining presence in American historical consciousness, seemed to lack the force of catastrophic memory demanded to even begin to render intelligible the defining visceral terror of 9/11. But the new structure of memorialisation does entangle the past and present anew, which at least offers a future on the basis of the security of the historical distance from and survival of prior catastrophic times.

Closure

However we characterise the contemporary immersion in and use of the representations of past conflicts – pseudo-nostalgia, melancholia, or as a stabilizing 'hook' in the face of new fears and uncertainties – I have argued that, in the developed world at least, mediatisation is a significant driver of a new structure to memorialisation.

There is a tension (and intersection) between the two dynamics here – what one might call the cultural memory of war and the mediatisation of emergent war – forging a new battleground of and for memory.

Mediatisation facilitates the persistence of a schematic cultural memory of earlier wars, colouring the lens of how emergent war is seen and not seen, legitimised and not legitimised; but also post-scarcity culture enables the seepage of the immediacy of the representation and the circulation of media content of new wars to reinscribe and reinforce cultural memory. I have employed the term 'structure' of memorialisation here, as there is a kind of virality or contagion to this process that makes it irresistible.

Finally, I will note that there is something of a paradox between post-scarcity culture and the schematisation of past conflicts. As Paul Virilio (1994, p. 13), perhaps somewhat prophetically, argued, a 'dependence on the lens' (mediatisation in my terms) has standardised 'ways of seeing' and thus has actually led to a 'reduction in mnesic choices' rather than being transformative in enabling new memorial imaginaries. The same pervasiveness, immediacy and volume of digital media content that deliver a post-scarcity present of incoming insecurities require more effective assuaging management. And it is this that, in one way at least, oddly perhaps, narrows and closes down cultural memory, rather than opening up a more diffused past.

Notes

1. *The Sun*, 8 July 2005, pp. 20–21.
2. 'David Blight discusses 9/11, part 3', at: http://www.youtube.com/watch?v=108DcwjA864 (accessed 17 August 2012). The Battle of Antietam of 1862 was the bloodiest single-day battle in American history, with over 22,000 casualties.

References

Blight, D. (2012) 'From the Civil War to Civil Rights and beyond: How Americans Have Remembered Their Deepest Conflict', Paper presented at *The Future of Memory* Conference, University of Konstanz, 5 July.

Brown, S. D. and Hoskins, A. (2010) 'Terrorism in the New Memory Ecology: Mediating and Remembering the 2005 London Bombings'. *Behavioural Sciences of Terrorism and Political Aggression*, 2(2), pp. 87–107.

Doss, E. (2010) *Memorial Mania: Public Feeling in America*. Chicago: University of Chicago Press.

Gilroy, P. (2006) 'Multiculture in Times of War: An Inaugural Lecture Given at the London School of Economics'. *Critical Quarterly*, 48(4), pp. 27–45.

Glass, C. (2005) 'The Last of England: Churchill Gave Londoners Courage, Blair Is Serving Them Fear'. *Harpers*, pp. 43–49.

Hoskins, A. (2004) *Televising War: From Vietnam to Iraq*. London: Continuum.

Hoskins, A. (2011) '7/7 and Connective Memory: Interactional Trajectories of Remembering in Post-scarcity Culture'. *Memory Studies*, 4(3), pp. 269–280.

Hoskins, A. (2014) 'Mediatization of Memory', in K. Lundby (ed.) *Mediatization of Communication*. Berlin: De Gruyter.

Hoskins, A. and O'Loughlin, B. (2007) *Television and Terror: Conflicting Times and the Crisis of News Discourse*. Basingstoke: Palgrave Macmillan.

Hoskins, A. and O'Loughlin, B. (2010) *War and Media: The Emergence of Diffused War*. Cambridge: Polity Press.

Huyssen, A. (2003) *Present Pasts: Urban Palimpsests and the Politics of Memory*. Stanford: Stanford University Press.

Kitzinger, J. (2000) 'Media Templates: Key Events and the (Re)construction of Meaning'. *Media, Culture and Society*, 22(1), pp. 61–84.

Le Goff, J. (1992) *History and Memory*. Translated by S. Rendall and E. Claman. New York: Columbia University Press.

Shandler, J. (1999) *While America Watches: Televising the Holocaust*. New York: Oxford University Press.

Silverstone, R. (2002) 'Mediating Catastrophe: September 11 and the Crisis of the Other'. http://www.lse.ac.uk/collections/media@lse/pdf/mediatingcatastrophe.pdf (accessed 20 January 2006).

Simpson, D. (2006) *9/11: The Culture of Commemoration*. Chicago: University of Chicago Press.

Sturken, M. (1997) *Tangled Memories: The Vietnam War, the AIDS Epidemic, and the Politics of Remembering*. London: University California Press.

Virilio, P. (1994) *The Vision Machine*. Translated by Julie Rose. London: British Film Institute.

Winter, J. (1995) *Sites of Memory, Sites of Mourning, the Great War in European Cultural History*. Cambridge: Cambridge University Press.

Winter, J. (2006) *Remembering War: The Great War between Memory and History in the Twentieth Century*. New Haven: Yale University Press.

Part III
Screened Nostalgias

9
Nostalgia Is Not What It Used to Be: Serial Nostalgia and Nostalgic Television Series

Katharina Niemeyer and Daniela Wentz

In the last episode of Season One of the television series *Mad Men* (AMC, 2007–), Donald Draper, creative director of Sterling Cooper Advertising Agency, pitches an advertising campaign for Kodak's new slide projector. Instead of concentrating on its technological newness, as the client wishes, Don emphasises the possibility of a 'sentimental bond with the product' and suggests that nostalgia is a powerful way to create this bond. He presents a slide show with photographs from his own family life and names the projector 'the carousel', a carousel that 'lets us travel the way a child travels, round and round, and back home again'. The scene condenses a lot of what the series is all about: reconstructing and reimagining the past visually, discursively and historically by portraying and referring to the key political, social, economic and aesthetic elements of former times. But, while *Mad Men* seems to be *the* paradigmatic example when it comes to the relationship between television series and nostalgia, it is by no means alone in dealing so overtly with the subject. In fact, there seems to be a trend towards the nostalgic in modern television: *The Hour* (BBC, 2011–), *Boardwalk Empire* (HBO, 2010–) and *Downton Abbey* (ITV, 2010–), for instance, are all evidently vintage in atmosphere. Svetlana Boym would call this pre-existent nostalgia 'prefabricated'; she would say that they obviate creativity for the future (2001, p. 351). But even a short look at the carousel scene shows that such a reading would be far too simplistic. This volume intends to show, via different theoretical and methodological approaches and via case studies, that media present several different notions and functions of nostalgia. Media can trigger nostalgic emotions, media are formative in the aesthetics of the nostalgic world they portray (through visual appearance, sound and narrative) and, at the same time, nostalgic media serve as a cure for the viewers' suffering and longing for a past era, the concept of which the media themselves may well have created. Media can also be technological objects of nostalgia and, by recalling their own past, they can even become nostalgic themselves. Hence, nostalgia offers the possibility and necessity of reflecting on mediation, media and their related technologies (Boym, 2001) and vice versa. In this context, television occupies a very important role, not only because of its capacity to imagine, evoke, quote, show or repeat aspects of the past, including its own, but also because it is simultaneously a medium of forgetting. Television cannot maintain the memory of everything, and not all broadcasts are automatically archived. Consequently, the notion of loss, closely associated with nostalgia, becomes an almost inevitable phenomenon: some pictures are gone forever. However, television can both renew 'real' past pictures, if they are archived, and invent an imagined past via the aesthetics and narratives of a series. Television in this sense is a complex time machine navigating in between an ephemeral present, an often unknown future and an intriguing past (Niemeyer, 2011). There is a trend of linking nostalgia to a more or less unrealistic past, adorning its portrayal exclusively with affirmative and positive feelings. But television in general and television series in particular have a more complex relationship with nostalgia. A nostalgic series is very often the object of its audience's longing. At the same time, nostalgia seems to be one of the preferred subjects for television series to engage with on multiple levels. Both these concepts (this is our assumption) are based on the fact not only that a series, due most notably to its structural and temporal characteristics, is particularly suitable to unfold the multiple dimensions of nostalgia, but also that nostalgia, through its modes of being and its tense, can itself be regarded as one of those characteristics. This chapter is dedicated to introducing and discussing different types of nostalgia that are generated and revealed through television series and the serial characteristics of television. *Mad Men's* carousel scene is used as the conceptual starting point for this chapter because it typifies the crystallisation of the different forms of nostalgia that fill the frames of *Mad Men* and expand its frontiers, offering a reflection on television, nostalgia and seriality on a broad and profound level.

Serial homesickness

The carousel scene does not portray nostalgia merely as being useful for emotional advertising campaigns. It also reveals the historical and psychological complexity of the notion of nostalgia, which Immanuel Kant and Karl Jaspers both discussed: that painful longing for a romanticised, stable and more innocent past, a past related to one's own biography and to the idea of childhood as an innocent and perpetually light-hearted state (Boym, 2001; Bolzinger, 2007). No less important than the mentions of the past in the carousel scene is the notion of what Don and many others regard as a particularly special place – the 'home', or, as Don describes it, 'the place where we know we are loved'. This recalls the initial meaning of nostalgia: homesickness. Don's mention of his Greek friend Teddy, from whom he learns that nostalgia in Greek means 'the pain from an old wound', combined with this notion of homesickness, immediately evokes Homer's *Odyssey*. The *Odyssey* is one of the very first serial narratives and tells the story of Odysseus' wanderings as he attempts to find his way home, only to realise, when finally coming home after ten years, that no-one recognises him. But the story Don tells is not exclusively an allusion to the *Odyssey*. It is also the story of Don himself, who lives and acts out every one of these dimensions of nostalgia. His old wound is his (at this moment in the series) still unrevealed and mysterious past as 'Dick Whitman'. What is evoked here as 'the place where we know we are loved', his actual home, the suburb where he lives with his family, is *not* the place he feels at home. The opposite is true: Don never feels at home, but always feels out of place, isolated, disconnected. In contrast to the apparently better times which are presented via the projected photographs, his marriage is in fact undergoing a deep crisis.

Mad Men, as already mentioned, is not the only series to overtly address nostalgia as a subject or as a function of its *modus operandi*. There are two examples from earlier decades, analysed in their political dimension by Marcus (2004). The first is the 1980s series *The Wonder Years* (ABC, 1988–1993), in which each year in the show's diegetic universe is presented as having taken place 20 years before the original air dates, and whose unseen and now adult narrator tells us in a bittersweet manner the story of his childhood and youth. The second is the sitcom *Happy Days* (ABC, 1974–1984), which aired in the 1970s and takes place in an idealised version of the mid-1950s and early 1960s, a version very different from the portrayal of these years in *Mad Men*. Other recent series that are not overtly labelled 'vintage' or nostalgic deal in a more subtle way with nostalgia by broaching the issue of homesickness and expressing the loss of identity, continuity or stability. Homesickness, loss and the notion of the home are the pivotal elements of *Lost* (ABC, 2004–2010). Exclusion from former life is a major basis of the narrative on the island, which itself becomes a new home-to-be and later even a place to be longed for (Niemeyer and Wentz, 2014). *Game of Thrones* (HBO, 2011–) often hides the notion of longing behind its emphasis on violence and intrigue: most of the protagonists leave their homes to protect and defend them, but the return they long and fight for is shown to be impossible, difficult or bound to fail. Sometimes this even includes the destruction of their beloved walls and castles. In *The Walking Dead* (AMC, 2010–), the last uninfected humans fight for survival against the backdrop of a zombie apocalypse. In one scene, two of the protagonists, Rick and Shane, walk through a forest talking and laughing about their high school loves and lovers (S01E05) until Shane states: 'We shouldn't talk about this stuff. That life has gone and everyone with it [...] Our people and stories are dead.' When Rick replies, 'Can't you just forget them?' Shane's answer is in the negative, saying, 'Digging up the past, I tell you what it is... Nostalgia, it is like a drug. It keeps you away from seeing things as they are and that is a danger. [...] Survival, Rick, it means making hard decisions.' Nostalgia creates bonds to one's personal history, but in doing so impedes work on and in the future. It is not a paradox that Rick and Shane discuss these two aspects of nostalgia, because, as has been noted, nostalgia 'can be both a social disease and a creative emotion, a poison and a cure' (Boym, 2001, p. 354). The protagonists realise that their former everyday lives are gone forever and that they need to reidentify themselves, an idea which Shane establishes in the very first episode when he states: 'We are surviving here. We are. Day to day' (S01E01). This is homesickness for a home that no longer exists and will never exist again. Disturbed and disrupted identities relating to nostalgia also appear in the television series *Homeland* (Showtime, 2011–), inspired and based on the Israeli version *Hatufim* (Il, Channel 2, 2010–). In both shows, the return of the protagonists from the war against terrorism is not a happy homecoming but entails a profound interrogation of what home and homeland mean, a very powerful question in countries where the concept of the home has historically always been central (Duyvendak, 2011, p. 17). The American version is a historical and geopolitical view on what happened after the September 11 attacks. There was not only an overwhelming eruption of institutional structures like the *Homeland Security Service*, but also a wider problem in redefining the values and attributes of what the home might be in contemporary times (p. 113).

But concepts of feeling at home or homecoming as responses to homesickness are not only important to the aesthetics or characters of a televisual narrative. They also concern audiences. Watching television can induce a homely feeling. A component of serials themselves is the necessity of habitual viewing, and this seems to strengthen the feeling of longing on the part of the audience.

Serial homecoming and longing

The carousel scene discloses that nostalgia is not just a vague emotion, but, rather, is intrinsically bound to its mediatised appearance and method of production: it cannot be separated from its mediated existence. The white rectangular projection surface at the end of the slide show stands in for this function of media as the projection space for our individual or shared nostalgic longings. Of course, this scene is highly self-reflexive, since the *Mad Men* slide projector overtly reveals nostalgia as having a specific function for media, where the evoking of nostalgic emotions, the symbolic charge of things, aims at turning those things into desirable commodities. Moreover, Don's description of the slide projector as a time machine, 'moving backwards, forward, round and round', can be assigned without restrictions to television, and television series in particular. With regard to television series, this description depends not only on the negotiation between cyclical and linear temporality, but also on the sentimental bond the viewers build with a series, which becomes one of the most important reasons to make them tune in repeatedly. Watching television series relates to personal habits based on new ways of organising the time and space of the viewing itself. The recent success and explosion of television series can at least partly be explained by the rituals they create in everyday life (Esquenazi, 2009), rituals that have already been analysed and discussed on a more general level as being central to television and correlated with the idea of a sharing community (Silverstone, 1988; Dayan and Katz, 1996). This assumption can be underpinned by Bolzinger's work (2007) about the history of nostalgia and the coining of the term by the doctor Johannes Hofer in 1688. Hofer's work underlines that nostalgia is mainly provoked by missing everyday life rituals and is itself a ritual disease. The hospitalised soldier, as Hofer and others found out, feels better when he can listen to the music of his homeland, or when he can interact with people having the same accent. His condition improves when the doctor tells him that he can go home soon. After a few days, if the promises are not kept, the soldier feels worse and may even die (Bolzinger, 2007, p. 140).

In our globalised world, the old, initial idea of nostalgia could explain why people are homesick or why they tend to want to leave the country which, whether voluntarily or involuntarily, they live in (Duyvendak, 2011). But these homesick people do not die, and progress in medicine and the healing capabilities of psychopharmacology might be the reasons for the fact that the old, initial meaning of nostalgia is rarely employed (Richard, 2004; Viennet, 2009). More pleasant symptoms of nostalgia, on the other hand, can be 'healed' or at least 'calmed' by objects or products of our consumer and media culture. In other words, the attributes of folklore and other traditions have mostly, or at least frequently, shifted to popular culture, a culture that creates common everyday shared life patterns, habits and memories. Television series that are common products of this popular culture take part in these rituals. Consequently, television series can become objects of longing themselves. As *The Wonder Years*, for example, still has not appeared on DVD, some viewers might wait for their cure, its rerun. One could even assume that nostalgic longing belongs intrinsically to the logic of seriality, and television takes advantage of this longing by several strategies: by endless reruns and by remakes of successful series like *Beverly Hills 90210* (Fox, 1990–2000, *90210*, the CW, 2009–2013), *Dr. Who* (BBC, 1963–1989, 2005), *Battlestar Galactica* (ABC, 1978–1980, Sky One, 2004–2009) or, one of the latest examples, *Dallas* (CBS, 1978–1991, TNT, 2012–). There are even whole networks whose programming is entirely based on the rebroadcasting of old television shows, especially series, for example *Nick at Nite* or the speaking '*Nostalgia television*' (Holdsworth, 2011). Nostalgia obviously has links to the inevitably mediatised past. It is based on the indivisible connection between one's own past and the media that accompanied that past. Media storage saves it and thereby makes it repeatable and memorisable today. As Don Draper puts it, 'It takes us to a place, where we ache to go again.' Series thus appear as the place where nostalgia can be healed, at least for a brief moment.

Over and above this, nostalgia seems to be a concept that fits without restrictions the structural characteristics of televisual seriality. Series can never (this is the hypothesis) *not* evoke a feeling of nostalgia, because they are based on the imperative to always leave a void. The void is inevitably present, whether in the form of the temporal gaps between episodes and seasons, the void a long-watched series leaves when it finally ends, or the never-arriving closure of an unfinished narrative. Series always create gaps that can never be filled, even by rewatching them. This longing, which pertains to the logic of seriality, clearly shows, once again, that nostalgia is not just the preserve of the past, but can be directed just as well towards the future or even the present (Boym, 2001).

Serial nostalgia

As we have mentioned, it would be considering the matter too narrowly if one linked the relationship between seriality and nostalgia only to a series' potential to evoke a nostalgic longing in either the viewers or the narrative. Rather, series, as they accumulate time, and thus a past and an imagined future, can be, and often are, nostalgic themselves. Hardly any long-running series gets along without flashback episodes, where the characters remember the series' past. *Friends* (NBC, 1994–2004) and *How I Met Your Mother* (CBS, 2005–), for example, have one or more in every season. Beginning with its title, the latter is even built on a continuous flashback that interlaces flashbacks of flashbacks and also imagined flashforwards that then become part of the fictional narrator's imagined memory. Nostalgia in *How I Met Your Mother* is located on a narrative level but is mainly created by the temporal and visual montage of the whole story. The longing to finally meet the mother concerns not only the two children, who are shown at the beginning of many episodes on their sofa listening to the story being told, but also the viewer (perhaps also sitting on a couch), who longs for this moment to come (cf. Wentz, 2009). This particular combination of narrative and interrelated montage is an element you can find, once again, in *Mad Men*. A strong parallel to the work of Edward Hopper, who coincidentally was himself an illustrator in advertising, can be drawn with the series' aesthetics. The recurring, long, almost photographic shots of Donald Draper sitting alone in a bar recall the famous work *Nighthawks* (1942). The melancholic glances of emptiness in offices recall paintings like *Office at Night* (1948) or *New York Office* (1962). Loneliness, alienation and longing percolate these nostalgic templates, which induce what Vera Dika (2003, p. 25) calls 'inner dialogue and memory'. The 'experienced time' (Ricoeur, 1993) of the epoch is incarnated via these 'tableaux of time', recalling Edward Hopper's work on an aesthetic and conceptual level. The very slow montage also emphasises these aspects of longing. These elements reinforce the idea and impression of the individual loneliness of beginning a stressful life in an advertising working environment and a modern world. As Gabriele Schabacher (2013) has recently emphasised, *Mad Men*, by referring to the 1960s, reanalyses an epoch which is already visually conventionalised and the self-conception and self-understanding of which are intrinsically linked to the processes of modernisation, and especially mediatisation. Of course, television and advertising are among the most important agents of that process. In this sense, serial nostalgia concerns not only the individual past of every series, but also the whole construct of an always already mediatised history. Another striking example of a television series dealing with this is *The Newsroom* (HBO, 2012–), the narrative centre of which is a news desk and the outstanding characteristic of which is the fictional news coverage of events that really happened in the very recent past. Every real event which is taken up by the series and whose coverage is still in our short-term memory serves as an example of journalism as it *should* be and also *could* be. This specific configuration is deeply nostalgic, as nostalgia means not only a melancholic memory of what was, but also the regret that it was not *different*, the fantasy of what *could* have been. Already the title sequence gives a clear idea of this melancholic–nostalgic attitude towards the past. It is divided into two parts. After the very first picture of a satellite circumnavigating the world, a very slow montage of black-and-white photographs unfolds, showing scenes and iconic figures of American television journalism. Among them, for example, is Edward Murrow, whose 1950s news show *See It Now* has shaped the image of critical journalism ever since. Chet Huntley and David Brinkley, the NBC News anchormen of the 1960s, also feature, as does Walter Cronkite, the main anchor of the *CBS Evening News* during the 1960s and 1970s and the 'most trusted man in America', who not only covered the Kennedy assassination and the landing on the moon, but was also a late but sharp critic of the Vietnam War. Text overlays like 'News Bulletin', 'Evening News', and so on repeatedly disrupt this montage. Subsequent to the black-and-white images, scenes from the first season of the series appear, only cut in a faster rhythm, and interrupted or overlaid by the same inserts signifying 'the News'. This second part differs from the first one in that it is in colour and uses some visual tricks, such as, at certain moments, translucent surfaces gliding over the images. More important yet than the *distinctive* features and effects of *Televisuality* (Caldwell, 1995), marking 'New Television', is the aesthetic feature that is *common* to both parts: all the images are overlaid by overarticulated horizontal stripes, instantly recalling 'interlaced video mode'. This was the prevalent technique before the invention of high-definition television, and one whose disturbing artefacts appeared in the form of this kind of stripe. The fictional news desk of *News Night*, a programme on the fictional news network *Atlantis Cable News*, places itself via this montage in the tradition of a television journalism understood as being investigative, educational and full of integrity. Such journalism is linked very clearly to a certain period, from the mid-1950s to the mid-1970s, exactly the same period of time covered by *Mad Men* and *Happy Days*. This period of American history has not been chosen randomly. It was the so-called *Golden Age* of the history of television, the time of big broadcast networks, prior to the invention of cable and target-group-specific television (it is not a coincidence that sitcoms from that time are among the most popular programmes for nostalgia television). The more recent television series *Desperate Housewives* is also a show which is set in the present, but re-enacts the relationship between television, its domestication after the Second World War and the socio-spatial formation of the suburb (cf. Spigel, 1992). *Desperate Housewives* can thus be regarded as portraying the very same 'critical nostalgia' as television critic Gary Edgerton describes for *Mad Men*, not simply towards the 'good old times', but towards 'the good old times' of (American) television (Edgerton, 2011, p. xxvii).

Television has recently begun to come under threat. Television and modern television series have started to transform and expand, or cross over entirely, into other media (cf. Maeder and Wentz, 2013). As television in its current form faces its potential end, it is possible to ask whether the nostalgic trend of modern television could be the expression of television's fear that it will lose its own place, its home, and soon become just a part of the past itself. The homely family feeling that television has inspired since the 1950s by occupying an important place in the living room or kitchen and being an important symbol for family life after the Second World War (Spigel, 1992) seems to be falling apart, which could be one of the reasons why this medium is entering a nostalgic cycle (Marcus, 2004) on all the levels described. It is nostalgic for its own past times and places, and television narrates and shows this nostalgia to provoke a response in its viewers. Nevertheless, it remains the projection space for this intriguing sense of longing that television series can mutually provoke and heal by their very particular status as both ritual-makers and ritual-breakers.

References

Bolzinger, A. (2007) *Histoire de la nostalgie*. Paris: Campagne Première.
Boym, S. (2001) *The Future of Nostalgia*. New York: Basic Books.
Caldwell, J. T. (1995) *Televisuality. Style, Crisis and Authority in American Television*. Brunswick: Rutgers University Press.
Dayan, D. and Katz, E. (1996) *La télévision cérémonielle*. Paris: PUF.
Dika, V. (2003) *Recycled Culture in Contemporary Art and Film – the Uses of Nostalgia*. New York: Cambridge University Press.
Duyvendak, J. W. (2011) *The Politics of Home – Belonging and Nostalgia in Western Europe and the United States*. London: Palgrave Macmillan.

Edgerton, G. R. (2011) 'Introduction. When Our Parents Became Us', in G. R. Edgerton (ed.) *Mad Men. Dream Come True TV.* New York: I.B. Tauris, pp. xxi–xxxvi.

Esquenazi, J.-P. (2009) *Mythologie des séries télé.* Paris: Le Cavalier Bleu Éditions.

Holdsworth, A. (2011) *Television, Memory and Nostalgia.* Basingstoke: Palgrave Macmillan.

Maeder, D. and Wentz, D. (eds) (2013) *Der Medienwandel der Serie. Navigationen.* Siegen: univeri.

Marcus, D. (2004) *Happy Days and Wonder Years: The Fifties and the Sixties in Contemporary Cultural Politics.* New Brunswick and London: Rutgers University Press.

Niemeyer, K. (2011) *De la chute du mur de Berlin au 11 Septembre 2001. Le journal télévisé, les mémoires collectivs et l'écriture de l'histoire.* Lausanne: Antipodes.

Niemeyer, K. and Wentz, D. (2014), 'The Island of the Day after. The television series LOST and the Post-911-Era', in B. Beil, H. Schwaab and D. Wentz (eds) *LOST in Media.* Berlin: LIT Verlag (to be published in 2014).

Richard, F. (2004) 'Temporalité, psychose et mélancolie'. *Adolescence*, tome 22, 4, Le Bouscat: L'esprit du temps, pp. 687–704.

Ricoeur, P. (1993) *Temps et récit. Le temps raconté*, t.3. Paris: Éditions du Seuil.

Schabacher, G. (2013) 'Mediatisierte Geschichte. Serielle Verfahren der Historisierung am Beispiel von Mad Men', in D. Maeder and D. Wentz (eds) *Der Medienwandel der Serie. Navigationen.* Siegen: univeri., pp. 13–30.

Silverstone, R. (1988) 'Television, Myth and Culture', in J. W. Carey (ed.) *Media, Myths and Narratives, Television and the Press.* Sage Annual Reviews of Communication Research 15. London: Sage, pp. 20–47.

Spigel, L. (1992) *Make Room for TV. Television and the Family Ideal in Postwar America.* Chicago: Chicago University Press.

Viennet, D. (2009) *Il y a malêtre. Essai sur le temps et la constitution du soi contemporain.* Paris: l'Harmattan.

Wentz, D. (2009) 'Das neue Fernsehen und die Historizität des Dispositivs', in D. Wentz and A. Wendler (eds) *Die Medien und das Neue.* Marburg: Schüren, pp. 151–165.

10
AMC's *Mad Men* and the Politics of Nostalgia

David Pierson

Nostalgia is an integral concept and appeal in AMC Network's popular TV series *Mad Men* (2007–). The series follows the exploits of several men and women who work for the fictional Madison Avenue advertising agency Sterling Cooper in early 1960s America. There are several different forms of nostalgia expressed in *Mad Men*. The first can be called the 'nostalgic imaginary' because the series represents the era as both alluring and repellent (Dove-Viebahn, 2013). Nostalgic pleasures can be found in the era's fashions and styles, the blissful unawareness of the dangers of alcohol and tobacco, and the impending promise of dramatic social change at home, in the workplace and in American society. But these pleasures come tempered with the period's most repulsive elements: sanctioned workplace misogyny, blatant racism and homophobia, rampant smoking, alcoholism and consumerism (Dove-Viebahn, 2013). The second nostalgia, as outlined by Niemeyer and Wentz (Chapter 8), is linked to the ways in which *Mad Men*, as a TV serial and mediator of the cultural past, evokes, through its visual appearances and narratives, an intense emotional loss and longing in the viewer, which in turn is 'healed' through its very representations. *Mad Men* intensifies these feelings by centring its narratives around a main protagonist, Don Draper, who repeatedly longs for a home he never had as a child and probably will never attain as an adult. In the series' first season, the audience learns that Don Draper is really Dick Whitman. A narrative flashback reveals that, during the Korean War, an enlisted Whitman took the dog tags and the identity of a Don Draper, an officer killed in an enemy attack. Whitman assumes this new identity to begin anew and to escape the shame of his illegitimate birth, along with his impoverished childhood. Throughout the series, Don is caught in a repetitive pattern of loss and displacement; he wants to be part of a family, but he is never able to accept it as a reality. The third form uses nostalgia to critically comment on the era as well as to make analogies with our contemporary culture. For example, Scott Stoddart (2007) asserts that the series deconstructs many of the reigning myths of the period, especially the white-collared, suburban American dreams embodied in Sloan Wilson's popular 1955 novel *The Man in the Gray Flannel Suit* and the Kennedys' mythic Camelot era. Stoddart contends that there never was a 'golden age of capitalism' and that the anxieties of this earlier period mirror those of our own (2007, p. 208). In this essay, I argue that *Mad Men* expresses a fourth form of nostalgia, a mode that employs nostalgia as an indelible resource for present-day cultural critique, and as a means of inspiration for social resistance and action against existing hegemonic domains of power in society.

For scholars such as Charles Maier (1999) and Michael Kammen (1991), nostalgia is a dubious emotion carrying with it implications of escapism and a dangerous longing for the mythical past. The basic value or function of nostalgia remains unacknowledged in much recent criticism of the phenomenon, criticism which tends to operate under the assumption that nostalgia is pathological, regressive and delusional. Hostility towards nostalgia is fuelled in particular by the recurrent co-option of nostalgia by conservative, reactionary politics (Lowenthal, 1985; Chase and Shaw, 1989; Heer, 2009). Feminist critics, such as Janice Doane and Devon Hodges (2013), have examined the ways in which nostalgic writers construct their visions of the golden past to authenticate woman's traditional place and to challenge outspoken criticisms of it. Liberal critics have pointed out how President Reagan used the nostalgic vision of preserving a small-town America and rugged individualism to dismantle the nation's welfare system and to build up its military forces to defend it. Stuart Tannock (1995) points out that these political critiques run the risk of conflating nostalgia and its use with conservative political groups. He maintains that nostalgia has always characterised the politics of the left and the right. During the 1960s, the youth counter-culture movement often relied on the nostalgic frontier vision of going 'back to nature' as a response to the mainstream consumer-based, bourgeois lifestyle. Peter Glazer (2005), in *Radical Nostalgia*, writes that Spanish Civil War commemorative events in America serve as examples of the progressive potential of nostalgia by animating and celebrating a historically significant moment for the American Old Left.

While nostalgia does approach the past as a source of value and meaning, this should not necessarily be confused with the desire for an established, traditional and hierarchised society. It is true that nostalgic individuals who find themselves in the face of an unstable present may long to return to a stable past, a past in which everything is held in its proper place, when social and gender roles were clearly and unambiguously defined. For traditional-minded viewers, *Mad Men* offers them a nostalgic vision of when social and gender roles were well defined in American society. In the series, men are presented as the family breadwinners and women mainly serve in supportive roles as either housewives or secretaries. White, college-educated males dominate the business realm and political and racial minorities are largely kept in the background. As the series progresses through the 1960s, Sterling Cooper does begin to experience changes in its office composition, with the hiring of a Jewish copywriter and an African-American secretary, and the return of Peggy Olson as head copywriter. With the exception of Joan Harris's (Holloway) inclusion as a partner for agreeing to sleep with a high-profile client, the firm continues with white men at the helm.

Nostalgic individuals may also, when faced with a present that seems overly fixed, static and politically immobile, long for a past when things were more open and could be put into play, opened up or provided with extra breathing space. The type of past, whether open or closed, stable or unstable, longed for by the nostalgic individual depends on his or her current position in society along with his or her fears and aspirations. Tannock (1995) calls for a more critical discussion of nostalgia, discussion that acknowledges the presence of multiple, distinct nostalgias among individuals and communities of social groups. More than mere sentiment, nostalgia is a complex conceptual and critical vision that responds to a diversity of personal needs and political desires in society.

At its core, nostalgia operates as the search for a continuity of specific values and meanings from the past. Nostalgia responds to an experience of discontinuity in the present; to the sense that something is blocking or threatening an agency or identity in the present and that this is leading to a separation from the cultural and communal traditions of a creatively remembered past, homeland, community or family (Tannock, 1995). By returning to a lost past with its people and places, the nostalgic individual seeks to reconnect with a sense of continuity with past values and ideals. Nostalgia is best understood not as an emotion or sense, but, rather, as a rhetorical practice in which discontinuity is as central to its position as any assertion of continuity. Tannock (1995) argues that the nostalgic pursuit of continuity with values and ideals from the past presupposes a lack of and a break from those same values and ideals in the present, which is represented as a period of discontinuity. While the designated break between an idealised past and a deficient present can be as close as a few years, there must be a supposed break for nostalgia to logically exist. Tannock asserts that nostalgia rhetorically functions through three emotive periods: the first part is the prelapsarian, utopic world before the Fall; second is the period of the break or the severance (the Fall); and third is the postlapsarian or present world, which is seen as deficient in some moral quality or value (1995, p. 454).

Herbert Marcuse (1987), in *Eros and Civilization*, relies on a periodic sense of discontinuity when he suggests that remembrance of past experiences can serve as a tool to examine and critique the present historical condition. A nostalgia that discovers a past of freedom and happiness puts into question the painful performances of alienated labour and assorted oppressions of everyday life. These memories are embedded in individual and collective experiences of a happier past and historical conditions that offered more and better freedom, gratification and happiness. Svetlana Boym (2001) points out that, though nostalgia appears to be a longing for a particular place, it is actually a desire to return to another time, a time in tune with one's imagination. Marcuse (1987) sought to explore the emancipatory qualities of memory blended with fantasy, and thereby posit that past cultural traditions contain embedded resources that can be mobilised to fight suffering and oppression in the present. The practice of recalling the pleasures of a previous period against the onslaught of modern industrialisation is undeniably future-orientated; it is looking to the past to construct a better future.

Similarly, Frederic Jameson (1974) asserts that there is no reason why a nostalgia conscious of itself, a clear dissatisfaction with the present on the grounds of a remembered plentitude, cannot be employed as a revolutionary stimulus for social change. Jameson gives as examples many of Walter Benjamin's written works, including his essay 'Paris, Capital of the Nineteenth Century' (1939), in which the writer uses descriptive, allegorical imagery to tacitly critique Western Europe's industrialisation and the rise of an authoritarian Nazi Germany. In Benjamin's posthumously published work *Berlin Childhood around 1900* (2006), he meticulously revisits his favourite childhood haunts (Berlin city zoo, parks, swimming pools, railway terminals), which now serve as a storehouse of utopian longing that contrasts with the industrial blight, urban poverty and reactionary politics of a modernising 1930s Germany. Ray Cashman (2006), whose work focuses on the uses of nostalgia in Northern Irish communities, maintains that nostalgia can be critical in an analytical way by enabling the evaluation of the present through contrast with the past. He adds that nostalgia can also be critical in the sense 'for inspiring action of great moral weight, action that may effect (sic) a better future' (Cashman, 2006, p. 138).

Upon close analysis, one can discover nostalgic aspects of *Mad Men* that can be used to question and critique our present social and economic situation. Despite its rigid hierarchical and patriarchal social structure and mind-numbing conformity, Sterling Cooper as an institutional entity represents the typical post-war modern American corporation. *Mad Men* is historically positioned (early 1960s) at a time when the American corporation was perceived as a 'secure, paternalistic, and globally-dominant organisation' and was clearly the preferred career pathway for newly emergent college graduates (Whitman, 1999, p. 1). During this period, roughly from 1950 to 1973, most corporations offered the middle-class professional stable employment, combined with incremental wage hikes, expanded benefits and job security, in exchange for improved productivity and dedication to the company (Ross, 2009). Richard Sennett (2007) argues that these older companies and organisations provided employees with an established sense of stability, and even a personal social identity, as long as it was closely aligned with the company's goals. Charles Heckscher (1996) states that most large American corporations followed an implicit policy of paternalism whereby the company would provide white-collar workers with steady employment and career advancement in exchange for complete employee loyalty. This paternalism was critical for the stable development and expansion of the post-war corporation into global markets (Heckscher, 1996). In *Mad Men*, corporate paternalism is evident in Don Draper's careful nurturing and promotion of Peggy Olson from secretary to first female copywriter, his acceptance of Harry Crane's concept of creating a television sales department, and his own promotion to firm partner at Sterling Cooper.

By the mid-1970s, increased global competition and several economic upheavals turned the American corporation into an institution vulnerable to short-term speculation, shifting world markets and increased boom-and-bust economic cycles. Whitman states that the intensified focus on bottom-line profits and economic efficiencies have led to 'a wave of what has been called downsizing, restructuring, re-engineering, and rightsizing, all terms that signify getting rid of people' (1999, p. 9). The implicit employer–employee pact of the older 'good corporation' of steadfast loyalty, job security, steadily rising wages, solid benefits and a guaranteed pension were replaced with workplace insecurity and corporate instability. The workplace relationship between company and employee is perceived today as contingent and probably temporary. Loyalty has been redefined to mean a mutual respect between employer and employee, and support is given as long as the relationship is beneficial for both parties. Jobs, pay increases and benefits are no longer assumed automatic entitlements for long-term employees, but, rather, are contingent on the employee's individual performance and contribution to the company's profit margin (Whitman, 1999). Andrew Ross (2009) states that, since the 1970s, contingent employment has steadily increased, from low-wage service positions to high-end skilled occupations, with no expected decline in sight. For white-collar workers, the corporate work environment often consists of longer work days, 24-hour on-call work status, reduced salaries and benefits, and new communication technologies, like smart phones and computer laptops, have led to virtual enslavement to the company, along with increased job insecurities (Fraser, 2002).

The series, however, does repeatedly disorient the audience's nostalgic expectations, especially those concerning Sterling Cooper. By the end of its second season, Sterling Cooper is sold to Putnam, Powell and Lowe (PP&L), a British firm, and the workers experience the usual instabilities and insecurities associated with modern corporate takeovers and global capitalism. At the end of the third season, Draper, Sterling, Cooper and a few other workers break their employment contracts with PP&L to begin a new start-up ad agency rather than become part of Sterling Cooper's absorption into a rival Madison Avenue mega-ad agency. Draper and his colleagues' actions are reflective of the post-1970s neoliberal entrepreneurial spirit that came to dominate American businesses, national politics and global economies in the 1980s and 1990s. In Season Six, Sterling Cooper Draper Pryce (SCDP) merges with another ad agency and contemplates going public by selling stock shares to amass enough capital to take on the larger Madison Avenue ad agencies. SCDP's possible venture into the stock market evokes Jameson's (2009) argument that the late twentieth-century growth of derivatives and arcane financial instruments ushered in a new period of financial capitalism. In our present era, the processes of production and consumption are subordinated to financial speculation, the global circulation of capital and the accumulated growth of money profits.

As mentioned earlier, *Mad Men* does re-present socially conservative images of the early 1960s as a period of 'lost' American innocence before the social and cultural movements that would soon overtake the nation. The series expresses the dominant sense that it was an era defined by social conformity, upward social mobility and hopeful optimism.

During *Mad Men*'s first three seasons, social dissent is primarily limited to urban bohemians and the early rumblings of the Civil Rights Movement.[1] *Mad Men*, however, also reveals the social resistance lurking just beneath the surface of the lives of its main characters. These moments of social conflict not only challenge hegemonic notions of the era, but also can be understood as 'counter-memories'. George Lipsitz (1990) adapts Michel Foucault's conception of counter-memory as a critical practice of re-examining history to determine and highlight moments of excluded historical memory. Lipsitz asserts that hidden histories excluded from dominant narratives constitute counter-memories that force revision of existing histories. Counter-memories can be employed to establish an oppositional consciousness critical of existing dominant social institutions and, thereby, promote social change for the future.

Although *Mad Men*'s moments of social resistance are fictional in nature, nevertheless, they do reveal actions that are plausible and expressible to people living within the social conformity of early 1960s America. One example of social resistance is expressed by the series' character of Peggy Olson, who continuously fights to be accepted as a fellow copywriter, to gain access to clients, all without alienating the other women who work at the male-dominated Sterling Cooper. In *Mad Men*'s pilot episode, 'Smoke Gets in Your Eyes' (19 July 2007), Olson, arriving on her first day of work as a secretary, stoically endures sexist remarks from the agency's male executives in an office elevator. In this same episode, when Olson tells her male gynaecologist that she wishes to go on the birth control pill, she must tolerate his patronising warning that she should not become 'a strumpet'. Later, in another episode, when she accidentally reveals to the men that she excels at creative brainstorming, Freddie Rumsen, a copywriter, both commends and humiliates her with one swift remark to his male co-workers. Freddie exclaims that seeing Olson in action 'was like watching a dog play the piano'. In the episode 'The Fog' (13 September 2009), Olson tells Draper that she wants a raise to equal pay with the men. When her request is denied, she replies to him: 'You have everything and so much of it.' While Olson does achieve success by accepting the position as copy chief at a rival ad agency, she still must contend with a male-dominated workplace. For feminists living in our relatively placid, post-feminist era, Olson's proto-feminist struggles can serve as a nostalgic source of continuity and inspiration to this earlier historical period. In terms of nostalgia, these acts of social resistance can be seen as moments of discontinuity or counter-memories with the hegemonic notion that the early 1960s was a period of limited social conflict.

Another example of female social resistance can be found in the character of Betty Draper, the unhappy, beautiful wife of Don Draper. Betty Draper, who once had a budding career as a fashion model, has resigned herself to being a suburban housewife and stay-at-home mother of her two children. The first physical signs of Betty's unhappiness appear in the series' second episode, 'Ladies Room' (26 July 2007), when her hands go numb and drop from the steering wheel of the family station wagon, which crashes into a bird bath on a neighbour's lawn. Following the accident, Don arranges for Betty to have weekly therapist sessions with the psychiatrist, who reports regularly to him. Betty's frustrations with her life are made manifest in the episode 'Shoot' (9/13/07), when her career as a model is almost revived by Jim Hobart, a McCann ad agency executive, who tells her that she might be perfect for his Coca-Cola campaign. Hobart's offer is a ploy to entice Don to consider moving up to the larger McCann agency. When Don declines Hobart's offer, Betty loses her chance to restore her career. Betty conceals her disappointment by telling Don that she didn't want to return to modelling after all. Betty expresses her frustrations by shooting into the air at her neighbour's pigeons with a BB gun, partly in retaliation for his threats against Polly, the Drapers' family dog, who grabbed one of his pigeons earlier in the same episode. The surrealistic image of Betty shooting her neighbour's birds ends the episode. At the end of *Mad Men*'s third season, Betty discovers that Don lied about his identity and his past, and subsequently divorces him. Betty's request for a divorce comes at the time of President Kennedy's assassination, which serves as a portent of drastic social changes in the series and in American society. As with Olson, Betty's visible frustrations and often rebellious acts of defiance in maintaining the patriarchal social role of housewife and supporter of her husband can serve as nostalgic points of continuity and potential political critique for feminist and other social critics who are frustrated with the stability of the current post-feminist political climate.

The men in *Mad Men* also exemplify moments of social resistance, including the lead character of Don Draper. Although Draper has established the ideal, middle-class family, he is reluctant to completely embrace the patriarchal role of father. Don is resistant against performing the role of disciplinarian, probably because it is too close to his own childhood experiences under his stern, callous father. He realises, at some deeper level, that his being Don Draper is just as much a social trap as being Dick Whitman. Don frequently escapes the conformity of his suburban life through sexual encounters with a host of uncommon women, from the bohemian Midge Daniels to the urbane, Jewish department store heiress Rachel Menken and the aggressive Bobbie Barrett, the wife-manager of comedian Jimmy Barrett. Following his divorce, Don moves to the city and marries Megan, a former SCDP receptionist, but soon continues his philandering with a neighbour's wife. Gary Edgerton (2012) maintains that Don Draper, who came out of the dark depths of the Great Depression, is not only a pretender, like John F. Kennedy with his Irish-American familial roots, to 'the WASP establishment and its values, but (he) is a harbinger of the new emerging educated class of today, steeped in an alternative sensibility that is more committed to meritocracy than nepotism (Roger Sterling) or social class (Pete Campbell)'.

As with Don, Pete Campbell is also resistant to assuming the dominant social role of father and parent. Pete's resistance creates intense tension and conflict between him and his wife Trudy. When Trudy learns that Pete's co-worker Harry Crane's wife is pregnant, she tearfully tells him that pregnant women are part of 'this big club' that she wants to join. In the episode 'The New Girl' (24 August 2008), Pete and Trudy see a fertility specialist to find out why they have been unable to conceive a child. The lab results reveal that his sperm is not the cause of the young couple's inability to conceive. Pete questions the rush to have a child and lists the drawbacks of parenting: 'You can't travel, you can't go to the movies.' Trudy responds by calling him immature and insensitive to her need to have a baby. In *Mad Men*, Don and Pete express resistance to what Ehrenreich (1983) has called the 'male breadwinner ethos', which places men as the dominant economic providers for the family. She argues that, since the 1950s, various social movements have emerged (largely generated by men), each defining a certain flight from commitment to the male provider image. In the 1950s, for example, there were attacks on social and corporate middle-class conformity, the *Playboy* celebratory and consumerist bachelor male model, and the beatniks, who outwardly rejected both work and marriage. In the 1960s, the youth counter-culture movement challenged the traditional conceptions of heterosexual love, sex, marriage and even family. These moments of social resistance can serve as nostalgic sites of continuity and potential political critique for present-day critics of the traditional patriarchal role for men. They can also be understood as counter-memories because they contradict popularly accepted notions of the early 1960s as an era of incontestable social conformity for white, middle-class men.

Perhaps more than fictional images, non-fictional, historical images can serve as a valuable nostalgic repository for historical stirrings and political practice. Benjamin (1969) argues that the past can only be seized and actualised by the present and conceptualised as a flashing image from the past. He asserts that an historical awakening occurs in the dialectical relationship between the historical image and the uses and needs of the present. Benjamin's notion challenges the dominant model of a universal, progressive and continuous history.[2] Through his conception of the dialectical image, he seeks to place the study of history at the centre of fostering social change (Buck-Morss, 1989; Berg, 2004). In *Mad Men*,[3] the recognisable televised image of President Kennedy can affect an historical awakening whereby the present liberal viewer can remember and contemplate the Kennedy years as a time of optimistic political liberalism and strong public trust in the federal government. This nostalgic remembrance can serve as both an emotional and an intellectual impetus for recovering a strong sense of progressive political liberalism to enact contemporary social changes. My use of the concepts of continuity and discontinuity in a critical nostalgia do not necessarily imply an acceptance of modern progress or a continuous history, but, rather, is intended to express the analytic connections or separations that nostalgic individuals or groups can actualise with their pasts. While the historical past is irretrievable for any individual or group, nevertheless, its imagery can act as a repository for contemporary historical stirrings and political action.

This study illustrates how nostalgic elements in popular culture can serve as a stimulus for politically liberal social and political change. Jameson (1974) and Marcuse (1987) argue that a nostalgia that reveals a past filled with freedom, happiness and rich cultural traditions can be employed to question and critique the social structures that comprise an oppressive historical present. In this respect, nostalgia serves as a revolutionary incentive for a critical and political practice that can be mobilised to transform oppressive social structures in our present historical condition. Popular culture representations that feature moments of excluded histories that counter or contradict hegemonic, traditional conceptions of a particular era can function as a source of continuity and inspiration for individuals seeking to alter present-day conditions. These individuals can discover and find a continuity of values associated with these excluded histories. Finally, Benjamin (1969) theorises that a dialectical relationship exists between images of the historical past and contemporary audiences. Through this dialectic, the past, whether understood as nostalgic or not, can be actualised and an historical awakening can occur whereby individuals can assess their social, political and historical place in contrast to the moment expressed in the historical image. For the critical scholar, nostalgia should not be understood as simply a politically regressive, precarious longing for a mythical past, but, rather, as an accessible resource available as an intellectual catayst for constructing a better tomorrow.

Notes

1. In Season Six, which takes place between December 1967 and November 1968, the growing social dissent and political events of 1968 affect many of the series' main characters. For instance, the episode 'A Tale of Two Cities' (6 February 2013) is set against the backdrop of the tumultuous 1968 Democratic National Convention and the ensuing conflict between protestors and police in Chicago. Megan, Don's wife, expresses anxiety when viewing TV footage of the Chicago street protests. In the episode 'Favours' (6 September 2013), Don helps a neighbour's son (Mitchell), who has dropped out of college and is classified as 1-A, obtain a position in the Air National Guard so he will not be drafted into the infantry and sent to Vietnam.
2. Miriam Hansen (2012) notes that Benjamin's critique of the nineteenth-century idea of progress runs throughout his early (*The Origin of German Tragic Drama*) to his later works (*The Arcades Project*). Although Benjamin is critical of the assumed nature of modern progress, he values the historical past as an essential stimulus for his concept of actuality, in which the past can only be actualised by standing outside of and against one's time to grasp the 'temporal core' of one's existence in the present. It is through this process of actualisation that one can begin to understand one's present social and historical situation, a necessary precursor to political action.
3. *Mad Men* makes judicious use of historical images from the time period, which may provide them with a stronger affective impact on audiences. The most prevalent images of the period are the consumer products and brand names (for example, Coca-Cola, Heineken, Jantzen, Lucky Strike, Volkswagen), many of which still exist today. This seems apropos for a series about the early architects of our incessant consumer culture. Although I have stressed visual images, nostalgic images would also include popular songs and recorded sounds from the time period, which frequently have stronger evocative and affective qualities with audiences.

References

Benjamin, W. (1969) 'Theses on the Philosophy of History (1940)', in H. Arendt (ed.) *Illuminations: Essays and Reflections*. Translated by H. Zohn. New York: Schocken, pp. 253–264.
Benjamin, W. (1977) *The Origin of German Tragic Drama*. Translated by J. Osborne. London: NLB.
Benjamin, W. (1999) 'Paris, Capital of the Nineteenth Century (1939)', in *The Arcades Project*. Translated by H. Eiland and K. McLaughlin. Cambridge, MA: Harvard University Press, pp. 14–26.
Benjamin, W. (2006) *Berlin Childhood around 1900*. Cambridge, MA: Harvard University Press.

Berg, O. (2004) 'Gilles Deleuze, Walter Benjamin and the Challenges of Film considered as Historical Research'. http://www.olafberg.net/forschung/dokumente/n-1deleuze-benjamin-v1-3.pdf (accessed 3 April 2012).
Boym, S. (2001) *The Future of Nostalgia*. New York: Basic Books.
Buck-Morss, S. (1989) *The Dialectics of Seeing: Walter Benjamin and the Arcades Project.* Cambridge, MA: MIT Press.
Cashman, R. (2006) 'Critical Nostalgia and Material Culture in Northern Ireland'. *Journal of American Folklore*, 119(472), pp. 137–160.
Chase, M. and Shaw, C. (1989) 'The Dimensions of Nostalgia', in M. Chase and C. Shaw (eds) *The Imagined Past: History and Nostalgia*. Manchester: Manchester University Press, pp. 1–17.
Doane, J. and Hodges, D. (2013) *Nostalgia and Sexual Difference: The Resistance to Contemporary Feminism*. New York: Routledge.
Dove-Viebahn, A. (2013) 'Mourning Becomes the Mad Men: Notes on Nostalgia'. *Invisible Culture* 17, http://ivc.lib.rochester.edu/portfolio/mourning-becomes-the-mad-men-notes-on-nostalgia/ (accessed 13 March 2013).
Edgerton, G. (2012) 'JFK, Don Draper, and the New Sentimentality'. *CST (Critical Studies in Television) Online*, http://cstonline.tv/jfk-don-draper (accessed 17 June 2013).
Ehrenreich, B. (1983) *The Hearts of Men: American Dreams and the Flight from Commitment*. Garden City, NY: Anchor Press/Doubleday.
Fraser, J. A. (2002) *White-Collar Sweatshop: The Deterioration of Work and Its Rewards in Corporate America*. New York: W. W. Norton & Company.
Glazer, P. (2005) *Radical Nostalgia: Spanish Civil War Commemoration in America*. Rochester, NY: University of Rochester Press.
Hansen, M. B. (2012) *Cinema and Experience, Siegfried Kracauer, Walter Benjamin, and Theodor W. Adorno*. Berkeley, CA: University of California Press.
Heckscher, C. C. (1996) *White-Collar Blues: Management Loyalties in an Age of Corporate Restructuring*. New York: Basic Books.
Heer, J. (2009) 'The Uses of Nostalgia'. *Sans Everything*, http://sanseverything.wordpress.com/2009/06/28/the-uses-of-nostalgia (accessed 13 June 2012).
Jameson, F. (1974) *Marxism and Form*. Princeton, NJ: Princeton University Press.
Jameson, F. (2009) *The Cultural Turn: Selected Writings on the Postmodern, 1983–1998*. London: Verso.
Kammen, M. (1991) *Mystic Chords of Memory: The Transformation of Tradition in American Culture*. New York: Knopf.
Lipsitz, G. (2001, 1990) *Time Passages, Collective Memory and American Popular Culture*. Minneapolis, MN: University of Minnesota Press.
Lowenthal, D. (1985) *The Past is a Foreign Country*. Cambridge: Cambridge University Press.
Maier, C. (1999) 'The End of Longing? Notes toward a History of Postwar German National Longing', in J. S. Brady, B. Crawford and S. E. Wiliarty (eds) *The Postwar Transformation of Germany: Democracy, Prosperity, and Nationhood*. Ann Arbor: University of Michigan Press.
Marcuse, H. (1987) *Eros and Civilization, a Philosophical Inquiry into Freud*. New York: Routledge.
Ross, A. (2009) *Nice Work If You Can Get It: Life and Labor in Precarious Times*. New York: New York University Press.

Sennett, R. (2007) *The Culture of the New Capitalism.* New Haven, CT: Yale University Press.
Stoddart, S. (2007) 'Camelot Regained', in S. F. Stoddart (ed.) *Analysing Mad Men, Critical Essays on the Television Series.* Jefferson, NC: McFarland & Company, pp. 207–233.
Tannock, S. (1995) 'Nostalgia Critique'. *Cultural Studies,* 9(3), pp. 453–464.
Whitman, M. V. N. (1999) *New World, New Rules: The Changing Role of the American Corporation.* Cambridge, MA: Harvard Business Review Press.
Wilson, S. (1955) *The Man in the Gray Flannel Suit.* New York: Simon and Shuster.

11
The Television Channel ARTE as a Time Machine and Matrix for European Identity

Aline Hartemann

This chapter examines the French–German, European-oriented, cultural television channel ARTE and its roles as a 'nostalgia policy maker' and a 'European identity contractor' (Cohen, Dezalay and Marchetti, 2007). ARTE is no stranger to nostalgic trends. Over several years, ARTE featured a special summertime programme entitled the 'Summer of...' series. Launched in 2008, it revisited the past by playing musical hits from former decades. It began with 'Summer of the Sixties' (ARTE, 2013a), followed by 'Summer of the Seventies' (ARTE, 2013b) in 2009 and 'Summer of the Eighties' (ARTE, 2013c) in 2010. The 1990s being, perhaps, too close in time, the decision was made to discontinue the 'decades' theme and replace it with something more up to date. 'Summer of the Girls' came out in 2011 and 'Summer of Rebels' (ARTE, 2013e) in 2012. This sudden change illustrates the ambiguity of the nostalgic theme: where are the acceptable limits, especially in terms of time, of this sort of looking back? What content should be featured in trips back in time? How can these endeavours be successfully made relevant to the present? This example also raises the questions of what each 'generation' is all about (that of the 1960s, for instance) and, furthermore, which generation this type of programme is aimed at. This chapter studies the way ARTE functions as a 'time machine' by examining its policy of nostalgia within its concern for shaping European identity.

Through its programmes, ARTE embodies a primary function of nostalgia: it recounts the past and it discusses origins. A short analysis of the focus of the *Parallel History* (*Histoire Parallèle*, ARTE, 1989–2001) programme will demonstrate this point. When one recalls certain events or facts, one necessarily excludes others: media both remember and forget (Luhmann, 2004). In this sense ARTE not only recalls the past, but also points to the accompanying notions of oblivion and memory. The programme *Ce qui me manque* ('What I Miss') will be a case in point in this chapter, underpinning the position it occupies in ARTE's policies of nostalgia. In a third and final section, this chapter will focus on ARTE's forms of 'counter-nostalgia'. If the channel tries to construct a tale based on European identity, with recourse to pictures of the past and to the power of oblivion, it misses its goal. A study of the programme *Karambolage* and the hybridisation phenomenon it features reveals the anticipation of a reality in the making, namely the reality of European identity.

Remembering the past

ARTE, founded nearly 20 years ago by a French–German partnership, can be regarded as the embodiment of a primary function of nostalgia. Its main objective is to recount the past, stressing the memory of the painful events shared by the two nations in question (Mink and Neumayer, 2007). The channel is well known for furthering the cause of reconciliation between the former enemies who fought against each other in both World Wars. Even today, ARTE specialises in documentaries dealing with this burdensome past. The former *Histoire Parallèle* programme, for instance, was emblematic of this early form of a 'grand' narrative of the past. *Histoire Parallèle* was particularly interesting insofar as it not only recalled and commemorated the past but also connected it with the present. The programme followed the events of the Second World War day by day, several decades after they happened. ARTE stands for 'Association Relative à la Télévision Européenne', and the purpose assigned to the institution by its supervisors was to provide programmes intended for a 'European' public which ARTE was hoping to help bring about. One can, therefore, see this channel as a sort of 'European identity contractor', tasking itself with meeting the terms of a contract. The way it uses the past is part of what once was called counter-nostalgia. It stages a past which is seen as a foil, fraught with horror, and is thus rejected.

However, the channel is unable to state unequivocally what the 'European identity' actually is: it has not stabilised fully and seems to be constantly in the making, forever in the womb, in a way that is close to anthropologist Marc Abélès's idea of 'presentism' (2000). Defining European identity from the standpoint of this painful past while maintaining a view of what is to come is the most interesting feature of

ARTE's 'nostalgia policy', which I propose to analyse with a particular focus on a number of productions of ARTE France's Research Workshop, such as *Karambolage* and *Ce qui me manque*. *Histoire Parallèle* can be classified as a 'brown soup' production. Programmes that deal with the World Wars are famous for attracting large audiences. This 'brown soup' was and is part and parcel of ARTE's nostalgia policy and is in tune with its sense of melancholia. *Histoire Parallèle* has a dark tone and, like most of ARTE's 'brown soup' productions, is in black and white. As emphasised by an article about *Histoire Parallèle* which appeared in *L'Express*, 'the War was for ARTE a flagship product' (Schifres, 2001). The programme was designed to attract an audience at minimal cost. *Histoire Parallèle* used to boast 1.5 million regular viewers. It seems to have been more than just a way to carry ARTE to the top of the ratings (Rostain, 2001): it appears to have been conceived as a staple of the nostalgia policy, designed to alleviate suffering. The programme aired weekly from May 1989 until September 2001 and was conceived by German and French historians, in particular Marc Ferro and Klaus Wenger. Its purpose was to show on screen, on either side of the Rhine, first on La SEPT, and later on ARTE, 'what the average Frenchman and the average German were allowed to see of the outside world 50 years ago, during the Second World war and in its aftermath, when television still did not exist' (Ferro, 1995). The programme was structured around three main guiding principles. The German title, *Die Woche vor 50 Jahren* ('A week, 50 years ago'), points to the first. It purported to show quite accurately, exactly 50 years on, what ordinary people used to see on the cinema screen. The programme's second important principle was that of integrity, the documents being delivered in their original condition without any cuts or editing. The third guideline was that of the 'French-German dual outlook' (Wenger, 1993), with images coming from German and French but also Soviet, American Japanese and other European newsreels (Ferro, 1993). Occupied France, under strict Nazi censorship, produced no news programmes of its own. Interestingly, the two presenters, Ferro and Wenger, were from different generations. The latter was born just after the Second World War, but the former lived through it, both as a witness and as a resistance fighter, and experienced its consequences (Garçon, 1992).

The historian Matthias Steinle offered an in-depth study of these questions at a symposium on history and the cinema which took place in Paris in 2010 (Steinle, 2010). The first principle upon which *Histoire Parallèle* was built is all-important to ARTE's nostalgia policies. As it told of events which occurred exactly 50 years ago to the day, *Histoire Parallèle* impacted the contemporary viewer's present (Ferro and Planchais, 1997). In Steinle's (2010) words, the revolutionary thing about *Histoire Parallèle* is that it is inscribed in another temporality; it is history in keeping with present-day life, history in real time, week after week. This original concept interlocked the past with the present, which caused a journalist to write that, while French lorry drivers were disputing points on their driving licences, Hitler was launching his attack against the Caucasus (Schifres, 2001). It also came closer to the format of a television series or serial, with moments of suspense and tension. However, it had one remarkable feature: the events seemed fresh, since they were being revisited 50 years later and shown in a novel way, but they were also predictable, since they were part of a story whose outcome was known to all viewers. Marc Ferro summed up this paradox very well when he said, in his introduction to the first episode of *Histoire Parallèle*, 'In some ways, I experienced the war twice, once as a resistance fighter and a witness, and once as a historian, and it is almost like the second time is proving the harder' (*Histoire Parallèle*, 1). The nostalgia policy implemented by ARTE turned the channel into an investigative tool for understanding the past. It was history in the Greek sense of 'istoria', which Herodotus saw as an 'inquiry', an 'exploration'. Steinle seems to be right when he says that the images of *Histoire Parallèle* at once gained and lost meaning. They could be considered simultaneously as active with regard to history and as a framework for what was observable and communicable. He calls them 'palimpsest images' (Steinle, 2010).

Media are time machines: They remember and forget

When one recalls certain events or facts, one necessarily leaves others aside. ARTE's programmes showed nostalgia as feeding on oblivion, on a feeling of something missing, the frustration of remembering what once was but is forever gone. With *Ce qui me manque*, the channel tried to explore that complex feeling. This aspect of their nostalgia policy was conceived by ARTE as a means to lend consistency to the 'European identity' they desired to bring about. *Ce qui me manque* came as two distinct series. In Part I, two individuals, one German and one French, no longer living in their native countries but across the Rhine from them, were asked to evoke in a few words, then to present on screen, an object they missed, explaining how it was used. Here was a television format that palliated oblivion by showing the absence of something causing a person to feel nostalgic. In the conversations I had with the producers, they explained that the TV presentation of these missed objects was significant on two levels: first on a subjective level, as they belonged to one person in particular, and second on a social level, as they reflected their owner's membership of a certain group. In *Ce qui me manque* Part I, several German and French expats presented one particular object that they missed in their adopted countries in order to help viewers on either side of the Rhine grasp an aspect of their identities. Part II confirmed and broadened this line of action. At first limited to French and German objects, the concept widened to include all countries of the European zone. From March 2007, on the occasion of the 50th anniversary of the Treaty of Rome, these small modules were vested with a greater mission: to show a European identity not only based on the French–German link but extended to the other European member-countries. Part II, in the words of Claire Doutriaux, the promoter of the programme, displayed 'small pieces of Europe, with all its cultures, of its languages, its life. *Ce qui me manque* embodies Europe in its various aspects' (ARTE, 2013f). Two features emerge from this analysis. Bringing to the fore objects that people had forgotten about was the way ARTE, as the contractor first of a German–French identity and later of a European one, designed its second nostalgia policy. It was by adding up these nostalgic moments, these missed objects, that a draft of European identity was constituted, like a mural showing many faces. The notions of a mural and of an addition were clearly emphasised in the travelling video exhibition that Claire Doutriaux designed and presented (for instance, in Paris during such events as the Nuit Blanche at the Maison de l'Europe on 4 October 2010): 'We are trying, as a complement to the broadcast on ARTE, to organise a travelling exhibition across Europe for this series, with two dozen screens showing 20 fixed faces becoming animated in turn, and forming a one-hour loop.' Claire Doutriaux could be seen as a European identity contractor. The latter concept seems to be particularly appropriate: it designates a group of individuals, or social groups, assuming a political role at the service of all. They embrace an idea and find ways to make it fruitful. Political scientists such as Cohen, Dezalay and Marchetti (2007), Aldrin and Dakowska (2011), as well as the ethnologist Mazé (2010), make use of this concept. For instance, the thesis is all about the emergence of so-called European museums on the Continent. Mazé (2010) found a number of museum curators who were applying the concepts of European memory and identity to their particular realms.

ARTE is like an identity contractor with a mission to represent Europe and to reveal its many aspects to the public. It thus implements different forms of nostalgia policies. This chapter has shown how the channel tried to explore the past in a new way by looking back at recent history and linking it with the present, thus offering a form of 'real-time history'. That first reflection singled out memory, oblivion, emptiness and longing for the past as being inherent in the channel's sense of nostalgia. Thus, in a way, ARTE seems inescapably hesitant about the formulation of the European identity it was hoping to promote. To conclude, I will now shed light on one final modality of nostalgia: ARTE's 'counter-nostalgia'.

Counter-nostalgia

When I was inquiring into the matter, interviewing ARTE staff members and attending their meetings, I was struck by their recurring concern with exactly how to define their 'European mission'. The topic was repeatedly broached and was the source of great perplexity. Even today, this question remains quite problematic for a number of ARTE programmers (Turner, 1974). One strategy they often used to elude the question was to relegate it to the very end of meetings (Hartemann, 2011). Time constraints then meant that they would put it off to the next meeting, and so on, again and again. The question could thus be kept pending over a long period. I noticed another way of solving the 'European identity' dilemma. It consisted in agreeing on at least one thing, namely that European identity is as yet unfinished, and ARTE is the matrix or mould in which it will be shaped. So, short of being able to adopt a common position on what definition to give for Europe, the managers of ARTE agree to see it as 'still in progress'. And so, at the end of their meetings, they keep raising, almost ritually, the question of the contents to be given to European identity: 'and about Europe, what do we do?' I call this attitude 'counter-nostalgia', or 'presentism', in reference to the notion developed by Abélès (2000) and Zawadzki (2008). It clarifies the issue and suggests that now, as we speak, European identity is still evolving, still pending. For some ARTE executives, meanwhile, it seeks its definition through this very process. Yet these reservations should be toned down. Various valid projects have been designed and have given birth to such productions as the *Visages d'Europe (Faces of Europe)* documentaries. In the introduction to the catalogue *Faces of Europe*, Jose Durão Manuel Barroso writes: 'I am delighted that ARTE has completed the Faces of Europe-collection that was successfully launched for the 50th anniversary of the Treaty of Rome. The catalogue contains 135 documentary portraits of citizens from every country in Europe, of all ages and conditions' (ARTE, 2008). But other elements of 'counter-nostalgia' are conspicuous in the creations and hybridisations devised by the creators of such programmes as *Ce qui me manque* and *Karambolage*. The idea that governs these counter-nostalgic programmes is the desire to project a hybrid image, showing European identity as a mix of cultures. This is no longer to be found solely in the German–French relationship, or only in membership of the European continent. *Ce qui me manque* and *Karambolage* have also discussed objects brought here by people from outside Europe. Take the case of Alice Diop (ARTE, 2013g), a French woman aged around 20 and of Senegalese origin. Alice discussed her traditional African wide-toothed comb. These programmes cast a new light on the question of European identity by focusing on items from outside the European continent. The presentation of these objects creates cultural hybridisations. Diop explains how her comb travelled from Senegal to France and was responsible for changes in the behaviour of both French-born women of African descent and hairdressers. The comb can be seen as a new European object, setting new programme topics and helping to shape European identity. Although ARTE implements nostalgia policies in order to accomplish its mission of building a European identity, the channel nevertheless seems unable to decide between various options. It is unsure whether it should be offering a vision of the past, emphasising oblivion, struggling with 'presentism' or looking forward to a Europe that still does not exist. Because of the complexity of its relation to time, ARTE rightly deserves to be seen as a time machine.

References

Abélès, M. (2000) 'L'Europe: un objet conceptuel mal identifié', in A. Abensour (ed.) *Le XXème siècle en France, Art, Politique, Philosophie*. Paris: Berger Levrault, pp. 67–83.

Aldrin, P. and Dakowska, D. (2011) 'Légitimer l'Europe sans Bruxelles? Un regard sur les petits entrepreneurs d'Europe, entre décentrement et recentrages'. *Politique Européenne*, 34, pp. 7–35.

ARTE (2008) *Visages d'Europe/Faces of Europe: The Human Face of Europe*. Catalogue, with an introduction by Jose Durao Manuel Barroso, D. G. Communication, Service audiovisuel, ARTE Edition.

ARTE (2013a) *Summer of the Sixties*, http://www.arte.tv/fr/summer-of-the-sixties/3194472.html (accessed 31 May 2013).

ARTE (2013b) *Summer of the Seventies*, http://www.arte.tv/fr/2012036.html (accessed 31 May 2013).

ARTE (2013c) *Summer of the Eighties*, http://www.arte.tv/fr/a-l-antenne/2616674.html (accessed 31 May 2013).

ARTE (2013e) *Summer of the Rebels*, http://www.arte.tv/fr/summer-of-rebels/6648126.html (accessed 31 May 2013).

ARTE (2013f) *Ce Qui Me Manque*, http://www.arte.tv/presentation-generique/1506550.html (accessed 31 May 2013).
ARTE (2013g) *Karambolage*, http://www.arte.tv/fr/europeens/karambolage/Emission-du-26-juin2011/3980748,CmC=3980902.html (accessed 31 May 2013).
ARTE, *Histoire Parallèle*, numéro 1, Marc Ferro, Klaus Wenger, *Emission Histoire Parallèle*, shown 3 September 1989.
Cohen, A., Dezalay, Y. and Marchetti, D. (2007) 'Esprit d'Etat, entrepreneurs d'Europe', in *Actes de la Recherche en sciences sociales*, 166–167, pp. 5–13.
Ferro, M. (1993) *Cinéma et Histoire*. Collection Folio/Histoire, 55. Paris: Gallimard.
Ferro, M. (1995) *Revivre l'histoire autour d'Histoire Parallèle*, with the cooperation of Claire Babin. Paris: ARTE Editions/Liana Levi.
Ferro, M. and Planchais, J. (1997) *Les médias et l'histoire, le poids du passé dans le chaos de l'actualité*. Paris: CFPJ Editions.
Garçon, F. (1992) 'La réussite d'Histoire Parallèle'. *Cinéma et Histoire. Autour de Marc Ferro, CinémAction*, Vol. 65, pp. 58–61.
Hartemann, A. (2011) 'Les relations franco-allemandes au sein de la chaîne culturelle à vocation européenne ARTE. Dissensions et modes de résolution des conflits au prisme de l'analyse stratégique et de la sociologie des organisations'. *Trajectoires*, http://trajectoires.revues.org/818 (accessed 31 May 2013).
Luhmann, N. (2004) *Die Realität der Massenmedien*. Wiesbaden: Verlag für Sozialwissenschaften.
Mazé, C. (2010) *Mettre l'Europe au musée: une affaire d'État? Ethnographie et sociohistoire du chantier des « musées de l'Europe (1980–2010) »*, PhD defended 22 October 2010, EHESS-ENS.
Mink, G. and Neumayer, L. (2007) *L'Europe et ses passés douloureux*. Paris: La Découverte.
Rostain, S. (2001) 'La fin de l'histoire en temps réel'. *Libération*, le 01.09.2001, http://wwwliberation.fr/medias/0101384945-la-fin-de-l-histoire-en-temps-reel (accessed 31 May 2013).
Schifres, A. (2001) 'La fin de l'histoire'. *L'Express*, http://www.lexpress.fr/informations/la-fin-de-l-histoire_645421.html (accessed 31 May 2013).
Steinle, M. (2010) 'L'expérience d'Histoire Parallèle'. Intervention dans le cadre du colloque international *Le cinéma au prisme de l'histoire. Les laboratoires 'Cinéma et Histoire'*, EHESS, 20–21 May 2010, Paris.
Turner, V. (1974) *Dramas, Fields and Metaphors. Symbolic Action in Human Society*. New York: Cornell University Press.
Wenger, K. (1993) ' "Histoire parallèle", eine Dokumentationsserie über den Zweiten Weltkrieg von hoher Aktualität', in U. Koch (ed.) *Deutsch-französische Medienbilder: Journalisten und Forscher im Gespräch/Images médiatiques franco-allemandes*. München: R. Fischer, pp. 243–246.
Zawadzki, P. (2008) 'Les équivoques du présentisme'. *Esprit*, Vol. 6, pp. 114–134.

12
Nostalgia, Tinted Memories and Cinematic Historiography: On Otto Preminger's *Bonjour Tristesse* (1958)

Ute Holl

Historiography, colour and cinema

Colour in film is a matter of subtle photochemical processes and inscriptions on delicate skins, called *pellicula* in Italian and *pellicule* in French, indicating proximity of physical and chemical procedures in the perception of the world. Inscriptions of light on film surfaces can create pleasant effects of shades and tones, but when applied excessively they ruin the surface and destroy the image. A similar phenomenon occurs on human skin. If exposed to the sun, Caucasian skin may stage a play of colours from pink to dark red. Colour films that have made an issue of the sunburn, usually on female skin, closely parallel the experience of seeing colours and that of feeling colours, giving a painful reminder of the physical basis in all filmic perception. It reminds the spectator that memory, as Nietzsche insisted, is always linked to a trace and a pain that remembers.[1] Colour in films, then, can be discussed as a special form of relating the technological, the physical, the aesthetic and the social side of cinema. Colour is a barely perceivable yet affective thread in the texture of cinematic historiography.

Colour sensation is an unstable element, especially in the case of cinema perception. Although colour film stock is usually durable, colours are perceived differently over the course of time, since their cultural impressions are subject to change. Film colours that appeared to be bright in the 1950s have become dull since more brilliant chemical colours have taken over the surfaces of things, textures, exteriors and, for that matter, cinematic looks. On the other hand, when in 2012 a digitally restored version of Meliès's *Le voyage dans la lune* (1902) was shown in theatres and on television screens, audiences were taken aback by the neon-coloured images, which did not at all fit with what colours were expected to look like around 1900. Colour perception is relational, linked to temporal and spatial environments, even if these are imaginary or virtual. Colour in cinema is a matter of giving consistency to a fictional world, as Stanley Cavell asserts (1979, p. 81). Memory as triggered by colour is linked to a historical and culturally moulded spectrum on the one hand, and on personal reminiscences on the other. Historical films exploit these impacts of colour (the greenish tones of the 1930s, the specific reds of the 1940s) to evoke the feeling of a certain historical time. Acting as parasites on colour-memory, those films create a sense of 'pastness' through stylistic connotations, which Fredric Jameson in his essay on postmodernism has called nostalgic (1984, pp. 67ff). While nostalgia etymologically refers to a disease incited by the wish to return home, in the case of colour this malady has temporal rather than spatial ramifications. Specific colours evoke the wish to return to the familiar order of things as they are supposed to have been in the past. Nostalgia's time is the *futurum exactum*. While history as 'real history' is erased, colour perception marks the present as historical time, a symptom of the present's 'imprisonment in the past' (Jameson, 1983, p. 116).

Although colour obviously links historical, personal, cultural and psychological elements, it often escapes critical analysis. From the Renaissance onwards, knowledge has relied on the calculable, on the mathematical index of *disegno*, line, form, geometry and perspective as forms of controlling space. Colours and tones belong to the incalculable, are a matter of feelings and emotion, of involuntary associations, often associated with female approaches, with uncertainty and fading. Since Goethe's *Farbenlehre* and his discussion of physio-psychological effects in colour perception, the after-image for example, colours have, in psychology as in art history, been related to a form of automatism or an unconscious in human thinking, operating halfway between the wishful and the compulsive. No wonder, then, that uncontrollable phenomena of sudden and involuntary memories should be associated with indistinct yet striking sensuous perceptions, not only taste and smell, as in Marcel Proust, but also with light, lighting and, eventually, colour. A striking example is the flashback, both a technical and a psychological term. In its techniques of flashback, cinema's aesthetics are able to simulate mental procedures, as Hugo Münsterberg argued very early on in film theory (Münsterberg, 1916, p. 46). Cinematic flashbacks are often put into practice through effects of light, flash frames or a changing of tones or colours. They not only represent a change of mental mode in the film's characters or plot, but also actually act on the minds of the audience, operating just below the level of conscious perception. Film aesthetics thus link the cultural and individual forms of remembering. Especially through colour, cinema relates, mixes and confuses personal and social memory. The analysis of this entanglement is difficult, since colour, as opposed to the logics of the line in *disegno*, generates its effects though interrelations, differences and vicinities, which are not easy to describe.

In cinema, a transformation from present reality to the past, to memories, dreams, visions or otherwise altered mental states in a film, may be achieved by a change of material from colour to a sudden black and white, or the other way around. The classic case is MGM's *The Wizard of Oz*, released in 1939, which starts in a grey monochromatic world called Kansas (or, for that matter, 'home') from where the main character, Dorothy Gale, is blown away by a tornado into the colourful world of Oz. Seemingly pure fantasy, this world will in the end be called 'a real, truly live place'. The girl Dorothy in this film is not nostalgic, not homesick for a place better than Oz. The misery of Kansas, depicted as dull, as in documentaries from the Depression years, is obvious to her and to the spectators. The film in its dual colour structure is illusory and disillusioning at the same time, as expressed in the *double entendre* of the girl's final statement: 'there's no place like home.' In the case of Victor Fleming's film, the difference between black and white and colour distinguishes two mental states of the protagonist uncannily meandering around the threshold of adulthood: while dressed as a child, actress Judy Garland is definitely a maturing young woman, something that definitely should have remained hidden in the toy-story of Oz.[2] Uncanny, then, is the return of the drives beyond the narrative plot. Desires and anxieties are present in the colours of the film, while the restraints and denials of real life are shot in shades of black and white. Spectators participate in the changing mental states of the protagonist through the film's colour dramaturgy. But audiences will do so differently today than at the time of the film's first release.

As well as the diegetic form of flashback, there is an extra-diegetic one. In this case, personal and biographical memories are triggered by film colour. An excellent example is Salman Rushdie's essay on *The Wizard of Oz*, in which he keeps involuntarily floating back into his own childhood memories through the colours. His meticulous analysis of the film is repeatedly interrupted by memories of his childhood in India triggered by the specific Technicolor of Oz. 'Thinking back once more to my Bombay childhood in the 1950s, a time when Hindi movies were all black-and-white, I can recall the excitement of the advent of colour' (Rushdie, 2002, p. 32). Looking at old films in their specific colour qualities, spectators are likely to be drawn into personal flashbacks, as trips down the memory lanes of their own biographies. While watching old Technicolor films, or while looking at the specific colours of Super-8 films or the strange colours of early video formats, different age groups will be differently drawn into their own biographical colour environments, into a specifically tinted childhood imaginary. These memories are ambiguous in themselves, since remembering those colours is remembering the times when they did not attract our attention, when they seemed normal, transparent, just representing the real. As soon as colour ceases to be transparent and appears as a quality in its own right, it indicates 'pastness' in Jameson's sense: it communicates the illusion of returning home and opens personal doors of perception to historiography.

Membranes and memories

Just as Victor Fleming in 1939 had used black and white to show the reality of depression in the US, Otto Preminger, in his *Bonjour Tristesse*, a film released both in Europe and in the US in 1958 as an adaptation of François Sagan's bestselling novel, used black and white to distinguish a depressed perception of the present from reminiscences of an untroubled past, a vacation by the Mediterranean sea which was interrupted by a dramatic, possibly even traumatic, incident. In *Bonjour Tristesse* these flashbacks are shot in Technicolor. A good deal of the nostalgia this film evokes today is due to the design, the fashion, the music, the acting and the moving bodies of the 1950s. Jean Seberg is the protagonist, Cécile, a sun-tanned strong and sporty party girl in a variety of fancy 1950s bathing suits, mingling associations of Greek physical ideals with anticipations of the 1960s' athleticism and libertinage. Seberg is the first American cinema girl to remodel European femininity through the American youth cultures that were broaching the issue of sexual relations. Sex, in all its bourgeois varieties, from pubertal innocence to incestuous compulsion, melancholy and sadism, Americanness and Frenchness, rules the plot. As Jean-Luc Godard had it in his *Histoire(s) du cinema*, 'Bonjour Tristesse -Le fond des choses- le cul' (Godard, 1999, p. 39). Another major part of the film's nostalgia is related to the Technicolor material itself, to its lighting and cinematic surfaces. The deeply tinted colours of the landscape, the sky and sea are contrasted with the frangibility of surfaces of dresses, skins and faces. This heightens the perception of vulnerability that creates the film's impact. The restored, digitally remastered version in the original Cinemascope format was celebrated at major film festivals throughout 2012. It communicates an immediate impression of the specific surface design and colours of the 1950s. Yet the colour perception of current festival audiences probably differs greatly from what contemporaries saw in 1958. As documents prove (Hirsch, 2007; Fujiwara, 2008), even contemporary reception differed significantly between American and European audiences. Reality and its approach through cinematic forms, conveyed in colour or shades of black and white, obviously is a different matter for different people and audiences. And even individual distinctions are indisputable. While the film seems a feast of bliss and *bonheur* to some, others are irritated by its disturbing elements, which are also triggered at the level of colours. The presentation of sunburnt skin is not the least of irritations here. The fissure which colour dramaturgy provokes in the film is not just a chronological one between past and present. Colour, rather, exposes layers of both the film's and the girls' skins, addressing the issue of membranes of memory. Here, history and the return of various repressed issues come into play, which link historical, aesthetic and personal aspects. Preminger's views on European post-war society are communicated through colour and its irritating effects on perception.

The distribution of black and white and colour as signatures of the real, on the one hand, and signatures of fantastic dream worlds, on the other, is not historically stable. While colour in early films indicated a mode of spectacle, attraction and illusion (Gunning, 1995), it was only later conceived of as a necessary completion to represent reality. As Edward Buscombe stated: 'We perceive the world as coloured, after all, and therefore an accurate representation of it should also be coloured' (1985, p. 88). This statement itself could only have been made in the 1970s, in the decade of colour TV's triumph over cinema. Colour is a matter of industrial standards rather than of the real or fantastic.

But, even in the longer course of history, colour had never been a simple or reliable indicator of the distinction between reality and imagination. Film styles change with technological innovations. The first complicated forms of colour film demanded several cameras, and later a single camera which was heavy and hard to handle. Colour film stock was expensive and difficult to process. Colour demanded meticulous planning in terms of lighting and acting. But it allowed surprising effects in a consistently composed world. Genre styles that relate to the utopian or to the lost, musical, Western or melodrama, have always relied on strict colour schemes. Until the 1970s black-and-white material had indicated mobile and journalistic forms of filming, reminded audiences of photojournalism and reportage, and was aesthetically closely connected to the retrieval of social and political evidence. But as soon as 16 mm colour reversal films entered the scene of news coverage in television, this relation was inverted. Only through time is the historicity of colour and colour relations conveyed. Usually, every contemporary form of technical and photographic image is perceived as transparent and apt to represent reality. This is as true for black-and-white photography as it was for the images of Technicolor in their unlikely shades and tones. In retrospective, it is irritating to think that they were once conceived of as adding realism to films, albeit an *enhanced* one, as Natalie Kalmus, wife and on-set controller of Technicolor inventor Herbert Kalmus, put it in her famous article *Colour Consciousness* from 1935: with chromatic sensations, 'motion pictures are able to duplicate faithfully all the auditory and visual sensations. This enhanced realism enables us to portrait life and nature as it really is' (Kalmus, 1935, p. 139). Instead, different colour schemes transform the logics of plot, character and impact. Discussing what cinematic reality could be, Stanley Cavell asserts that the use of colour in his contemporary cinema had a 'de-psychologizing and de-theatricalizing' effect on its subjects (1979, p. 89). Discussing the films of Michelangelo Antonioni, the cinema of the Nouvelle Vague and of Alfred Hitchcock, Cavell observes that these directors were constructing reality through the inventive use of colour, as opposed to Jean-Luc Godard, whom he accuses of adopting a dramaturgy of colours that is close to advertising. Godard does, in fact, draw our attention to the fact that advertising and its colours are exactly where urgent and emergent collective imaginaries come into view. In an article on colour strategies of the Nouvelle Vague, Alain Bergala points out that Godard's use of colour created new forms of spatio-temporal relations in cinema. In this sense, Godard seems to have been the first after Méliès to use colour as a deliberately untransparent mode of depiction. He strove for an impression of reality by emphasising the artificiality of colour and consequently marking the film as screen and medium between the world and the viewers. Preminger's strategy of colour, especially in the film *Bonjour Tristesse*, is radically formalistic and surprisingly close to Godard's own. While it is well known that Godard, as author of the *Cahiers du cinéma* that featured Seberg on the cover in February 1958 when the film opened (De Baeque, 2010, p. 120), directly picked Seberg from the set of *Bonjour Tristesse* to star in *A bout de souffle*, Godard's debt to Preminger's work with colour seems underrated. Richard Brody related the structure of Godard's *Eloge de l'amour* (2001) to Preminger when he remarked that 'the film's colour scheme, with the present shot in black-and-white and the flashback in colour, is derived from Otto Preminger's *Bonjour Tristesse*' (2008, p. 606), stressing the fact that *Eloge de l'amour*, too, is dealing with the presence of the past in personal, political and cinematic terms, 'a film of history in which the past is revealed to live in the present' (p. 588). Apart from this overall structure, Preminger's work with primary colours, which adds a layer of chromatic relations to the chronic plot of figures and forms, antecedes Godard's colour dramaturgy. Preminger and Godard use colours in an alienating way and to accentuate film and screen as transformative media devices. In Preminger's film, primary colours are used to combine ineffable relationships: the incestuous ties between Cécile and her father, which Preminger and his cameraman Georges Périnal manage to keep constantly present by focusing on identical, corresponding, complementary or contrarian patterns of colour in Raymond's and Cécile's clothing. On another level, these colours are embedded in the surrounding or environmental colours, in natural or urban textures. On a third level, vectors are construed towards semantic or symbolic codes of colour: whiteness for presumed innocence, blue, white, red for the French tricolour, and an insistent green for the dresses of those who don't fit in with the bourgeois environment. Repeatedly colour is applied to irritate, to disturb and to point out an irreconcilable element.

The element of control of colours is addressed in the character of Anne Larson (Deborah Kerr), the fashion designer who joins the vacationing crowd and who, as a false but dictatorial mother-figure, will be the victim of Cécile's machinations. Anne Larson fails in her effort to control. An inscription of colour turning evil or even malign is achieved by repeatedly focusing on the sunburn of the father's young mistress, Elsa Mackenbourg (Mylène Demongeot), clearly depicted as an Eastern European figure by look, behaviour and language. This sunburn, the apparent destruction of a *jeune fille en fleur* who has not stayed in the shade, already appears in Sagan's novel. But the film stages it in a downright sadistic way, the burnt and oversensitive skin relating both to the excessive desire of the girl to please elderly gentlemen and to her visible vulnerability. Thus, the vulnerability of all membranes involved in cinematic perception is envisioned. In Preminger's film, two levels of colour schemes interlace: sadistic games of physicality and surface, and schemes of primary colours that introduce abstraction and a larger social matrix of symbolic colourings.

In view of the close resemblance of Preminger's and Godard's operations with film colours, the question of the real in those aesthetics can be reconsidered. Preminger's film *Bonjour Tristesse*, which in its title already evokes the notion of the nostalgic, that is, an operation of erasing history in favour of a feeling of 'pastness', reveals a new layer of meaning if it is perceived according to colour. The film was produced, directed, shot and post-produced over the course of Preminger's post-war return to Europe. Being Jewish and fed up with German cultural politics, Preminger had left Europe in 1935 on the invitation of Joseph Schenck and Twentieth Century Fox. After the war, Preminger's adaptation of George Bernard Shaw's *St. Joan*, shot in black and white, for which he had discovered the actress Jean Seberg, was a first step to working with British personnel according to the post-war Eady plan devised to distribute a share of the American production capital within England (Fujiwara, 2008, p. 198). *Bonjour Tristesse*, shot just a year later and mostly on location on the French Riviera and in the seaside villa of publisher Pierre Lazareff, differs fundamentally from *St. Joan* in all aesthetic categories. Its colour dramaturgy evokes differences of perception between audiences in Europe and in the US, between audiences then and now, between the feeling of post-war *bonheur*, definitely a symptom of nostalgia, and the discomfort of those who returned from voluntary or involuntary exile.

Colours of the real

Preminger's *Bonjour Tristesse* opens with Saul Bass's titles in their specific watercolour look characteristic of the 1950s, pans over the roofs of Paris in black and white, accompanied by the theme of *tristesse* George Auric composed for the film, to continue with a first scene in a tone of existentialist risky carelessness. Seberg's character in *Bonjour Tristesse*, Cécile, meanders through galleries, restaurants and clubs, mingles with society people, to eventually meet and dance with her rather sybaritic bachelor father and afterwards to fall into a very depressive mood, remembering a vacation on the French Riviera and her loss of innocence in all respects. Stunning in this first black-and white scene is the long enduring gaze of Seberg directly into the camera; later a leitmotiv of *A bout de souffle* (Figure 12.1).

Thus violating the Hollywood laws of framing, Preminger is literally penetrating the surface of the film. And, while crossing the invisible fourth wall of classical cinema space, Seberg's interior off-monologue mixes imperceptibly with Juliette Greco's voice singing the words of the title song, beginning with 'I live with melancholy', another mental illness that can also imply grappling with the past. Here, then, Seberg

Figure 12.1 Direct gaze of Seberg into the camera (Bonjour Tristesse, screenshot)

pronounces the central sentence of the film: 'I am surrounded by an invisible wall of memories.' In his film, Preminger construes this with colours, visible yet not likely to be perceived. The gaze into the camera will be constantly repeated in the film's black-and-white scenes, but it never occurs in the colour sequences. Thus, the flashy Technicolor scenes seem to represent objectively perceived reality, while the black-and-white scenes maintain the connection to the affectivity of an interior protocol. Then, during the extended interior monologue, colour gradually enters the frame like liquid being poured into it. At first blue spaces and the sea, then red objects and textures, then the white of the villa's architectural backdrop and finally the colours of the French Riviera landscape and nature, mainly shades of green, are filled into the scene. The coloured past enters as an insistent element of reality, while the monochrome present appears as an unreal, subjective and emotionally tinted layer of the film.

The film's drama and narration play on the mathematics of the number three. This is true for the magic triangle of daughter, father and his changing girlfriends in the film, but also in terms of colour structure. Three basic colours form the drama: red, blue and white. But then there is always one more, one colour too many. Sometimes a sudden green or pink, sometimes another less saturated colour is added to the primary tricolour. The structure of the film is thus based on three plus one. Three form a harmony, and every additional one causes disturbances and irritation in the story. In his colour dramaturgy, Preminger deliberately confuses the familiar mode of representing chronological time, which would depict the present tense of narration in affective coloured images while diffusing memories in the distancing aesthetics of black and white. When asked by Peter Bogdanovich why he decided to 'use colour for the memory scenes and black-and-white for the present' in *Bonjour Tristesse*, Otto Preminger answered: 'I am not particularly fond of flashbacks, so I probably tried to make it more agreeable or interesting by doing *that*' (1997, p. 629). Through this central structure of the film, though, Preminger has made a peremptory statement concerning history and cinema.

Changing the chronological order of black and white and colour in the film's narrative contests a notion of cinema's history, which is usually conceived of as a development from black and white to colour. The reverse is true, though. Early cinema was full of colours and colouring systems, hand-painted and stencilled, tinted and toned. Only in the 1920s did cinema systematically develop the art of black and white, its mastery of light in expressionism, constructivism and film noir, until, in the mid-1930s, colour processes eventually returned to the studios, prominently in the *Wizard of Oz* in 1939 – and then to Salman Rushdie's India. Approximately at that time, in 1935, Preminger left Europe for Hollywood. Since then, colours have come and gone in different shades and tonalities, subjected to rules of fashion or economics. Preminger's strategy to switch from black and white to colour images deceives the viewers into perceiving a movement from the highlighted presence of the holidays at the French Riviera back to the gloomy times of wild days in Clichy or Paris; at least, for contemporary audiences. Chronologically, of course, the dark nights in Paris are the tinted present of Preminger's film, or else the tinted future of the past perfect of the lost time. Melancholy, even more than nostalgia, loses track of a chronological order of narration to highlight the story around the concealed traumatic incident. But, beyond the individual traumatic triangle of family relations (after all, the 'real' mother is missing altogether), another broader social and historical layer of memory and trauma of the film comes into sight. In the post-war politics of cinema, colour once more joins the personal and the social.

Due to conventions of representation, the mode of showing a collective past would be in black and white, complying with the conventions of most historical documentary films. But, while it is true that most newsreel material was shot on black-and-white stock, this is certainly no general rule linked to technological standards, national taste or cultural politics. Cinematic memory in post-war Germany, for instance, had for a long time preserved the past, and especially the years of fascism, exclusively in black and white, while colour usually indicated post-war normality. Germans, so it could be claimed, preferred to remain in a colourful dreamlike post-war present, displacing evidence of the crimes committed into the distance of a black-and-white perception of the past. When colour newsreel films of Nazi Germany surfaced in the 1970s, audiences were shocked. Through colour, the horror had come closer, had become more real. For the same reason, in his *Nuit et Brouillard*, Alain Resnais interlaced colour material with the black-and-white footage of the concentration camps as they were shot in the war, thus finding a film form that would realise the presence of the past. Resnais solved the problem primarily through his montage of material – even if the text and voice of Jean Cayrol as well as the music of Hanns Eisler congenially interweave past and present in their disturbing composition of acoustic layers and overtones. Resnais's film was released in 1955, shortly before Preminger started working on *Bonjour Tristesse*.

Jean-Luc Godard has made a crucial point of the colour case in cinematic memory. In the first part of his *Histoire(s) du cinéma* (1988) he deals with history, film industry and aesthetics. In this section Godard discusses a 'resurrection of the documentary' in 1944, writing in verses: 'and if George Stevens | hadn't been the first to use | the first sixteen millimeter colour film | at Auschwitz and Ravensbrück | there's no doubt | that Elizabeth Taylor's | air of well-being | would never have found | a place in the sun' (Godard, 1999, I, 15, p. 43).

There are slight and probably intended inaccuracies in this. The film director and cameraman George Stevens, who had directed comedies and musicals in his earlier career, went to Europe as a lieutenant colonel in the US Army Signal Corps. Like John Ford, Samuel Fuller and others, he had filmed the liberation of concentration camps, in his case Dachau, using 16 mm colour film stock. As far as the protocols show at the Imperial War Museum, where his material is archived, he had not been to Auschwitz or Ravensbrück. Godard is obviously condensing matters in order to refer to Theodor W. Adorno's statement that there can be no poetry after Auschwitz, a position Godard has always severely contested. George Stevens compiled the material he had shot in Dachau in his film *Nazi Concentration Camps*, which was projected as evidence at the Nuremberg Trials. This introduction of colour into the reality of atrocities, or, rather, the introduction of atrocities as evidence in colour, according to Godard, fundamentally changed the idea of the documentary. With Stevens's films, the relation between film colour and reality became contingent, touched people, perpetrated the safe screen and screening of memories. The reference to atrocities was less formalised, the images had an immediate effect, albeit a culturally mediated one. This rupture in the documentary relation was not caused by montage, but by the film stock itself. It seems that Martin Scorsese in his film *Shutter Island* (2010), set in the year 1954, takes his cue from Stevens, Resnais and Godard. The plot of the film deploys the trauma of a soldier who had been part of the US Army unit discovering the prisoners in Dachau, which in post-war times leads to an inverted and barred memory. *Shutter Island* also employs the dramaturgy of colour as of false, tinted and toned Technicolor memory when it cinematically transfers and communicates the disturbed forms of post-war memory.

In the 1940s, colour film stock on 16 mm had been widely used for home movie formats. George Stevens's images proved that the two realities, the documentaries and the home movies, the camps and the homes, had always existed side by side. Therefore, Godard continues in the *Histoire(s) du cinéma*: 'thirty-nine | forty-four | martyrdom and resurrection | of the documentary O how marvelous | to be able to watch | what one can't see | o sweet miracle of our blind eyes' (Godard, 1999, I, 15, p. 43).

In 1945 nobody really wanted see what Stevens had recorded on colour film stock. Bergala in his essay on the Nouvelle Vague writes: *'L'horreur en couleur de ce que l'on n'avait pas voulu voir'* (1995, p. 128). It was primarily the colour of the films that produced a disturbing moment and thus fundamentally questioned the possibility of representing the horror of history. With colour, historical memory broke through the controlling fourth wall of nostalgic cinema. Instead of representation, colour was conceived of as an instant affect connecting present and past. Godard then links this with George Stevens's most successful movie from 1951, again shot in black and white: *A Place in the Sun*. As opposed to Theodore Dreiser's original novel *An American Tragedy*, the hero in Stevens's film, a young ambitious person who will be tried for murder in the end, played by Montgomery Clift, is called George Eastman. The hero is thus named after a famous pioneer of film technology who had invented perforation and worked on film stock. In Eastman's factory in Rochester, Eastmancolour had been invented in 1939, as the first monopack colour film stock, which made filming much more flexible and mobile. In Stevens's movie *A Place in the Sun*, the Eastman factory is transformed into a factory for swimming suits. The film begins with a huge billboard showing a girl in a bathing suit, in the sun, together with the caption 'This is an Eastman'. Despite references to *Eastman, in other words, to the development of colour film stock* throughout the film, colour is markedly absent, remaining a blind spot of post-war perception, albeit an insistent one. In Stevens's film, as Godard has underlined, the emotions turn out to be an issue of the intimate as well as of the industrial. Again, colour and girls' skin are closely linked. And they are linked to industry as the masterplan of representation: 'But otherwise the cinema is an industry | and if the First World War | had enabled | the American cinema | to ruin the French cinema | with the birth of television | the Second would enable it to finance | that is, ruin all the European cinemas' (Godard, 1999, 1, 16, p. 44). Godard's argument on film colour is not one of distinguishing the real and the fantastic, or truth or fiction; he is discussing the instability, the vulnerability and destructibility of perception in terms of the personal, the industrial and the political at the same time.

Tricolours

Film colour after the Second World War was no longer a matter of feelings and emotions, but a matter of industries, as well as politics and ideologies. Andrew Dudley (1980), in his seminal essay on 'The Postwar Struggle for Colour', underlines that the war between political systems in the Second World War extended to the aesthetic realms of the US system of Technicolor and the German Agfacolour. Film colour and film sound, those very affective and emotional aspects of cinema that strongly shape and mould memories as nostalgic feelings, are entangled with industrial plans, market strategies and imperial politics. Interestingly, and this escapes Dudley's attention, the German chemical and colours industry IG Farben, also producer of the gas for the death chambers, held a subsidiary company in California throughout the Second World War. In 1945 the French film industry wavered in its decision over a film colour system, since the development of a proper French colour film production was unlikely. In 1945, then, as Dudley writes, 'there was the assumption that the natural colour sense and good taste of the French would be able to choose one or another foreign process and put it to uses never before imagined. Choices seemed to be between Technicolor and Agfacolour' (1980, p. 63). When Preminger began to shoot *Bonjour Tristesse* on colour stock in July 1957, he did so in the midst of this historical tension, although, as an American in Paris and on the Riviera, there was little doubt that he would use the Technicolor system. Still, he addresses the issue of colour and memory in his film in a subtle and probably not altogether conscious way.

In one of the most stunning scenes of the film, which on first sight seems to stem from the tradition of the musical, the complete cast of characters meets at the harbour of a little fishing town, supposed to be St Tropez. Again, introduced by a melancholic black-and-white shot of Cécile looking at the audience, at us, through the reflection of a mirror, where she remembers: 'we did have fun then, and everybody was so nice to everyone else', Preminger cuts to a Cinemascope long shot of the colour scene of a huge summer party where tourists and the town's people join in dancing and drinking. The image here is composed nearly exclusively of blues, reds and whites forming the dizzying image of the French tricolour turning into a wild vortex. When eventually everybody gets up to form a Polonaise, this is led by a bearded and dark-skinned young man wearing a Phrygian cap, which historically marked the opposition to Greek culture, a sign of those from the margins, of the peripheral people. Later it was worn by the Republican opposition in the French Revolution. In the film, the scene and its music it is linked to Eastern European cultures. The dancing, too, turns out to be not French at all but some sort of carnival movement, performed by all sorts of people and peoples. As the diverse dancers pass, a carnival of old European souls seems to spread across the marketplace. Gradually the colours of the people's costumes mix and the tricolour dissolves. Among the dancers, the sunburnt Elsa in a green dress keeps appearing and disappearing in the crowd. Again, her skin marks the vulnerability of *bonheur*, well-being, and significantly she says: 'The music is brilliant, it has even made me forget the last of my sunburn.' Truffaut, in his homage to the film, ends by stating: 'His [Preminger's] vision of Saint Tropez is not very strict. *Bonjour Tristesse* is not France as seen naively by an American, but France as shown to the Americans the way they like it, by a European who is clear minded and very contemptuous' (1958, pp. 166–167). It is significant that for Truffaut this scene should betray Preminger's attitude. Full of contempt, *méprisant*, will also be the way Godard in his later film *Le Mépris* dismisses those directors who cooperate with the American film industry. Against the American destruction of French cinema, Godard, in 1963, called Fritz Lang and his Greek Project of Ulysses to his set, prominently featuring fake Technicolor cameramen in the final shot, trying in vain to capture the invisible Greek gods for the screen. What Truffaut perceives is that Preminger's staging of the scene is not trying to simulate Frenchness, but, much rather, the failure ever to be French again. Obviously, the French themselves liked this estrangement, as Preminger remarks: '*Bonjour Tristesse* [...] was a very big success in France and in America the critics said it wasn't French enough which is very funny' (Bogdanovich, 1997, p. 629). What is striking here is that the colours themselves negotiate the Frenchness of the scene, but in a double sense. Technicolor is pretending to do the tricolour. Colour perception as sensuous is contrasted with colour as a sign or signal. Colour as intrinsic to film stock is contrasted with the signal level of colour, which is insensitive to film stock, and thus the political side of perception. Of course, the two cannot be separated. But, in Preminger's film, the sensuous colour perception, colour as physiological affect and memory is highlighted by constantly referring to the burnt skin.

Altogether de-psychologizing the plot, colour on this level acts as a political force. The American colours themselves introduce a condescending view of Frenchness, since French cinema does not have its own colours. While using French design (the robes and swimming suits of Givenchy), it shows it on American and British actresses, imposing American sexuality through the depiction of girls and their skin and membranes. And Technicolor appropriates the French Riviera, sea and landscape. Astonishingly enough, French audiences liked the slight estrangement of the view on France, opening in the film with Juliet Greco singing her chanson in English, albeit with a sweet French accent. There is, indeed, nostalgia in this film, because Preminger is not addressing European or French history as it really was, the traumatic, the genocide, but he is conceptualising a Europe that would have integrated and sheltered all its peripheral people: a Europe that would have been like Preminger's US. This nostalgic plan is sketched out on the skin of the film and the skin of the American girl Cécile. Through its colour structure, the film reveals that Preminger's return to Europe is not a homecoming, not a *nostos*, and in no way nostalgic. Coming back, Preminger found 'a place surrounded by an invisible wall of memories', which he renders visible through the colours in his film. The issue of the surface of the girl Elsa's burnt skin keeps reminding the audience of the fact that light is not only a metaphor for enlightenment or reconnaissance, but can also be destructive. There is a wound; something traumatic is indicated where the film's skin becomes dysfunctional. It is the colouring that resists closure in the film.

Notes

1. Friedrich Nietzsche (2001) 'On the Genealogy of Morals', in *Basic Writings of Nietzsche*. Translated by Walter Kaufmann, introduction by Peter Gay. New York: Random House, Modern Library Edition, p. 497:

   Perhaps indeed there was nothing more fearful and uncanny in the whole prehistory of man than his *mnemotechnics*. 'If something is to stay in the memory it must be burned in: only that which never ceases to *hurt* stays in

the memory', this is a main clause of the oldest (unhappily also the most enduring) psychology on earth.
2. Cf. Sigmund Freud, 'The Uncanny[1919]', in *The Standard Edition of the Complete Psychological Works* of Sigmund Freud, translated from the German under the General Editorship of James Strachey. In collaboration with Anna Freud. Assisted by Alix Strachey and Alan Tyson. 24 volumes. Vintage, 1999, 17: 217–256.

References

Bergala, A. (1995) 'La Couleur, la Nouvelle Vague et ses maîtres des années cinquante', in J. Aumont (ed.) *La Couleur en cinema*. Milano, Paris: Edizioni Gabriele Mazzotta, Cinémathèque française.
Bogdanovich, P. (1997) *Who the Devil Made It: Conversations with Legendary Film Directors*. New York: Alfred A. Knopf.
Brody, R. (2008) *Everything is Cinema: The Working Life of Jean-Luc Godard*. New York: Metropolitan Books, Henry Holt and Company.
Buscombe, E. (1985) 'Sound and Colour', in B. Nichols (ed.) *Movies and Methods. An Anthology Vol. II*. Berkeley, Los Angeles: University of California Press, pp. 83–92.
Cavell, S. (1979) *The World Viewed: Reflections on the Ontology of Film*. Boston: Harvard University Press.
De Baeque, A. (2010) *Godard: Biographie*. Paris: Grasset & Fasquelle.
Dudley, A. (1980) 'The Postwar Struggle for Colour', in T. de Lauretis and S. Heath (eds) *The Cinematic Apparatus*. London, Basingstoke: The Macmillan Press Ltd., pp. 61–75.
Fujiwara, C. (2008) *The World and its Double: The Life and Work of Otto Preminger*. New York: Faber and Faber.
Godard, J.-L. (1999) *Histoire(s) du cinéma*. Vol. 1–4., ECM Records.
Gunning, T. (1995) 'Colourful Metaphors: The Attraction of Colour in Early Silent Cinema'. Fotogenia, http://www.muspe.unibo.it/wwcat/period/fotogen/num01/numero1d.htm (accessed 26 June 2013).
Hirsch, F. (2007) *Otto Preminger: The Man Who Would Be King*. New York: Alfred A. Knopf.
Jameson, F. (1983) 'Postmodernism and Consumer Society', in H. Foster (ed.) *The Anti-Aesthetic. Essays on Postmodern Culture*. Seattle, Washington: Bay Press, pp. 111–125.
Jameson, F. (1984) 'Postmodernism, or the Cultural Logic of Late Capitalism'. *New Left Review*, 146(July–August), pp. 53–92.
Kalmus, N. (1935) 'Colour Consciousness'. *Journal of the Society of Motion Picture Engineers*, 25(2), pp. 139–140.
Münsterberg, H. (1916) *The Photoplay: A Psychological Study*. New York and London: Appleton.
Rushdie, S. (2002) *The Wizard of Oz*. London: BFI Classics.
Truffaut, François (1958) 'Bonjour Tristesse', *Les Film de ma vie*. Paris 1975, pp. 163–167.

Part IV
Creative Nostalgias

13
Creative Nostalgia for an Imagined Better Future: *Il treno del Sud* by the Migrant Filmmaker Alvaro Bizzarri

Morena La Barba

This chapter will illustrate the idea of nostalgia in *Il treno del Sud*, which was the first film by Alvaro Bizzarri, a migrant filmmaker who arrived in Switzerland in the late 1950s to serve as an apprentice blacksmith and became a typical and essential figure in Swiss film history (Buache, 1978; Schaub, 1985; Schlappner and Schaub, 1987; Dell'Ambrogio, 2004; Dumont and Tortajada, 2007; La Barba and Mayenfisch, 2009). As part of a larger research project in progress about cinema and Italian migration to Switzerland, this paper tries to sketch a hypothesis about the concept of *migrant nostalgia*, which stems from a cultural crisis of the present caused by ambivalence and conflict between different values, spaces, times and relationships. It enacts memories of the past and the imagining of a better future. *Migrant nostalgia* concerns persons, groups and nations, and migrants and non-migrants of a country of origin and a host country. In the late 1960s, Switzerland had a massive presence of foreign labour, the majority of whom were Italian. The consequences of Switzerland's economic policies were quick to affect the socio-cultural dimensions of the nation. The old fears of *Überfremdung* (infiltration), as well as the 'spiritual defence' of the nation, reappeared. After the birth of an anti-Italian political party in the early 1960s, the xenophobic movement gave rise to several anti-foreigner initiatives throughout the 1970s. In this context, the Italian migration to Switzerland strengthened its tradition as an association movement. The Federation of Free Italian Colonies in Switzerland (FCLIS), the most important Italian migrant association in Europe (Ricciardi, 2013), engaged in social welfare activities, but also served as a cultural movement (La Barba, 2013a). Founded in 1943 by anti-fascist refugees in the 1960s, the FCLIS, in addition to fighting for the social rights of Italian workers, developed cultural policies for the training and emancipation of Italian migrants (La Barba et al., 2013c). Alvaro Bizzarri, leader of the local film club movement, and other members of the FCLIS were the protagonists of a unique experience in the migratory movement of post-war Europe (La Barba, 2013a): the production of a feature film on the 'immigrant condition' (Castelnuovo-Frigessi, 1978).

As summarised by Bizzarri in his notes,

> *Il Treno del Sud* is the story of a young Italian trade unionist who immigrated to Switzerland and tries to organise his compatriots around the local union to obtain a larger contractual force and to claim fairer living conditions for all workers.[1]

In the xenophobic atmosphere of the late 1960s, before the 'Schwarzenbach initiative' against the Italian migrants, Paolo il Rosso, the protagonist of the film, who is an Italian blacksmith and the alter ego of the director, chooses to return to his country of origin. Why? Is it *Heimweh, mal du pays*, nostalgia, homesickness, or the need to fight for a better future? When he finds himself impotent in realising his project, his deep feeling of injustice against the 'immigrant condition', his disappointment about the lack of solidarity, and his disillusionment with his former comrades lead the protagonist to take a train back to the South, in the hope of being able to resume his struggle for a better world. However, before choosing to return to Italy, Paolo becomes, or, rather, looks sick. Why? Is the 'immigrant condition' a pathological condition, as doctors and psychiatrists contend? Is it possible that nostalgia, in a historical context of conflict, can become a source of political and artistic creativity? We chose to analyse and understand nostalgia in this context more from a medical and psychiatric view, rather than from a cinematic point of view (Dika, 2003; Casetti and Di Chio, 2009).

Il treno del Sud: Go away and return home

Alvaro Bizzarri, the *eccezionale normale* (Grendi, 1977) of Italian migration, was born in Tuscany in 1935, and in 1955 he migrated to Switzerland to work as a blacksmith. In the 1960s, he became an activist for CLI Bienne and was in charge of the organisation's cultural activities and movie club. In 1968, he began to engage in amateur filmmaking. Between 1970 and 1998, after he returned to Tuscany, he produced 12 films (La Barba, 2013b).

Paolo il Rosso, the protagonist of the film *Il treno del Sud*, is an amateur photographer and the alter ego of the director, an amateur filmmaker. In a recent interview about his film, Bizzarri says (La Barba, 2009, p. 85):

> *Il treno del Sud* is a personal film. A man, thanks to the help of a cousin, comes to Switzerland to work, but he soon discovers that the cousin is a debauched man who does not share his moral choices. The environment of the Italian trade unionists is not an easy one. The protagonist is accustomed to certain forms of struggle in Italy, such as opposition to the Vietnam War (he had covered his room with posters of revolutionary heroes), so he decides to leave Switzerland and takes the train back to the South.[2]

The film is personal and collective at the same time. The actors in the film are migrants themselves and members of the CLI association, as well as family members and friends. Bizzarri works according to the rules of Italian neorealism (La Barba, 2009): by participating in a collective project, migrants re-enact their lives, their problems and their hopes. The film is about Paolo, the protagonist, who arrives in Bienne, a Swiss town undergoing rapid industrial expansion, in the late 1960s to work in a factory on the invitation of his cousin Bruno, who welcomes him at the train station. Bruno, an amateur photographer like Paolo, engages in an illicit activity with his Swiss boss: he covertly makes pornographic pictures. He offers Paolo the opportunity to develop the pictures, without revealing the true kind of work he is offering. While Bruno plays cards with his photography models in a bar, Paolo tries to meet with his old friends, one of whom is Salvatore, who lives in a dilapidated house. Paolo asks Salvatore to commit himself to the struggle for the rights of migrants. However, Salvatore does not want to, because he feels responsible for his family and does not want to take risks, including that of being expelled, since migrants have no right to engage in political activities in Switzerland. Instead, he proposes hunting for other comrades in the workers' barracks. Then, Paolo visits Bruno, who is secretly shooting pornographic pictures at home. He tries to get rid of Paolo by pretending to be sick. Paolo leaves and walks alone through the city, while meditating on the sunset. After Paolo develops the first film, he finally discovers what is going on. He condemns Bruno and his immoral activity, slams the door, and rejects the opportunity to earn easy money. Paolo then goes to the workers' barracks and meets his friend Aldo, who explains that, following a divorce, he lost his residence permit and the ability to rent a house. Aldo tells Paolo of his past activism and expresses his disappointment and resignation over the present state of things. He invites Paolo to return to Italy because there is a risk of being expelled from Switzerland, which had happened to many other communist activists. Aldo meets with his comrades, who are mostly early migrants. While drinking alcohol and playing cards in a desolate and bleak environment, Paolo listens to the stories of these migrants, who are aware of their situation but resigned to their fate. While Bruno continues his work as a photographer, Paolo works with Antonio on a site where the Italians are given the most dangerous work to do. When Paolo encourages Antonio to leave and vote in Italy to assert his civil rights, Antonio shows him a document stating that he has been removed from the voting list of his place of origin because he had emigrated; thus, he now has no political rights in either Italy or Switzerland. In the meantime, Bruno meets his boss and his boss's wife at a painting exhibition for Italian artists and seduces the woman, who is fascinated by the artistic sensibility of the Italians. Alone in the streets, Paolo becomes aware of the injustices suffered by the Italians: 'the negroes of Europe' have no right to live in the houses they build. With the passing of the seasons and the arrival of Christmas, Paolo finds himself looking through the windows at scenes of Swiss family life, which stimulate memories of his family in Italy. At this point, he decides to write to his wife, in order to express his regret for being unable to participate in the *Autunno Caldo* (Hot Autumn) labour movement taking place at home. Doubting his gesture, he throws the paper into the trash and directs his thoughts to the Vietnam War and its innocent victims. Instead, he writes a poem dedicated to the children and mothers of Vietnam. He thinks back to his past in Italy as an activist in the labour movement and the March for Peace.

While his imagination seems delirious, with confused images of his family in Italy, his daughter and his wife, and train rails all mixed up, his cousin rings the doorbell. Bruno notices the political posters hung around the room, and they begin a discussion, in which their different visions of life and of the past emerge. Bruno wants to forget the suffering of the war and to enjoy the pleasures of life, while Paolo wants to continue to keep the memory of the suffering and injustice and to fight the horrors of the war. He finds that Switzerland lives outside reality and seems to ignore the authenticity of the war. Bruno says that Paolo is sick; he refuses to carry the world's problems on his shoulders and makes an appointment for the next day, Sunday, with a model to distract himself. However, the next day, Paolo firmly decides to take a train to the South because he does not want Schwarzenbach, the leader of the Swiss xenophobic movement, to pay for the return ticket for him. Bruno runs to the station in a vain attempt to stop his cousin, but the train passes him by, and, in the end, he is forced to accept the decision of his cousin: 'Switzerland is not made for ideals.'

Nostalgia: A Swiss or Italian disease?

During the Italian mass migration to Switzerland in the 1960s and 1970s, doctor and psychiatrist Michele Risso and sociologist Delia Castelnuovo-Frigessi (1982) published a book about emigration, nostalgia and mental illness. By reviewing a series of international studies on the link between migration and mental illness, the two researchers aimed to explain *why*, rather than *how*, the disease develops. Alterations in the behaviour of migrants were attributed to different social norms, rather than individual health. The disease of the migrant is only the visible tip of the social structure's iceberg. In their book, they translate many excerpts from the *Dissertatio Medica*, by Alsatian doctor Johannes Hofer, as well as the work of other physicians from the past. In the *Dissertatio* of 1688, nostalgia was introduced in medical nosology as a typically Swiss disease: 'from the Greek *nostalgia*, from *nostos*, the return, and *algos*, pain or suffering' (Castelnuovo-Frigessi and Risso, 1982, p. 10). At that time, the German term *Heimweh* indicated the pain of the Swiss mercenaries in Europe who were far from home and feared that they would never see their homeland again. After observing the Swiss affected in France by this misfortune, the French coined the term *mal du pays* (p. 10). *Heimweh, mal du pays* or nostalgia was then considered to be a deadly disease. The only remedy was to return home (p. 14).

By observing the attitudes of the Swiss mercenary soldiers, Hofer lists the specific behaviours that permit diagnosis of the disease (p. 13):

> tendency toward sadness, intolerance toward foreign customs, an aversion to social relations, violent displeasure shown in response to every joke or to the smallest injustice, an inclination toward avarice, constant expressions of praise of their countries, and contempt for any other region or district.[3]

Where does nostalgia come from? In the opinion of Dr Hofer, nostalgia comes from 'a distorted force of imagination'. According to its scientific explanation, the 'idea of the homecoming' is caused by the juices of the nerves that 'always take one and only one direction through the brain' and thus first evoke an idea. Homecoming is an idea 'related to sometimes violent, sometimes milder signs and accidents' (Castelnuovo-Frigessi and Risso, 1982, p. 10). According to him, 'the power of imagination' can generate suffering when the part of the brain where 'images of those objects that evoke nostalgia' are set in motion (p. 10).

Does Paolo, the protagonist, suffer from this distorted idea? Do Paolo's attitudes correspond with the symptoms of the original Swiss pathology? In the behaviour of the protagonist of *Il treno del Sud*, we can actually see some of these symptoms. Paolo is serious and does not like jokes, he is not ironic, and he is responsible and passionate about his ideals. He feels empathy for the plight of his suffering compatriots. He has a high sense of justice, and he despises his host country because Switzerland is responsible for gross injustices against his migrant compatriots. His languor and longing for his homeland are caused by nostalgia for his family, as well as for a place and a time when he could fight against injustice. In his room, Paolo reviews the images that remind him of the past: family photos, Italian newspaper articles, posters of political leaders, and leaflets from his previous political battles. His cousin Bruno jokingly calls him 'the decorator'. After his first attempts to socialise with his colleagues, Paolo starts walking alone in the streets of the city, thinking about the condition of his compatriots, and then he retires alone to his room and ponders his situation. Is Paolo disillusioned?

In a more recent treatise about the mental health problems of migrants, family psychotherapist, medical anthropologist and sociologist Natale Losi (2000, p. 33) observes that, as a result of multiple breaks, we can often see in migrants 'self-abandonment, neglect, and disillusionment', which are frequently connected to 'surprise, guilt, and inadequacy' for not having understood a situation before their departure. Losi addresses the 'sense of injustice' and the collective 'demand for justice' (p. 33):

> For anyone who is in exile, a wound is formed by the most profound sense of injustice and resentment for his lack of understanding and sharing. The demand for justice is not only individual, but also collective and joint, and does not necessarily need a sense of revenge.[4]

Paolo is probably disillusioned because of the betrayal, the trap of his cousin Bruno, and his unsuccessful attempts to involve his companions in a collective project. Since he finds it impossible to act in the present, he decides to return to Italy.

Paolo il Rosso: Pathological or creative nostalgia?

Paolo experiences conflict through clashing values, which affects his relationships. He defends justice, civil rights, legality, integrity, solidarity, responsibility, truth, consciousness, compassion, work, peace, love and memory. His cousin Bruno is corrupt, irresponsible, individualist, sarcastic and indifferent; he defends illegality, money, sexual desire, consumption and oblivion. Salvatore, Aldo and Antonio, Paolo's friends, are assimilated, afraid and disillusioned. Paolo admires international revolutionary heroes, and in Switzerland he confronts a conservative and reactionary leader of a xenophobic movement. Paolo lives between contrasting spaces (Italy and Switzerland, his country of origin and the host country; North and South; barracks and houses; streets and rooms) and between different times: past, present and future. The conflicts in his present produce a need to remember in Paolo. For migrants, one of these forms of injustice concerns memory, as they are 'particularly opposed to clearing the memory and the ability to transmit it' (Losi, 2000, p. 33). This need for memory pushes Paolo to escape in the future. He begins to develop symptoms of the disease. Is his imagination altered?

Due to his crisis, Paolo remembers his personal past and collective history in his room. His decision to leave Switzerland is not an individualistic solution. Paolo and some of his comrades idealise other time–space dimensions and human relations. He refers to a memory of an imagined past. Paolo and his migrant companions are affected by the tragic experience of the Second World War: some of them lived in concentration camps, while others lived through the war and participated in the resistance movement. They keep the memory of the horrors of war and injustice. Paolo imagines a different future of militancy and the struggle for peace, justice, human rights and building a new society. A song inspired the film soundtrack and title: *Il treno che viene dal Sud*, by Sergio Endrigo. The lyrics speak about hopes and dreams; they are not only about a private dream, such as a house for one's family in Italy, but also a collective one: the dream of a beautiful new society. In the lyrics, the migrant worker has a pessimistic point of view (Endrigo, 1967):

> Fatigue is harder without love, but at night, it's always the same dream: I'll have a house for you and me. From the train coming from the South, dark men get off with hope in their pockets, but in their hearts, they feel that this beautiful new society, this new, great society, will never be accomplished, will not be done.[5]

Is Paolo this kind of pessimistic, nostalgic migrant? During his last night in Switzerland, Paolo has blurred vision and fuzzy images of his family, his wife and his daughter. Is he an idealist, a dreamer, a visionary, a utopian or an artist? He is probably all of these, but, primarily, Paolo has become ill, and his cousin is the first to notice it. He has various opportunities. First, his becoming ill and being a migrant in Switzerland are not a coincidence, as shown in several studies published at the time on the cause–effect relationship between migration and disease (Risso and Böker, 1964). Other opportunities include returning home, as 300,000 Italians did in the same period. In the end, Paolo also decides to return to Italy, though for different reasons from those of his compatriots, who are unable to face the hardships of such a life. He chooses to fight for his own rights and for those of his comrades.

Is *migrant nostalgia* a pathological or creative nostalgia?

The migrant symbolises and gives body to the figures of rootlessness, cultural shock and homesickness that produce several diseases among Italian migrants. Nevertheless, the departure of the protagonist of the film (more specifically, his desire to go back) is explained as a revolt against the injustices and inequalities of his migrant status. The protagonist of Bizzarri's film embodies other nostalgic characters. He feels the loneliness of his life and melancholic memories of his family; however, his desire to return is linked with the possibility of participating in the struggle to assert alternative visions of society.

As the honorary president of FCLIS, Zanier emphasises (2004, p. 132),

> the first wave of migrants had certainly come to Switzerland to work, and Switzerland was in great need of their labour, but they also had a 'project': the project for a new society. [...] All in all, they had 'subversive' ideas on political and trade union rights, on the redistribution of wealth, and on the welfare state.[6]

Paolo il Rosso, the protagonist of the film, is aware of the political and historical moment he is living in, given the rise of the emancipation movements of youths, women, workers and blacks, the beginning of anti-colonial liberation struggles, and the peace movement and the mobilisation against the Vietnam War. Because the opportunities to participate in the transformation of the present and the affirmation of a different future are denied to him in Switzerland, he decides to return to

Italy. His nostalgia as a migrant is also nostalgia for an idea: a vision of the future and a vision of a society that rejects the principle of war and affirms the equality of human rights. We could say that it is nostalgia for a imagining a better future, as well as the possibility of affirming the values of justice, humanity, equality and solidarity. Seen from this point of view, nostalgia can be not only pathological, but also creative and innovative.

As the leaders of FCLIS's movie club movement argue, the film becomes an opportunity to challenge the problems of the Italian immigrant workers and provoke a process of cultural creativity (La Barba, 2013a). Psychotherapists Giuseppe Cardamone and Maridana Corrente (2000) argue that nostalgia in the historical horizons of a migrant can be a source of terrible disappointment, but, at the same time, a positive illusion. For migrants, the hope of going back to their place of origin, as well as to their memory and history, can help them not to feel as if they are without a home or without a sense of belonging. Nostalgia, then, can become not only 'a distorted force of imagination' or a possible source of pathology, as Dr Hofer argued in 1668, but also 'the transforming energy for the quest for a place to live' (Cardamone and Corrente, 2000, p. 313). Nostalgic migrants can contribute and participate, according to their own intentions, possibilities and imagination, in building a new and more just society.

Paolo, the alter ego of the director, returns to Italy to fight for a more just and peaceful society; likewise, Bizzarri, the director, decides to make a movie about the migrant condition in Switzerland for the same reasons. They are faced with different political expressions of the same form of nostalgia, a *migrant nostalgia*. Why did Bizzarri begin to make films? As he says in an interview (La Barba, 2009, p. 85),

> when you go through emigration, something occurs in you: when you become aware of your condition, in a place very different from the one you came from, your relationships with others change. Shortly after I arrived in Switzerland, I realised that they treated us like underdeveloped people, people of *cincali*, pigs.[7]

However, far from being the end, this is the beginning of a long story. In his second film, *Lo stagionale*, the Italian migrant protagonist Giuseppe, his clandestine child and the comrades of FCLIS choose to demonstrate for their rights in Switzerland, against their status as seasonal workers. In 1970, outside the Italian embassy and the Swiss federal parliament building, the fiction of film meets the reality of the documentary, political actors reach film actors, and political imagination adjoins artistic creativity for a better imagined future in Switzerland.

Notes

1. Translated by the author of this chapter: Alvaro Bizzarri's private notes: 'Il Treno del Sud, c'est l'histoire d'un jeune syndicaliste italien émigré en Suisse lequel essaye d'organiser ses compatriotes autour du syndicat local, dans le but d'obtenir une force contractuelle plus importante et pouvoir revendiquer des conditions de vie plus justes pour tous les travailleurs'.
2. Translated by the author of this chapter:

    Il treno del Sud est plus personnel. Un type arrive en Suisse grâce à son cousin et se trouve confronté à un dépravé qui ne partage pas ses choix. Même parmi les syndicalistes italiens, il ne trouve pas un terrain facile. Lui qui était habitué à certaines formes de lutte en Italie, comme contre la guerre du Vietnam (il avait tapissé sa chambre d'images de révolutionnaires), il préfère ficher le camp et reprendre le train du Sud.

    La Barba, M. (2009) 'Alvaro Bizzarri: Migration, Militance, Cinema'. *Décadrages – Cinéma à travers champs*, 14, p. 85.
3. Translated by the author of this chapter:

    tendenza alla tristezza, l'insofferenza verso i costumi stranieri, il disgusto verso i rapporti sociali, la violenta avversione verso ogni scherzo, verso la benché minima ingiustizia; una certa inclinazione all'avarizia; le costanti espressioni di lode nei confronti del proprio paese e di disprezzo nei confronti di ogni altra regione o contrada, in Castelnuovo-Frigessi, D. and Risso, M. (1982) *A mezza parete. Emigrazione, nostalgia, malattia mentale.* Torino: Einaudi, p. 13.
4. Translated by the author of this chapter: 'Per chi è in esilio una ferita in più è costituita dal profondo senso d'ingiustizia subita e dal risentimento per la sua non comprensione/condivisione. La richiesta di giustizia non è solo individuale, ma collettiva, di gruppo, e non riveste necessariamente un significato di vendetta'. Losi, N. (2000) *Vite altrove. Migrazione e disagio psichico.* Milano: Feltrinelli, p. 33.
5. Translated by the author of this chapter:

    Senza amore è più dura la fatica. Ma la notte è un sogno sempre uguale, avrò un casa per te, per me. Dal treno che viene dal sud, discendono uomini cupi che hanno in tasca la speranza. Ma in cuore sentono che questa nuova, questa bella società, questa nuova grande società, non si farà, non si farà.

    Endrigo, S. (1967) 'Il treno che viene dal Sud', in *Endrigo*, Fonit Cetra.
6. Translated by the author of this chapter:

    molti di quegli uomini, quelli della prima ondata, certamente erano venuti in Svizzera per lavorare e che di quella manodopera la Svizzera aveva gran bisogno, ma avevano anche un 'progetto'. Un progetto di società. [...] Insomma avevano esattamente le idee 'sovversive': sui diritti sindacali e politici, sulla ridistribuzione della ricchezza, sullo Stato sociale.

Zanier, L. (2004) 'Fiches', in E. Halter (ed.) *Gli italiani in Svizzera. Un secolo di emigrazione*. Bellinzona: Casagrande, p. 132.

7. Translated by the author of this chapter:

> quand tu vis l'émigration, quelque chose se passe en toi: lorsque tu prends conscience de ta condition, dans un milieu très différent de celui d'où tu viens, ton rapport aux autres change. Peu après mon arrivée en Suisse, je me suis rendu compte que l'on nous traitait comme un peuple sous-développé, un peuple de «cincali», de cochons.

La Barba, M. (2009) 'Alvaro Bizzarri: Migration, Militance, Cinema'. *Décadrages – Cinéma à travers champs*, 14, p. 85.

References

Buache, F. (1978) *Le cinéma Suisse*. Lausanne: Editions l'Age d'Homme.
Cardamone, G. and Corrente, M. (2000) 'Diversità, stati di coscienza e relazione terapeutica', in N. Losi (ed.) *Vite altrove. Migrazioni e disagio psichico*. Milano: Feltrinelli, pp. 311–324.
Casetti, F. and Di Chio, F. (2009) *Analisi del film*. Milano: Bompiani.
Castelnuovo-Frigessi, D. (1978) *La condition immigrée*. Lausanne: Editions d'en bas.
Castelnuovo-Frigessi, D. and Risso, M. (1982) *A mezza parete. Emigrazione, nostalgia, malattia mentale*. Torino: Einaudi.
Dell'Ambrogio, M. (2004) 'I viaggi della speranza. L'immagine dell'immigrato italiano nel cinema svizzero', in E. Halter (ed.) *Gli italiani in Svizzera. Un secolo di emigrazione*. Bellinzona: Casagrande, pp. 261–269.
Dika, V. (2003) *Recycled Culture in Contemporary Art and Film – the Uses of Nostalgia*. New York: Cambridge University Press.
Dumont, H. and Tortajada, M. (eds) (2007) *Histoire du cinéma suisse 1966–2000*. Lausanne: Cinémathèque suisse, Hauterive: Gilles Attinger.
Endrigo, S. (1967) *Il treno che viene dal Sud*. Italy: Ed. Fonit Cetra Music Publishing.
Grendi, E. (1977) 'Microanalisi e storia sociale'. *Quaderni storici*, 35, pp. 506–520.
La Barba, M. (2009) 'Alvaro Bizzarri: Migration, Militance, Cinema'. *Décadrages – Cinéma à travers champs*, 14, pp. 79–89.
La Barba, M. (2013a) 'Les ciné-clubs de la *Federazione delle Colonie Libere Italiane in Svizzera*: naissance d'un mouvement culturel dans la Suisse des années 1960', in M. La Barba, C. Stör, M. Oris and S. Cattacin (eds) *La migration italienne dans la Suisse d'après-guerre*. Lausanne: Antipodes.
La Barba, M. (2013b) 'Alvaro Bizzarri et la naissance d'un cinéaste migrant: scénario d'une rencontre', in M. La Barba, C. Stör, M. Oris and S. Cattacin (eds) *La migration italienne dans la Suisse d'après-guerre*. Lausanne: Antipodes.
La Barba, M. and Mayenfisch, A. (2009) *Accueillis à bras fermés. Travailleurs immigrés dans la Suisse des années 70: le regard d'Alvaro Bizzarri* [DVD]. Lausanne: Les Amis d'Alvaro Bizzarri/TSR/AB.

La Barba, M., Stör, C., Oris, M. and Cattacin, S. (eds) (2013c) *La migration italienne dans la Suisse d'après-guerre*. Lausanne: Antipodes.
Losi, N. (ed.) (2000) *Vite altrove*. Migrazioni e disagio psichico. Milano: Feltrinelli.
Ricciardi, T. (2013) *Associazionismo ed Emigrazione. Storia delle Colonie Libere Italiane in Svizzera*. Bari-Roma: Laterza.
Risso, M. and Böker, W. (1964) *Verhexungswahn: ein Beitrag zum Verständnis von Wahnerkrankungen süditalienischer Arbeiter in der Schweiz*. Basel: S. Karger.
Schaub, M. (1985) *L'usage de la liberté: le nouveau cinéma suisse 1964–1984*. Lausanne: l'Age d'Homme.
Schlappner, M. and Schaub, M. (1987) *Cinéma Suisse. Regards critiques 1896–1987*. Zurich: Centre suisse du cinéma.
Zanier, L. (2004) 'Fiches', in E. Halter (ed.) *Gli italiani in Svizzera. Un secolo di emigrazione*. Bellinzona: Casagrande, pp. 131–136.

Historical source

Alvaro Bizzarri's private archives.

14
Nostalgia and Postcolonial Utopia in Senghor's *Négritude*

Nadia Yala Kisukidi

Négritude took shape as a plural movement, at the nexus of theory, literature and politics, in the 1930s and after the Second World War, in Paris, around the figures of Léopold Sédar Senghor, Birago Diop, Aimé Césaire and Léon Gontran Damas. The concept of *Négritude*, such as Léopold Sédar Senghor theorised it, was received with hostility but also with passion. For many it still appears as outdated and obsolete. Stanislas Adotevi, Marcien Towa, Mongo Beti, to name only a few, have rejected the concept of Senghor's *Négritude*. Senghor's theorisation of *Négritude* is twofold. The term *Négritude*, which was first coined by Césaire during the 1930s, consists of subjective and objective aspects in Senghor's view. Subjectively, it refers to an experience lived by Blacks and grounded in the historical form of their human condition in the face of the violence of slavery and colonisation. It comprises 'all the values of the black civilisation' (Senghor, 1988, p. 158). In Senghor's early writings, this so-called objective *Négritude* was based on the assertion of a dichotomy between European rationalism and emotion, usually ascribed to the black man. This aspect was prominent in an early essay published in 1939, 'Ce que l'homme noir apporte', exemplified in the now famous phrase: 'Emotion is black as much as reason is Greek.'[1] This dichotomy appeared as an avatar of the Lévy-Bruhlian thought of 'primitive mentality', as if Senghor's *Négritude* 'accepted colonial stereotypes' (Jones, 2010, p. 131), thus encouraging a discourse that implies a racial and absolutised approach to difference.

The revival of this racial dichotomy between reason and emotion led some to reject the possibility of reading Senghor's theory of *Négritude* as one of emancipation. The concept of *Négritude* does not, at first glance, appear to withstand Mongo Beti's scathing analysis: Senghor's universalism and his philosophy of the melting pot are represented as highly suspect notions that are embedded in a lyrical and mystical enterprise for conciliation, before building up as anti-colonial projects (Beti and Tobner, 1989, p. 206). However, in reality, this little opening does not break through an ordinary practice. As Francis Abiola Irele ironically notes, in the wording of Lydie Moudelino, the evocation of Senghorian *Négritude* always involves the assertion of its necessary and now effective replacement (2008 p. 12). But this hides the multi-dimensionality of Senghor's *Négritude*. *Négritude* may well have been a 'State ideology' (p. 73) during Senghor's time in power, but it also allowed an underground stance to emerge that was both political and ethical. This position was based on a transvaluation with true critical potential: by proposing the construction of a shared world, the despised and dominated group, assuming that it does not consider itself to be the exclusive owner of suffering,[2] may hold the promise for a form of emancipation in which it is certainly the object, but also the subject.

This ethical underground stance in Senghor's *Négritude* finds expression in a peculiar experience of nostalgia in his poetry, especially in the collections *Chants d'Ombre* (1945) and *Hosties Noires* (1948), but also through his theoretical texts. The expression of this stance, however, cannot be understood in Jankelevitch's sense of 'unreal chimeras' that are inextricably tied to the idea of 'reviving the already-lived' (Jankélévitch, 1974, p. 69).[3] While Senghorian nostalgia emphasises the development of the myth of Africa and of the race it was once based on, it also plays an important role in the development of an anthropological and political thought that aims at the construction of a shared world.

How does the affective experience of nostalgia help in producing a cosmopolitical and postcolonial utopia in which the myths of Africa and Negro-African civilisation play an important role? This problem finds a twofold mediation, in both Senghor's theoretical discourse and his poetic voice (especially in *Chants d'ombre* [1945] and *Hosties noires* [1948]). These mediated forms, which we will examine now, contribute to the construction of an experience of nostalgia that is more than a simple affective experience of recollection, but also becomes a discursive and ethical proposal.

The 'Kingdom of Childhood'

Senghor's constructions of the myth of Africa and Negro-African cultures have contributed to the creation of a 'metaphysics of essence', as shown by Edward Said (1994) in *Culture and Imperialism*. But, first and foremost, this mythical construction in Senghor's thought takes shape within a narrative of the Self that requires the mediation of poetic language and of philosophical discourse in order to be articulated. It is underpinned by an ethical and political urgency: namely, to resist the ontological and axiological negation comprised in the colonial reality and the slave trade in Africa. Senghor and Césaire respectively express their opposition to this negation. In a text published in 1952, Senghor writes: 'Slavery and colonisation emptied the negro of his virtues, of his substance to make him an "assimilated one", this negative of the White where appearance supplanted being: a nothingness' (1964b, p. 167).[4] And Césaire also notes in his book *Toussaint Louverture*: 'Thus was the colonial society: better than a hierarchy, an ontology: the white man at the top – the being in the full sense of the term and down, the black man [...] the thing, in other words nothing' (1981, p. 33).[5]

The Senghorian experience of nostalgia was precisely formed to defeat an ontology and the model of civilisation[6] that supports it. Such an experience is a 'commonplace' in *Négritude* literature (Irele, 2008, p. 12). In Senghor's work, this experience leads to the project of a hermeneutics of the subject in the first person, a subject rooted in a position of the existing Self, that is caught in the density of temporality: *I am a being and not nothing* – and if I am, it is precisely because *I have been*. Historicity of the Self is connected to spatial experience: beyond Europe, *I have been*. Density of subjective experience is not limited by space or, more specifically, continental boundaries. Nostalgia enables the obliviousness of the present and the disruption of the hierarchies that structure geographies.

In the poem 'Tout le long du jour', from the collection *Chants d'Ombre* (1945), forgetting Europe is at the heart of the experience of nostalgia: 'Here I am seeking oblivion from Europe at the pastoral heart of Sine' (Senghor, 1964a, p. 11)[7] – Sine being one of the regions of the former kingdom Serere, the location of Joal, Senghor's birthplace; the same oblivion from Europe is also evident in this other poem from *Chants d'Ombre*, 'Que m'accompagnent Kôras et balafongs': 'Paradise my African childhood, which used to keep Europe's innocence' (Senghor, 1964a, p. 26).[8] The theme of the 'Kingdom of Childhood' ('lost paradise' or 'Eden') runs through Senghor's entire œuvre: it underlines an effective connection between time and space, in this case between history and Africa. The density of subjective experience is enabled by this spatio-temporal connection, through which alone the subject can access the awareness of what s/he really is, namely by withdrawing from the process that seeks to deny his/her being through assimilation. The experience of nostalgia consists first of all in recovering what has been and what cannot have been destroyed by colonial domination: this process requires going beyond the irreversibility of time and the irrevocability of events.

Senghor's experience of nostalgia is, however, built on an undeniable tension. The first moment of the hermeneutics of the Self is transformed, by a singular movement, via an ethnological theory of culture that is centred on the concepts of Negro-African culture or civilisation, and of race. Paradoxically, the poetic introspective movement, written in the first person, is an expression not only of a collective experience, but also of the objective thematisation of a culture. This introspection, at first poetic, turns into an essentialist theory of Negro-African culture and personality, based on a singular transposition of Bergsonian 'intuition' (Jones, 2010; Diagne, 2011). In his essay *Introduction à la métaphysique* (1903), Bergson's theme of 'intuition' features a mental exertion that is typically human, defined as sympathy, this 'simple act of moving oneself into the inner being of an object to grasp what is unique and ineffable within it' (Bergson, 2009, p. 181).[9] Based on the theoretical assertion of the concept of creation in *L'Evolution Créatrice* (*Creative Evolution*), written in 1907, this intuition promises to recapture things from within their movement of creative evolution, of internal growth (p. 95). In 1922, 'intuition' is understood as the experience of capturing the 'participation of things, even material ones, in spirituality' (p. 29).[10] The mind, as defined by Bergson, is this reality that gains more than it can contain in creative activity. Senghor considers Bergson's philosophy of intuition to be a philosophical event because it rejects the primacy of intelligence in the true understanding of the real (Diagne, 2008, p. 127). This event is named by Senghor the 'Revolution from 1889' – the same year in which Bergson released *L'essai sur les données immédiates de la conscience* (*Time and free will*). But Senghor reinterprets this philosophy of intuition: a universal spiritual effort becomes a racialised cognitive inclination. This is the meaning of the text written in 1947, 'L'Afrique noire. La civilisation négro-africaine':

> It is thus how the Negro is essentially defined by its ability to be moved. [...] But what moves the Black, is not the outward appearance of the object, this is the *reality*, or rather [...] its surreality. So he is therefore affected by the surreal. But with such an essential violence that he must abandon his own Self in order to bond with the object.
> (Senghor, 1964b, pp. 70–71)[11]

Despite repeatedly warning us not to believe in the pre-logical mentality (p. 43), this racialisation nonetheless remains a persistent tension in his discourse. The use of recollection, of memory and nostalgic evocations appears more than suspect. Nostalgia emphasises, of course, a childhood that has not been harmed by the process of colonial assimilation. But, if it is first of all personal and subjective, it becomes collective and objective: it immerses one in the origins of a civilisation and discloses values that were hidden and covered up by colonial expansion. Of course, the experience of nostalgia promotes the rehabilitation of the black man and Africa, but the objective values such as the primacy of emotion over rationality, which are supposedly disclosed, nevertheless reinforce a discourse that once belonged to the colonial prose and in which *Négritude* is thus trapped, Wole Soyinka has shown (1976, p. 127). Despite rejecting the racist rhetoric of hierarchy, to which he opposes the idea of the 'co-belonging to humanity' (Mbembe, 2000b, p. 27), *Négritude* does not seem to succeed in discrediting the meanings of signifiers such as 'Negro' and 'Africa' that were used by European racialist doctrines of the nineteenth century.

One must nevertheless avoid losing sight of the ethical orientation that characterises the Senghorian experience of nostalgia, even if many intellectuals, such as Mongo Beti, for example, rightly criticised this double dimension of introspection. Another reading is possible if one cares to identify multiple intellectual genealogies through Senghor's thought. It is the emphasis on these genealogies that highlights the critical, underground potential of Senghor's concept of *Négritude*. Senghorian nostalgia wavers, indeed, between two major trends: the experience of the loss of identity as a personal drama, on the one hand, and the experience of cultural alienation as a collective drama, on the other hand. The famous poem 'Message' in *Chants d'Ombre* recalls the experience of the self in the context of a culture destroyed by slavery and colonialism. It is also embodied in the experience of community shaped within the lyrical construction of a myth of Africa and Negro-African civilisations, resulting in an aestheticisation of the colour line. It is also based on the peculiar appropriation of some European philosophy from the interwar period and of some ethno-philosophical material from Father Tempels's reflections on Bantu philosophy (Diagne, 2007, pp. 67–70). Taking this lyrical and theoretical constellation into consideration enables us to outline a new understanding of the various uses made of nostalgia throughout the 'Kingdom of Childhood', and to reinscribe them in their multiple intellectual genealogies.

First, the function of nostalgia is to criticise the individualism of European capitalist countries, which is usually based on the conception of an independent and conquering subject. The introspective movement of nostalgia reveals an alternative conception of the subject, when viewed in its attachment to the community. Senghor's understanding of the subject does not aim at reviving old 'African cultures', which are supposedly based on a holistic view of the community that denies the individual. It is, rather, more related to the duality between 'person' and 'individual', such as was theorised by the French Christian philosopher Emmanuel Mounier: the 'individual' is the product of a culture of quantification; it is distinct from the person 'caught' in a network of relationships (a community), whose destiny is spiritual. This duality illuminates the Senghorian perspective of a struggle against alienation: true liberation must be material, but also spiritual, allowing everyone to become a person, able to give and host.[12]

Second, Senghor's use of nostalgia aims at dismantling the Hegelian prejudice of 'facticity' (Africa exists just because it is) and of the 'arbitrary' (the African subject cannot claim universality) (Mbembe, 2000a, p. 11): the *used to be* mode of nostalgia reveals the existence of a past and a history. Africa does not exist in this infinite present, nor is it closed to the indeterminacy of the future.

The Senghorian experience of nostalgia is a lyrical and theoretical construction, mediated by resources of poetic language, philosophy and anthropological discourse. It has a precise meaning: the desire to return home (*homesickness*) is not reflected on a political level by the desire to restore an old social order. The 'Kingdom of Childhood' draws fantasised spaces and cultures, but it also involves the building of a cosmopolitical project, grounded in both the experience of nostalgia and a philosophy of creation.

Creation and nostalgia in Senghor's *Négritude* as basis for a postcolonial utopia

The poetic experience of nostalgia, as well as the myth of Africa and Negro-African civilisations that comes with it, can also be found in other *Négritude* poets. It produces a set of anti-values that challenge some features of European modernity. From an economic, political and cultural point of view, the expression of this modernity is considered deadly, as shown by the dialectic of death and life in *Chants d'Ombre* and *Hosties Noires*. This can be seen in the poem written in 1940, 'Camp 1940', for example. As Francis Abiola Irele (2008) shows in *Négritude et Condition Africaine*, the poetic experience of nostalgia and the myths of Africa and the Negro-African civilisation are romantic myths in Senghor's poetry and thought. The theory of 'Negro-African civilisations' has nothing to do with objectivity and does not produce positive knowledge about the African continent. These are personal constructions, products of a hermeneutics of the Self. But this point, which signals the death of Senghorism for such writers as Mongo Beti and Odile Tobner (Beti and Tobner, 1989, p. 206), deserves to be explored. Senghor's *Négritude* starts from the experience of nostalgia and builds a romantic myth of Africa, which has an ethical and political function. His promotion of the past does not express a will to revive traditional values against the future. The valorisation of the past does not inscribe Senghor's *Négritude* within a policy of partition that would be feeding the illusion of repetition. Senghorian nostalgia is a creative nostalgia that opposes one of the processes of material and cultural destruction caused by colonialism. It describes the dreamt direction of a universal *polis*, which must be embodied in what Senghor calls, repeating Césaire's words, the 'encounter of giving and receiving'. While this encounter has indeed found an institutional and political expression through the ideology of 'Francophonie', it also took shape through a postcolonial utopia, understood as what Teilhard de Chardin called the 'civilisation of the Universal'.

The inclusion of an emotional experience of nostalgia in the production of a cosmopolitical utopia, which is based on a fantasised myth of Africa, is an important point of Senghor's thought. Questioning Senghor's *Négritude* leads one to understand the depth of this myth as a romantic one – in the sense that Michael Löwy and Robert Sayre give it in *Révolte et Mélancolie* (1992). For both authors, European romanticism, this heterogeneous movement, is characterised by an analogous critique of modernity, that is to say, modern capitalist civilisation, in the name of the values and ideals of the past (Löwy and Sayre, 1992, pp. 29–30). Since this critique of modernity is related to the experience of loss, one can see why the experience of nostalgia can come to play a key role in the rejection of the present social reality.

We thus come to understand the romantic undertone of the anti-modern and anti-capitalist values developed by Senghor's *Négritude*, as criticising modernity in the light of past values and ideals, driven by a myth of Africa and a fictionalisation of 'Negro-African' civilisations. Like the myths of Ancient Greece, or the fantastical re-enactments of the Middle Ages produced by nineteenth-century European romanticism, Senghorian myths function by opposing qualitative values to the exchange values that defined European and colonial capitalist exploitation. *Négritude* produces anti-values, which are in opposition to the crisis of civilisation sweeping European modernity.[13] As such, it defends

- creative life against mechanisation,
- spirituality and qualitative values against the quantification and the world of money,
- intuition and emotion against the rationalist abstraction,
- the effective capacity of the community to act against the dissolution of social ties,
- vivifying religiosity against the disenchantment of the world.

These five anti-values, which characterise Senghor's *Négritude* and its thematisation of Negro-African civilisation, in fact coincide with the five specific romantic orientations, according to the method of Weber's ideal-type, as suggested by Sayre and Löwy (1992, pp. 46–64). These anti-values are implemented in the lyrical and theoretical construction of a Negro-African civilisation that Senghor's *Négritude* offers: the features of the black man are emotion, fulfilment of the person inside community, spirituality, religiosity and creative life. Senghor's Negro-African civilisation is an anti-modern romantic construction. Its purpose is the critique of European capitalist modernity, whose designs were exacerbated in the commodification of people, colonisation and conquest.

This critique is driven in Senghor's work by the production of a cosmopolitical utopia, based on the feeling of nostalgia and a philosophy of creation. As such, Senghor's nostalgia is not an experience of de-temporalisation of time that would reduce, as Jankélévitch claims, the becoming to a coming back or souvenir (1974, p. 34). If any experience is, in fact, the moment of a *futurition*, this 'sense of the irreversible becoming' (p. 77), Senghorian nostalgia takes full responsibility for its place in the direction of this *futurition*, which is, paradoxically, its real purpose. Löwy and Sayre, moreover, remind us that the transformation of the attachment to the past in relation to the future is paradoxical only in appearance: 'the memory of the past is used as a weapon in the struggle for the future' (1992, p. 37).[14] Not all romantic longings are necessarily politically restorative or conservative: they can be creative and progressive. The purpose of Senghor's nostalgia is to foreshadow the possibility of a 'living together' that defeats all forms of humanity's negations, including those that the peoples of Africa, as well as those of other empires, and Europe itself, had to endure. This ethical proposal, however, will be possible only to the extent that what might have appeared to be nothing is recognised as a being. This recognition is here based, theoretically, on the articulation of the experience of nostalgia with a philosophy of creation. This approach finally enables a further understanding of Senghor's theoretical and lyrical uses of the experience of nostalgia, one which serves to deepen the first.

First, the evocation of the 'Kingdom of Childhood' refers to a territory and reveals a place where works of art can be found. Art shows that creation has occurred, that there have been unexpected bursts of novelty and being. As creative activity presupposes a subject, art cannot be a production of the nothingness. There is no creation *ex nihilo*. Thus, to paraphrase Senghor, the black man did contribute! Second, nostalgia reveals a temporality made of rhythms and dances that embrace life. The emphasis on rhythm, dance and life does not necessarily and exclusively perpetuate Gobineau's racialist categories. Instead, they are the conceptual contents of a metaphysical anthropology that is based on an ontology of the *force vitale* (Diagne, 2011, pp. 47–48): life is associated with a movement of creative growth. This anthropology, inspired by the philosophies of Bergson, Teilhard de Chardin and the ethnophilosopher Father Tempels, considers creativity to be the eminent task of human destiny (Senghor, 1964b, p. 203). Third, the 'Kingdom of Childhood' highlights the ethical and political vocation of the poet of *Négritude*. Art is the assumption of creative life against all forms of cultural and material reification. That is why the poet has 'to prophesy the City of Tomorrow' (Senghor, 1964b, p. 221).[15] The polity of tomorrow is not the universal society that reduces *Négritude* to merely a weak moment in the dialectical process that calls for its own overcoming, as Sartre interprets it in 'Orphée Noir', the preface to *Anthologie de la nouvelle poésie nègre et malgache de langue française*, which was edited by Senghor in 1948. The polity of tomorrow must be understood as a self-creation, that is to say, a gradual enrichment of the creation and the creator as the work takes shape. This is the real meaning of Césaire's expression, the 'encounter of the given and receiving', and of Senghor's melting pot as an ethical aim.

Senghorian nostalgia thus signals first of all the oblivion of Europe as a desire to return home. But it should be understood, in the wording of Barbara Cassin, as a longing for a place where one is welcomed (2013, p. 132). It is not the will to withdraw into one's essentialised identity, rooted in the earth and the dead. It is, instead, the nostalgia for a 'world of hospitality', or, to put it in Senghor's words, a nostalgia for a world where 'all the peoples of the earth [are] solemnly invited to the Catholic feast' (1964a, p. 54).[16]

This last point raises two concluding remarks. First, Senghor's *Négritude* does not insist exclusively on finally rediscovering a pre-colonial essence. The construction of a shared postcolonial world implies an act of recognition, rejecting any process that equates being with nothingness. The second comment relates to the status of a critique anticipated by Senghor's *Négritude*. His thematisation of nostalgia is based on the idea that we have to invent our humanity through a process of self-creation. What begins as a personal and subjective feeling becomes, in Senghor's use of nostalgia, fuel for political myths. Mediated by poetry and the theoretical discourse of *Négritude*, whose intellectual genealogies are many, the Senghorian nostalgia cannot be understood as a melancholic pathology, expressing the mere desire to return home and to be confined in 'self-segregation'. Senghorian nostalgia summons a desire as the expression of a postcolonial and cosmopolitical utopia: free our home of territory so that we may feel at home everywhere (Cassin, 2013, p. 106).[17]

Notes

1. Translation by the author of this chapter: 'L'émotion est nègre comme la raison héllène'.
2. We are here referring to the thematisation of the outcast rebel, performed by Eleni Varikas (*Les rebuts du monde. Figures du paria,* 2007, Paris: Editions Stock).
3. Translation by the author of this chapter: 'revivre réellement le déjà-vécu'.
4. Translation and comment by the author of this chapter: 'L'esclavage et la colonisation ont vidé le nègre de ses vertus, de sa substance pour faire de lui un "assimilé", ce négatif du Blanc où le paraître s'est substitué à l'être: un néant.' Assimilation was the project of the French colonial enterprise.
5. Translation by the author of this chapter: 'Telle était la société coloniale: mieux qu'une hiérarchie, une ontologie: au sommet l'homme blanc – l'être au sens plein du terme – en bas, l'homme noir...la chose, autant dire rien.'
6. The translation of this civilisation model was political and material, and formed the act of colonial violence. This violence is condemned in Senghor's poem 'Prière de paix' from the collection *Hosties Noires* – a long indictment against colonial violence, but partly grounded in a rhetoric of love and forgiveness.
7. Translation by the author of this chapter: 'Me voici cherchant l'oubli de l'Europe au cœur pastoral du Siné'.
8. Translation by the author of this chapter: 'Paradis mon enfance africaine, qui gardait l'innoncence de l'Europe'.
9. Translation by the author of this chapter: 'se transporter à l'intérieur d'un objet pour coïncider avec ce qu'il a d'unique et d'inexprimable'. The English translation of this book is: *An Introduction to Metaphysics*; authorised translation by T. E. Hulme, New York: 1955.

10. Translation by the author of this chapter: 'saisir dans les choses, même matérielles, leur participation à la spiritualité'.
11. Translation by the author of this chapter: 'C'est ainsi que le nègre se définit essentiellement par sa faculté d'être ému. [...] Mais ce qui émeut le Noir, ce n'est pas l'aspect extérieur de l'objet, c'est la *réalité*, ou mieux [...] sa *surréalité*. Le surréel l'atteint donc. Mais avec une telle violence *essentielle* qu'il quitte son moi pour adhérer à l'*objet*'.
12. Senghor's dimension of liberation, both spiritual and material, focuses on the future-person subject. This was highlighted by Souleymane Bachir Diagne, especially during a conference held at the University of Geneva on 14 June 2012, entitled 'Senghor et la question qui se pose toujours'.
13. Léopold Sédar Senghor (1964b, pp. 173–174). The critique of a novel by Camara Laye highlights some of Senghor's political framework: what makes a Black is that he opens 'the door to hope' (p. 173), whereas Europe is agonizing under its 'modern myths', which are 'money', 'productivity' and 'progress' (p. 174). Translation by the author of this chapter.
14. Translation by the author of this chapter: 'Le souvenir du passé sert comme arme dans la lutte pour le futur'.
15. Translation by the author of this chapter: 'prophétiser la Cité de demain'.
16. Translation by the author of this chapter: 'À tous les peuples de la terre conviés solennellement au festin catholique'.
17. I am grateful to Aurélie Noël and Cécile Malaspina for their help in translating this article from French to English.

References

Bergson, H. (2009) 'Introduction à la métaphysique' (1903), in A. Bouaniche et al. (ed.) *La pensée et le mouvant*. Paris: PUF Quadrige.
Beti, M. and Tobner, O. (1989) *Dictionnaire de la négritude*. Paris: l'Harmattan.
Césaire, A. (1981) *Toussaint Louverture*. Paris: Présence Africaine.
Cassin, B. (2013) *La nostalgie. Quand donc est-on chez soi?* Paris: Editions Autrement.
Diagne, S. B. (2007) *Léopold Sédar Senghor, l'art africain comme philosophie*. Paris: Riveneuse éditions.
Diagne, S. B. (2008) 'Bergson in the Colony: Intuition and Duration in the Thought of Senghor and Iqbal'. *Qui parle*, 17(1), pp. 125–145.
Diagne, S. B. (2011) *Bergson Postcolonial*. Paris: CNRS.
Irele, F. A. (2008) *Négritude et condition africaine*. Paris: Karthalla.
Jankélévitch, V. (1974) *L'irréversible et la nostalgie*. Paris: Champ Flammarion.
Jones, D. (2010) *The Racial Discourses of Life Philosophy*. New York: Columbia University Press.
Löwy, M. and Sayre, R. (1992) *Révolte et mélancolie. Le romantisme à contre-courant de la modernité*. Paris: Payot.
Mbembe, A. (2000a) *De la postcolonie*. Paris: Karthalla.
Mbembe, A. (2000b) 'A propos des écritures africaines de soi'. *Politique africaine*, vol. 77, pp. 16–43.
Sartre, J.-P. (1964) 'Orphée Noir', *Situations V*. Paris: Gallimard.
Senghor, L.-S. (1964a) 'Poème liminaire', *Poèmes, Hosties Noires*. Paris: Seuil.

Senghor, L.-S. (1964b) *Liberté I. Négritude et humanisme.* Paris: Éditions du Seuil.
Senghor, L.-S. (1988) *Ce que je crois.* Paris: Grasset.
Soyinka, W. (1976) *Myth, Literature and the African World.* Cambridge: Cambridge University Press.
Varikas, E. (2007) *Les rebuts du monde; Figures du paria.* Paris: Editions Stock.

15
Impossible Nostalgia
Itzhak Goldberg

For Mona and Marek Zamdmer.

Like Kiefer or Lüpertz, Baselitz is one of the leading German artists who has been deeply marked by feelings of guilt regarding history, together with attempts to tackle an unbearable past and to reconsider a dialogue with the history of their country. In theory, two solutions arise, representing two almost diametrically opposed ways of achieving a collective amnesia, of banishing the fearsome ghosts that threaten to resurface at any moment. Schematically covering over or erasing the dividing line between these two options represents the border that separates pre- and post-war Germany. This was as much an ideological as an aesthetic choice, one that intensified after 1947 and the beginning of the Cold War. Henceforth, Western art joined the international avant-garde, and socialist realism ruled the art of the East. The German Democratic Republic's (GDR) artistic policy, under Soviet 'inspiration', sought to develop a progressive approach to usher in a better future. The hastily cleared-away ruins belonged to the past and, once again, a construction project for building the New Man was launched. Such was the context in which Baselitz, who was born in the GDR, began his artistic training. He quickly felt suffocated, and came in for the now-mythic episode of being sent down from the Berlin-Weissensee School of Art for 'social and political immaturity'. After a few months of going back and forth, he moved definitively to the Promised Land, Berlin, that island of modernity.

Arriving in West Germany, Baselitz was faced with an intolerable situation, caught in a double bind between the world of aesthetics and the world of politics. On the one hand, he had turned his back on a new version of socialist realism as representation, characteristic of creation that is in the service of totalitarian ideology. On the other hand, the abstract painting that dominated the West German artistic landscape also refrained – albeit in a quieter manner, under a modernist pretext – from speaking of the historical context and its consequences. Recent memories, whether of National Socialism or its destruction, faded away. 'Wiping out the past by abandoning images that threatened to reflect it, such was the role that non-figurative painting could fulfil perfectly [...] what remained of Germany was amnesiac, without a past, and depersonalised', wrote Violette Garnier (1997, p. 115). With no other goal than to highlight its self-proclaimed autonomy, such art (at least on the surface) seemed to guarantee unlimited artistic freedom. Very quickly, the motifs of Baselitz, a member of the generation born during the war, declared an end to both lying and repression. Borrowing from traditional German imagery and painting without any taboo whatsoever, he took aim at the glorious symbols of German history, forever sullied by Nazi propaganda. Eagles, mythical forests and figures of giants made appearances. In order to avoid any ambiguity and to make plain the critical element of his oeuvre, the artist breaks the taboo and uses two concepts that are clearly in opposition to a totalitarian aesthetic: ugliness and irony.

Irony finds full expression in a series of paintings that Baselitz entitled 'Heroes' and 'New Types', a mark of derision with respect to all ideologies that seek to create a new, heroic type of human being. These 'glorious' titles are immediately refuted by the figures wandering aimlessly in desolate landscapes: 'anti-heroes' with a pathetic air about them, in search of unlikely deeds of gallantry. Baselitz's work revives a connection with the tradition of historical genre painting, but one in which history is absent and the figures perform no exemplary actions and offer no moral lessons. These colossi, these giant marionettes (with their monumental trunks topped by tiny heads, and their theatrical poses and lack of expression), are both disturbing and brittle. And yet, another language takes over from the expressionless faces, the language of hands, which are never depicted in a conventional position, and which no longer play the role of tools with which human figures manipulate the world around them. Their disturbing, non-functional and sometimes incomprehensible gestures resist attempts to codify them, becoming the focal point of the painting. Sometimes held away from the body, as if it wished to rid itself of this cumbersome organ, sometimes caught in a dowsing rod that drips with blood, the hands seem to escape any control by their 'owner'. Everything leads one to think that these hands, turned towards the viewer, as if caught in a gesture of powerlessness, signify the extreme helplessness of these grotesque knights errant, adrift in a desolate landscape. Even if the bodies here are not yet fractured and dismembered, we can see the initial indications of a renunciation of the body's position of a subject acting on the world. Is it mere chance that, in the series of paintings 'Forward Wind' (1966), the exhausted hero needs to lean heavily on a tree to keep himself upright?

In 'The Great Friends' (1965), a signal work from this period that was accompanied by a provocative manifesto, the two roughly sketched and shredded figures, frozen against a black background, are depicted with empty, open hands. The impossibility of action of any kind, the banning of any uprising, takes on anguished tones in other paintings, in which the crushed and bleeding hands of the 'heroes' have been definitively condemned. Although every society gets the great figures it deserves, the German pantheon takes on the air of a purgatory inhabited by tragic vagabonds. We know that the 'Heroes' series was influenced by Mannerist works that Baselitz discovered during his stay in Florence, Italy. The disproportionate bodies, the elongated forms, the figures turned in on themselves in nearly autistic fashion, the unbalanced space, these are all stylistic clues to a period which saw the erosion of the certainties of the Renaissance. Making reference to Mannerism in this way allowed Baselitz to take his place in a classical artistic tradition, but one that contained latent signs of modernism. This desire was made all the stronger since it, like an entire young German generation, was cut off, in its own artistic tradition, from all modernism.

In the world of the German artist, symbols pertaining to his specific culture are never far away. With his pathetic 'Heroes', Baselitz seizes not only the archetype of the human being deprived of all reference points, but also the place of his country in the face of history, both glorious and shameful. Among the constituent parts of German identity, there is one symbol that, both literally and metaphorically, dominates the horizon: the tree. It is, of course, a universal, cross-cultural symbol. Nevertheless, the forest and the tree seem to have left a particular mark on the history of the German people. In *Crowds and Power*, Elias Canetti devotes a chapter to what he calls national crowd symbols. The German crowd symbol is the marching forest, the army, the ordered crowd of peers. According to Canetti, 'in no other modern country has the forest-feeling remained as alive as it has in Germany. The parallel rigidity of the upright trees and their density and number fill the heart of the German with a deep and mysterious delight. To this day, he loves to go deep into the forest where his forefathers lived; he feels at one with the trees, faithful, and upright as he himself wanted to be. The effect of this early forest romanticism on the German must never be underrated. He absorbed it from countless poems and songs and the forest that appears in these is often called "German" ' (Canetti, 1966, pp. 183–184). Canetti's proposed symbolism is based on ancient tradition. Thus Schelling reminds us that, according to Tacitus, the Germans had no temples, but they worshipped their gods in the open air, beneath the trees. This is the same Tacitus who told in great detail the seminal event of German identity, the battle between the Germans and the Romans, in which the Germans, led by their chief Arminius, lured the Roman army into a dense forest and massacred them. The so-called Battle of the Teutoburg Forest became the symbol of German resistance, the patriotic – and even nationalist – emblem of Germany down through the centuries. Anselm Kiefer painted this battle several times. These include 'Varus' (the name of the defeated Roman leader), a canvas depicting a distanced version of Caspar David Friedrich's 'The Hunter in the Forest' (1814). At once an ironic allegory of the rout of Napoleon's Grande Armée and the Teutoburg battle, the framework of the painting is a forest of bare trees, without the slightest hint of greenery. On the ground, dirty snow is stained with blood and, in the place of heroic soldiers, one finds only the names of various military and political leaders who forged the German nation. Kiefer's choice of Friedrich is not an innocent one, because Friedrich's isolated trees, often perceived only in their psychological signification, are part of what has been called national romanticism. From this perspective, they are transformed into metaphors for political misery, but also for patriotic stirrings in the wake of Napoleonic hegemony, as the decomposition of the country was the source of profound confusion.

With 'The Ways of Worldly Wisdom' (1976), a clearly ironic title, Kiefer depicts a confused and ghostly family tree in flames, in which the myth of Germanism burns, fed by the great works while also feeding the dangerous pathos of nationalism. By jumbling up the portraits and names of celebrated German figures in the midst of the forest, the painter shows us how two wars have destroyed the European ideal: the cruel irony of the title flies in the face of any sort of reassuring concept of history. Here we may conclude that Kiefer's entire oeuvre is aimed at destroying the power of myth, in order to give the Germans back their trees and their works. This is, we might add, not without a certain light-headed, sometimes grandiloquent, ambiguity.

In the work of Baselitz, the tree appears to be present at every crucial moment, both to mark stylistic transformations and to introduce new metaphors. Thus, it is no mere coincidence that, in the midst of the 'Heroes' series, when Baselitz confronts for the first time an unspeakable past, a painting appears with the title 'The Tree I' (1965–1966). Immense, filling the entire canvas, with the tips of its branches broken and bleeding, the tree is an anthropomorphic version of the confused Teutonic knights. Elsewhere, in 'Trap' from 1966, the two trees form a sort of ironic triumphal arch in front of which is an exhausted figure. The man and the tree form a single body, because they share the same mutilations, the same bloody wounds. In yet another painting, 'Two Meissen Woodsmen' (1967), the trees are turned horizontally, as if in the initial stage of a complete overturning of the motif.

From here on, Baselitz undertakes a long process of systematically deconstructing traditional figurative painting, with, for its main target, the human figure, but the archaic symbolism of the tree and forest as well. The painter begins to divide his paintings, first in two, then into a great many horizontal stripes. The contours become less distinct, the lines more distorted, and stain marks partially erase the contrast with the background. The figures become fractured, their various parts are out of joint with each other, like a puzzle that is impossible to reconstruct. Despite its legibility, this 'sceptical figuration' eliminates any possible analogy between reality and the world of representation.

This is a crucial stage, marked by images in which the painter himself becomes inseparable from the tree. As Violette Garnier neatly describes it, 'The three stripes of "Three Stripes – The Painter in a Coat – Second Fracture Painting"' (1966) offer up two different motifs – the figure of the painter from the Heroes series is divided between the upper and lower strips; a heavy trunk of an oak tree, its branches sawn off, one end of which is reminiscent of an erect male member, occupies the central portion, replacing that part of the painter located between the breast and the legs. The mixture of a mobile human figure, with his foot leaving a red trail on the ground, and that of a motionless thing, the tree, underscores the desire for roots of one whom destiny has condemned to exile, and the mutilation of the original oneness of human and nature (Canetti, 1966, pp. 183–184). Speaking of a personal experience, Baselitz (2006) recounted that when he saw a painter working in nature for the first time, it was an extraordinary experience. He did not know that such a thing existed. He had seen reproductions of paintings, works hung on a wall in a house or at an exhibition, but for the first time he saw someone; painting an oak, it was quite the event. Without attempting risky psychoanalytic interpretations, one can venture that we are in the presence of a primitive artistic scene. The alliance between human being and tree proves to be a risky one. With increasing fury, Baselitz smashes the body into pieces. In 'B for Larry' (1967), scraps of flesh mingle with the truncated bodies of dogs and sawn-up pieces of trees, all of which hover above a background of imperturbable blue. The treatment is similar to that of 'Woodmen', painted the same year. Fracturing, shattering, these various means of introducing breaches into convulsive bodies are a way of stating that Germany cannot have a 'natural' national continuity. Finally, in 1969, Baselitz invented a stylistic figure that subsequently became his personal brand: the inverted motif. From then on, all of the figures were represented upside down, challenging the usual reading of the painting. Or, as Baselitz has suggested, the upending forces the viewer to create a distance from the content of what is being depicted, to be wary of obvious similitudes. 'If one empties the motif of its content,' Baselitz has remarked, 'no matter what type of content, then I can paint everything. This is the meaning of inversion'. This sounds like a far-off echo of Matisse, the other ardent supporter of motifs and of the human figure, who stated: 'I am not making a portrait, I am making a painting.'

Mundus inversus: the world turned upside down, linked with European literature when it deals with madness? No doubt. But, above all, this forest is the compact expression of Baselitz's problematic relationship with a History that has been repudiated. The strong attachment to the soil, invested with mystical virtues and a disturbing irrationality, this means of affirming continuity in the German identity, is treated with savage aggressiveness. How, indeed, can one claim one's roots in a territory that has been constantly occupied, in one's native land, after it has been contaminated by the fascist ideology of 'Blood and Soil'?

The violence is, however, underhanded, because the inverted depictions are not subjected to the distortions and fractures that Baselitz had previously employed. This is not due to some unlikely 'return to order', but, rather, a clear-eyed observation: if one is to effectively call art history into question, the inverted image must remain intact, easily identifiable and nameable.

If, in Baselitz's wrong-way-around work on memory, trees, and by extension forests and wooded landscapes, have such metaphorical strength, it is because German culture has 'recycled' a subject whose universal power extends far beyond Germany's borders. The tree is a component of nature endowed with a special ability to engender myth, and it is found as much in literature as in religion. As Mircea Eliade wrote,

> By its simple presence and through its evolution, the tree repeats that which, for the archaic experience, is the entire universe... if the tree is endowed with sacred forces, it is because it is vertical (linking the Ouranian and Chthonian worlds), because it grows, loses its leaves

and recovers, and that as a consequence it regenerates itself countless times.

(1949, pp. 275–276)

In this description we find the tree's principal qualities: its rootedness in the earth and its capacity to resist the natural elements, its verticality that makes it similar to the human form, its uninterrupted evolution from the very beginning of time, and its capacity for regeneration. Anthropomorphically, the tree often appears in metaphors in connection with human beings, as it presents a perfect screen for psychological projections. In the realm of the aesthetic, the tree is often assimilated with artists and their creative activity, which rises from roots to branches, a shining example of which can be found in Klee's famous speech. Above all, however, it is the evolutionary diagram of art history that is often compared with the concept of the family tree and the obsessive concept of descendants.

From this point of view, inverting the tree is a gesture that short-circuits several networks simultaneously, that undermines multiple traditions. The iconoclastic Baselitz, after introducing figurative painting against the officially recognised current of modernism, then proceeds to treat it with what appears to be the utmost casualness. With this affront to the laws of gravity, the painter claims to have attained total plastic freedom, to the detriment of any connection with History. This is also a way to pretend that the theme, despite its symbolic richness, can become a tool of plastic experimentation for exploring weightlessness within the pictorial space. This brings us practically back to Kandinsky's famous 'conversion' and the story of the upside-down painting that opened the way to abstraction. Viewing, in the twilight, a work 'of extraordinary beauty, glowing with an inner radiance', but whose subject was incomprehensible, the Russian painter understood at last that it was one of his own figurative paintings, 'leaning against the wall the wrong way up', and concluded that the subject was not an indispensable part of his art.

But, as Isabelle Ewig has remarked,

> Is the inversion of the theme sufficient to negate the content to the point of retaining nothing but the style? The response to this question is complex, and it would appear that certain subjects are too associative to be entirely stripped of their meaning, such as the eagle, the symbol of the Empire, and the forest, the founding place of German national feeling [...] By asserting a discourse on pure

painting, both Baselitz and Lüpertz uphold the paradox and establish an indirect way of questioning the past.

(Garnier, 1997, p. 117)

In reality, no matter what the painter's assertions, and one should be wary of his too-vigorous denials, in Baselitz's subjects there is an element of control over the work's structure. This subject, while perhaps escaping the law of gravity, nevertheless deals with weighty matters. The question of artistic bloodlines remains, despite all, secondary to the issue of identity. Inevitably, the impossibility of taking one's place within a generational lineage, the crucial need to deal a decisive blow to one's criminal fathers, is carried out in Baselitz's work by using a language that is equal to the task: an artifice that is all the more explicit as the inversion forces a sort of optical adjustment upon viewers, and (sometimes in spite of themselves) even closer inspection to the theme; the impossibility of forgetting the subjects, but also, as Maurice Fréchuret has written,

> the way in which they are treated, the charged technique, the colours – at once bright and muffled – are all elements that fight against their obfuscation. Perhaps they become even more apparent for being presented upside down, with no underneath beneath them. The worthiness of Georg Baselitz's oeuvre is found...in such uncertainty.

(Ewig, 2007, p. 255)

1980. The Venice Biennale. To the great surprise of the art world, Baselitz turns to sculpture, perhaps because he finds there an even more radical zone of discontinuity with the previous generation. A tree makes way for the immediacy of wood, a material that allows direct intervention, work with an axe. 'Model for a Sculpture' created a veritable shock. Emerging from an oblong, barely squared-off trunk are a rounded torso, a head and a raised arm: the sculpture is partly reclining, partially upright. With this provocative, figurative work the artist turns against the modernist tradition in order to rediscover the 'primitive' figures of the first Expressionist generation (Kirchner, Heckel, etc.). Even more provocative is the ambiguous hand gesture that brings to mind the Nazi salute. Irony and the drive to exorcise the weight of the past...Baselitz, as always, refuses these types of interpretations of his work. For Lüpertz, on the other hand, provocation is the core of his paintings when he declares:

European art has always known the idea of provocation... this idea is the beginning, the basis of art. Challenge not as a means, but as a goal. It was always one of the tasks of the painter to probe the limits of his time by trying the power of provocation. To see to what extent it is possible to cause injury by innocent means as a piece of paper and a pencil.

'Die Ärhe' ('L'Epi') is a work created in 1987 by Lüpertz. In appearance, it is an innocent subject. In another context, painted by an artist of a different nationality, one could look at it as the symbol of a lush countryside, a souvenir of an idyllic walk in the country. Unfortunately, this monumental painting, disproportionate, dithyrambique as Lüpertz would say, does not leave us the opportunity to believe this. German art has been locked for a very long time in the era of suspicion. It is hard, if not impossible, when facing some German works, not to think of the terribly apt words with which the filmmaker Hans Jürgen Syberberg addresses Hitler: 'You took away our sunsets, sunsets by Caspar David Friedrich. You are to blame that we can no longer look at a field of grain without thinking of you. You made old Germany kitschy with your simplifying works and peasant pictures... you occupied everything else and corrupted it' (Fréchuret, 2003, p. 164).

References

Baselitz, G., Mason, R. M. and Fondation de l'Hermitage (2006) *Baselitz: une seule passion, la peinture*. Lausanne: Fondation de l'Hermitage.
Canetti, E. (1966) *Masse et puissance*. Paris: Gallimard.
Eliade, M. (1949) *Traité d'histoire des religions*. Paris: Payot.
Ewig, I. (2007) *Néo-Expressionnisme, L'art moderne et contemporain*. Paris: Larousse.
Fréchuret, M. (2003) *Les années 70: l'art en cause*. Bordeaux: catalogue du CAPC.
Garnier, V. (1997) *L'Art en Allemagne, 1945–1995*. Paris: Nouvelles éditions françaises.
Royal Academy of Arts (1985) *German Art in the 20th Century*, London: Royal Academy of Arts.

16
Journeys through the Past: Contempt, Nostalgia, Enigma

John Potts

In this chapter, I consider a range of contemporary perspectives on the past, including that of nostalgia. I advocate a historicising perspective, against the largely de-historicised condition of consumer network culture. I focus on nostalgia as it is refracted through the media and consumer culture – that is, as it is commodified. I appraise the construction of the past in commodity culture as one of contempt: the present evinces an attitude of disdain for the inferior and 'primitive' conditions of earlier times; nostalgia functions within this particular emotional–economic circuitry.

I discuss alternative perspectives on the past found in the work of contemporary artists. Here the past is represented not as nostalgia or commodity, or object of contempt, but as part of an ongoing dialogue with the present. At the same time, in the work of Thomas Demand, Walid Raad and William Kentridge, the past has an enigmatic quality, devoid of the sentimentalising aspects of nostalgia, existing in the present in a complex, often unsettling manner.

Contempt

Consumerism is built on building blocks laid down in industrial modernity: progress, designed obsolescence, dismissal of the past unless rendered as nostalgia, a utopian sheen projected onto technology, commodity and product. Commercial culture fosters a love of the present and the near future, an allure intensified in the marketing of information technology: each new-generation Apple product offers the look of the future, rendering previous-generation products out of date. Consumer culture, in its relentless focus on the immediate present, encourages a cultural amnesia in its citizens, especially the young. This atrophy of memory is to the advantage of the market: it is easier to recycle music and films from the 1970s, for example, if the originals have disappeared from view. The temporal orientation of commodity culture remains as diagnosed by Fredric Jameson in 1983: a 'perpetual present' that 'obliterates traditions' (1983, p. 125). There are counter-currents such as recycling and conservation even within the market, but this is possible because no-one, since the environmental hazards beginning in the 1970s, is able to believe in industrial progress with anything approaching the zeal of the Futurist leader F. T. Marinetti or his modernist peers. In the wake of environmental disaster and global warming, progress has shifted to the domain of information and post-industrial technology. This has allowed the face of the market to remain resolutely set towards the future, guided by the imperatives of growth, development and progress in information technology. The technocratic ideology today emanating from Silicon Valley – that only information and network technologies offer the hope of changing the world for the better (Packer, 2013) – mirrors the technocratic programme pursued by industrial modernists in the early decades of the twentieth century. In this respect, the industrialist Henry Ford set the tone in 1916, speaking not only for his industrialist peers but also for his post-industrialist successors in the next century. Ford elevated technological progress while denigrating history as 'more or less bunk'. For Ford and his modernist colleagues, history was to be dismissed as stale tradition:

> We don't want tradition. We want to live in the present, and the only history that is worth a tinker's damn is the history we make today.
> (Cited in Cohen and Major, 2004, p. xxv)

What is true of consumer culture is even more apparent in media culture. Every night, commercial television news provides 'a cavalcade of events: isolated from process, removed from precedent, detached from history. Each news story is an instant, a spectacle, with minimal connection to other instants' (Potts, 2010, p. 192). Television news, or audio-visual news footage relayed on YouTube and elsewhere on the web, is a series of dislocated images. As a result, the procession of televised news events makes little sense. International news is rendered as a parade of violent spectacles, with no context or rationale. Bombings and other killings blend with natural disasters, with no historical depth to give them background or meaning. The cumulative effect on the viewer is bewilderment and anxiety; this reaction stimulates the desire to retreat from the world into a more comfortable insularity, or consumption, or nostalgia for a fondly reimagined version of the past. Commercial TV news has no (or exceedingly little) memory, and it does not 'desire' memory. When the televised events of the present have been broadcast, they are 'rarely' remembered, as they are readily replaced by a new barrage of images.

This is the triumph of event as smoke, the 'hasty' time disdained by the great historian Braudel in his tripartite model of historical time:

> Its delusive smoke fills the minds of its contemporaries, but it does not last, and its flame can scarcely ever be discerned.
> (Braudel, 1980, p. 27)

Braudel wanted to 'transcend the event' and 'the brief moments of awareness' experienced in the short time span (p. 67). For him, historical meaning could only be grasped at the level of the *longue durée*, which is 'the source, for each society, of its own internal logic' (p. 209). Yet, sadly, today, in the domain of both the general public and cultural theorists, the *longue durée* remains largely unGoogled.

Given the orientation to the present in the consumer media world, history is not welcome in this precinct. Occasionally, however, it may be wheeled out and given a starring role, if only as villain. In 2006, for example, Nike attached itself to the football World Cup – the world's biggest cultural event – with a series of advertisements for the Australian market featuring 'History'. In these ads, History was personified for our amusement, and disgust. As embodied in the Nike TV advertisements, History is ugly, unpleasant, cantankerous, foreign (some kind of European), of possible Goblin background, shrunken with age, consumed with memories, living in a dressing gown, consigned to a nursing home. He addresses the footballing New World with contempt, deriding its aspirations. Nietzsche may have had such an ogre in mind when he described, in 'The Uses and Disadvantages of History', the 'withered and dry' condition of one who is too weighed down with history (Nietzsche, 1983, p. 115). Yet even Nietzsche, in that essay of 1873, proposed a balance of active forgetting and remembrance. It is doubtful he would have embraced the abdication of memory and rejection of history found in the modern consumer society. Most definitely, as the Nike ad reports, History is 'against us'. Nike's rejoinder, on behalf of the New World, is to 'stuff History', a crude reprisal of Henry Ford's equally crude modernist dismissal of history as 'more or less bunk'.

The evaporation of the past in consumer culture is intensified by the overwhelming emphasis on the present found in Web 2.0. Social media organisations such as Facebook fund themselves by selling information on their users (their 'likes' and current obsessions) to advertisers, who are interested only in today and tomorrow, not yesterday or any further back. Social media is a ravenous beast hungry for the present in the form of status updates, likes and daily ephemera, all tapped as clues for advertisers to offer users the means of satisfying their current needs. As Evgeny Morozov has observed, the 'very architecture and business models of social networking sites' are oriented to 'what we are doing and thinking about right now' (2011, p. 228). He notes that Twitter and Facebook are not interested even in what we were doing or thinking five years ago; as a result, our lives are increasingly 'lived in the present, completely detached even from the most recent past' (p. 228). There is a commercial imperative for this 'fundamentalist preference for the present' (p. 229), as the advertisers who feed off social media aim to satisfy the immediate needs and preferences of users/consumers. The past, including the past of social media users, is irrelevant to the goals of the targeted market research available to advertisers in the form of 'likes' and current interests.

Lev Manovich has made the further observation that the structure of the social media apparatus privileges the now and the about-to-be over the past. Manovich describes the constant feed of information on Twitter, Facebook and other Web 2.0 outlets as a 'data stream', which he contrasts both with the database format established by the 1990s World Wide Web and with the older means of organizing information, the narrative (2013, p. 199). Facebook's News Feed and Ticker facilities display constant updates of friends' activities, while Twitter provides a continuously changing stream of information-bursts. The user experiences this information not through browsing or searching, as in a database, but as a 'continuous flow of events' (p. 199). The new is constantly displacing the not-so-new, as Manovich remarks: 'new events appearing at the top push the earlier ones from the immediate view'. In this system, 'the most important event is always the one that is about to appear next because it heightens the experience of the "data present"' (p. 199). The latest information event is the most privileged, as all other events 'immediately become "old news", still worth reading, but not in the same category' (p. 199). For Manovich, this data stream interface is a 'quintessential modern experience ("Make it new"), only intensified and accelerated' (p. 199). It is the Web 2.0 post-industrial version of the imperative to the new, first articulated in the age of industrial modernity by spokesmen such as Marinetti and Ford. As befitting the information age, the present is continuously updated as current information, consigning the past to the digital trash.

Nostalgia

The past serves a purpose in the consumer world only if mythologised or waxworked as nostalgia, when it can be used to sell something. As already discussed in this volume, nostalgia is a Swiss 'invention', or, at least, the word was coined by a Swiss doctor in the late seventeenth century, from the Greek *nostos* – 'homecoming' and *algos* – pain or ache; the condition was initially known as *mal du Suisse* or Swiss illness. There is even a loose connection between the newly identified disease of nostalgia and the founding of Australia as a European colony: the English botanist Joseph Banks wrote in his journal, on the long sea voyage to Australia in 1770, that the sailors were 'pretty far gone with the longing for home which the Physicians [...] esteem as a disease under the name of Nostalgia' (Beaglehole, 1962, p. 145).

Today nostalgia is understood as a personal emotional attachment to the past, or, rather, to a version of the past. Most individuals experience nostalgia to some degree: a longing for past childhood, family home, perhaps country of origin. But, when used for commercial purposes, it is an entirely sentimental construction of the past. Most importantly, it is an extremely lucrative construction of the past within the media industry. An individual may have an emotional attachment to the music of his or her youth and young adulthood, but radio stations capitalise on this charge of affect by programming music solely of this period. This is the domain of the Hits and Memories radio format, also known as Adult Classic, Original Hits and Timeless Memories, and Radio Recall. This commercial radio formatting freezes the flow of pop music into a museumised version of the past, selling the loyal listeners to advertisers. This form of commercial nostalgia sells and promotes the past as commodity.

Similarly, period TV series such as *Downton Abbey* (ITV, 2010–) or *Mad Men* (AMC, 2007–) construct a glamorised version of an historical period, which can fuel new vogues in retro-fashion or a fondness for earlier trends. The past is rendered as exotic in these period reconstructions, in which art design plays a leading role in evoking the design aesthetic of specific historical periods and cultures. Most viewers, of course, did not experience the 1910s or 1960s the first time around;

for them these reconstructions represent nostalgia for a time and place otherwise unknown. This is televisual nostalgia as simulacrum: an artfully constructed phantasmogoria of the past, for those who did not experience the original. The current vogue for televisual nostalgia indicates a fondness for peering back at these past worlds, however idealised and fictionalised they may be in construction. No doubt there are contradictory impulses at play as viewers negotiate the differences between past and present. The freedom of the 1960s, when a three-Martini working lunch functioned as a norm, may be contrasted with the greater restrictions of our more bureaucratic, health-conscious, regulated society. At the same time, our position in the present – morally superior due to the benefit of decades of social progress – is confirmed: we can look back and rebuke the earlier period for its shortcomings, the oppressive class system of early twentieth-century Britain, or the sexism and reprehensible attitudes to women of pre-feminist 1960s America. In this regard, nostalgia may be construed as the 'ideological twin' of progress, as Christopher Lasch has observed. The veneration of both progress and nostalgia constitutes an 'abdication of memory' (Lasch, 1991, p. 83), in that the past is represented as other, backward, superficially appealing but ultimately undesirable. Nostalgia as refracted through mass media is thus related not only to progress, but to contempt.

Enigma

What would an un-nostalgic representation of the past look like? Much recent art is concerned with the event not as an ephemeral moment, but as a political and social act, rooted in time and place, that reverberates far beyond its initial circumstance. Artworks play with contradiction, or expose the processes of meaning-making, national identity formation, or wilful acts of cultural forgetting. 'Where events may have been erased from national or collective memory, art may intervene to undo this willful forgetting; or the artist may challenge the official record by constructing alternative histories, following a counter-archival impulse' (Merewether and Potts, 2010, p. 6). These practices jostle with official narratives and orthodoxies in what has been described as the politics of memory. Recollection and archive, past, present and memory, may mingle here in a zone where, as the Atlas Group informs us, 'fiction is not necessarily the opposite of non-fiction' (p. 6).

Many contemporary artists are concerned with the process of memory, but this is not memory as a commodified dose of the past or as sweetened nostalgia. Memory is often revealed as partial, subjective, faulty, contested. The biologist Steven Rose, in *The Making of Memory*, remarks on the imprecise, essentially creative aspects of human memory. Unlike the various forms of artificial memory, especially computer memory, the human mind does not simply invoke information in its act of remembering. Rather, 'each time we remember, we in some senses do work on and transform our memories; they are not simply being called up from store' (Rose, 1992, p. 91). For Rose, the subjective, inaccurate nature of human memory contains an element of 're-membering', a variant of 'dismembering'. This is an active process, in which the past is refigured with each act of memory: 'Our memories are recreated each time we remember' (p. 91). The creative recasting of past events, experiences and processes, which for Rose is integral to the very nature of human memory, is made evident in many recent art works.

The South African artist William Kentridge mines the concerns of time, memory and the construction of the past in many of his works. His work *The Refusal of Time*, shown at Documenta in 2012, is a study of the imposition of standardised clock time in the nineteenth century by the European colonial powers and the resistance to this mode of time from within Africa. In the animated film works for which Kentridge is best known, he deploys deliberately old-fashioned techniques. His animated films are drawn by hand, in a manner that breaks with the conventions even of old-style hand-drawn animation. Kentridge adds layers of different charcoal drawings onto the same sheet, rather than on separate successive sheets. The result is that each image is composed of traces of previous drawings. The past and the present are compressed into the image by means of the very technique of creating the image. Each moment of the film is a palimpsest. This technique mirrors many of the concerns of Kentridge's art. The characters in his animated films play out some of the political and emotional struggles within South Africa. His more general theme, however, is erasure. He is concerned with forgetting, both willed and unintentional. His works evoke the suppressed or forgotten, lying beneath the surface of the present. In a note accompanying the work *Felix in Exile*, Kentridge wrote: 'In the same way that there is a human act of dismembering the past there is a natural process in the terrain through erosion, growth, dilapidation that also seeks to blot out events' (2003, p. 122). The ambiguity and uncertainties within Kentridge's art are conveyed within this constant engagement or rejection of the past. His technique in the animated films visualises the act of erasure, as the traces of previous frames remain evident to the viewer in the current frame: the past lingers in the present even as it is erased.

In a series of works, the Lebanese-American artist Walid Raad has focused on history as the process of interpreting events. The Atlas Group is a fictional archival organisation, created by Raad. Heavily detailed videos and performance works are Raad's creative version of an archival reckoning of historical process, with specific reference to the 1975–1991 Lebanese Civil Wars. Raad offers the Atlas Group project as a vast, all-encompassing archive of these historical events. The officious titles of the Atlas Group documentation connote ordered objectivity; however, those titles are apt to change their details and dates. The Atlas Group videos are narrated by a fictional character, yet the archived documents, the events and the city, are nevertheless held out to us as real. Raad exposes the difficulty, not with recording these events, but with ordering and defining them, that is, deriving meaning from them. The Atlas Group pronouncements gradually reveal themselves as harbouring lack of clarity and confusion. The Group's obsession with empirical detail, ordering and classification is presented as a parody of the objective mode of 'correct' state or official history. In performances, Raad presents some of the amassed historical detail of the Civil Wars in a dry archival tone – yet his surety dissolves into the repeated phrase 'It's unclear why...' when more complex issues of cause and effect arise.

The documentation of history as objective record is revealed as impossibly confounded by competing viewpoints, uncertain motivations and the labyrinthine nature of the causal chain. The Atlas Group project, beneath its objectivist surface, is an 'archive of traumatic experience', as Alan Gilbert has observed (2006, p. 80). Rather than a pristine and objective archive, the project is revealed as a repository of symptoms. The reverberations of a whole series of events are so charged, and so complex in their convoluted sequence, that the empirical record of history must fail to encompass their range and their consequence. Testimony is inadequate. Place and event are displaced within the very telling of their history, and the past remains enigmatic. The German artist Thomas Demand pursues a singular technique. His works are based on photographs, either from media or photographs of the object-world. He builds carefully crafted paper and card paper sculptures, based on the photographs. The sculptures are then photographed and destroyed. His work thus effects a series of displacements in the process of representation. The final image is a photograph of a model based on a photograph of an object. The final printed image will bear similarities to the original photograph, but the printed image will differ from the original in significant ways: details will be omitted or altered, so that the print is an approximation of the photograph, in the same way that our memories store approximations of remembered sights and events. If one were charged with the task of reconstructing a scene or space from memory, the result would be nothing more than a likeness: recognisable but lacking the details and fine points of an accurate representation. Demand's photographic images share something of this subjective, imprecise aspect of recollection, the re-membering/dis-membering process of active memory described by Steven Rose. Many works by Demand, based on images taken from newspapers, magazines and other media, have probed the slipperiness of memory and the construction of historical truths as forms of myth-making. The 'problematic of commodification' is also visible in Demand's works built on media images, as Tamara Trodd has observed (2009, p. 969). In contrast to these works, the images in Demand's recent series *The Dailies* are close likenesses of transient scenes, insignificant moments and objects, suspended in time and memory. Each of the Dailies is built up from scenes observed and photographed by Demand while walking the streets, each scene then filtered and edited in the painstaking reconstruction process. They are ordinary objects in simple settings, familiar as office, hotel, suburban yard or urban street. At times stark in their reduced simplicity, the images are contemporary still-lifes: banal, forgettable, yet bearing a hermetic appearance suggesting, as Sophie Forbat has observed, 'the bare compositions of dream, impressions or recollections' (2012, p. 5) (Figure 16.1).

The 2012 Sydney exhibition *The Dailies* was housed in the Commercial Traveller's Association Hotel, further accentuating the everyday aspect of the images as they may be processed, sorted and recollected in memory. Each of the photographed images was installed in a room in the commercial travellers' hotel, creating the impression that each work represented a brief recollection, a still-life witnessed by the room's inhabitant. As a component of the installation encompassing the cramped hotel room, the printed image suggested a moment captured from the previous day, reworked in memory, poised in the possibility of narrative.

The title 'The Dailies' refers to cinema and the daily rushes viewed in the editing room, selected for inclusion in the greater narrative of the film, or perhaps set aside or cut out altogether. They are glimpses of an everyday, a few of the multitude of images experienced, sorted and edited by the mind 'in the creation of its narratives' (Forbat, 2012, p. 7). They are the dailies of the mind's editing room, also known as memory. *The Dailies*, focused on the ephemeral and the quotidian, shows us a series of enigmatic instants in the process of being sorted. In common

221

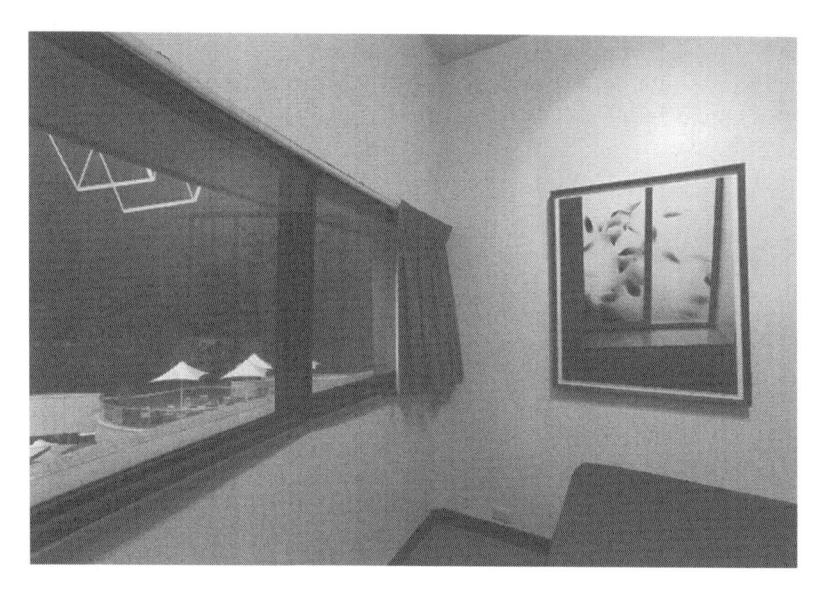

Figure 16.1 Installation View: Thomas Demand, 'The Dailyies', Kaldor Public Art Project 25, Sydney, 2012. Photo: Kaldor Public Art Projects/Paul Green (caption 1)

Figure 16.2 Installation View: Thomas Demand, 'The Dailyies', Kaldor Public Art Project 25, Sydney, 2012. Photo: Kaldor Public Art Projects/Paul Green (caption 2)

with the works of Kentridge and Raad, Demand's images are rigorous in their construction. They are representations of memory that are free of sentiment, free of nostalgia and free of contempt.

References

Beaglehole, J. C. (ed.) (1962) *The Endeavour Journal of Joseph Banks 1768–1771 Vol. II*. Sydney: Public Library of NSW/Angus and Robertson.
Braudel, F. (1980) *On History*. Translated by Sarah Matthews. Chicago: University of Chicago Press.
Cohen, M. J. and Major, J. (eds) (2004) *History in Quotations*. London: Cassell.
Forbat, S. (2012) 'Thomas Demand and the CTA' in *The Dailies* catalogue. Sydney: MACK and Kaldor Public Art Projects.
Gilbert, A. (2006) ' "It's Unclear Why..."/Walid Raad and the Writing of History' in Charles Merewether (ed.) *Zones of Contact: 2006 Biennale of Sydney Catalogue*. Sydney: Biennale of Sydney.
Jameson, F. (1983) 'Postmodernism and Consumer Society', in H. Foster (ed.) *The Anti-Aesthetic: Essays on Postmodern Culture*. Port Townsend: Bay Press.
Kentridge, W. (2003) 'Felix in Exile: Geography of Memory' (extract), in *William Kentridge*. Catalogue London: Phaidon.
Lasch, C. (1991) *The True and Only Heaven: Progress and its Critics*. New York: W. W. Norton.
Manovich, L. (2013) 'Future Fictions'. *Frieze* (156), http://www.frieze.com/issue/article/future-fictions/ (accessed 24 February 2014).
Merewether, C. and Potts, J. (2010) 'Introduction', in C. Merewether and J. Potts (eds) *After the Event: New Perspectives on Art History*. Manchester: Manchester University Press.
Morozov, E. (2011) 'What Do We Think About? Who Gets To Do the Thinking?', in J. Brockman (ed.) *Is the Internet Changing the Way You Think?* New York: Harper Perennial.
Nietzsche, F. (1983) *Untimely Meditations*. Translated by R. J. Hollingdale. Cambridge: Cambridge University Press.
Packer, G. (2013) 'Change the World: Silicon Valley Transfers its Slogans – and its Money – to the Realm of Politics'. *The New Yorker* 27 May 2013.
Potts, J. (2010) 'The Event and its Echoes', in C. Merewether and J. Potts (eds) *After the Event: New Perspectives on Art History*. Manchester: Manchester University Press.
Rose, S. (1991) *The Making of Memory*. London: Bantam Press.
Trodd, T. (2009) 'Thomas Demand, Jeff Wall and Sherrie Levine: Deforming "Pictures" '. *Art History*, 32(5), 955–975.

Poetic Transfer of a (Serious) Situation

Marine Baudrillard

Foreword

Jean Baudrillard passed away on Tuesday, 6 March 2007. In the months following, a German publisher asked whether I would be interested in publishing an interview I had conducted with the French philosopher in 2004. I contacted Marine Baudrillard, his widow, to obtain permissions for this publication. I met her in the summer of 2007 in Paris, the day on which she first shared with me and a mutual friend the audio version of the text you will encounter here. It was a strange moment because, oddly enough, Marine's voice on the recording reminded me of one of Emilie Camacho's dance videos. I later sent it to Marine herself. She also noticed the resemblance between Comacho's *Vertigo* and the recording, prompting me later to construct a montage of the two. We never published this montage, but she allowed me to show it in September 2012, on the last day of the *Flashbacks-nostalgic media and other mediated forms of nostalgia conference*, which I had organised at the University of Geneva. The video closed the conference as a nostalgic counter-nostalgia poetic reflection on the idea of creative nostalgia and our sometimes ambivalent and difficult relation to time and death.

Things have changed since 2007, and the following text should not be understood as a theoretical denial of death, reality or suffering. It is, rather, an expression of deep love and grief, appearing only a few months after the loss of a loved one. I would like to thank Marine Baudrillard for permitting its publication and Philippa Lewis for translating it from the French.

Katharina Niemeyer

Poetic Transfer of a (Serious) Situation
Marine Baudrillard

We must not talk about others, we must talk to others.
We must not talk about the dead, we must talk to the dead.
All our troubles come from having lost contact.
Jean Baudrillard is my husband, and much more besides...
I offer him this little love song which I could call,
  in all complicity:

Death... For the two of us, as for all of us, it had always been there. From the beginning it followed us about like a shadow, but at 4 p.m. on Tuesday 6 March 2007, it eventually gave in to you. You liked that idea, Stanislas Lec's aphorism: 'Death resists us. It tries as hard as it can but, in the end, it gives in to us.' And that's what happened that day: death gave in to you, and you left me. A minute before and you were still there, all smiles, something of a double already, and then, pff, you were gone. You left me. These things happen...

It was time for the Great Abstraction.

You had slipped a few instructions into one of your last pieces, doubtless anticipating the approaching end:

> Dying is nothing, knowing how to disappear is what counts. To die is a chance matter of biology, it isn't important. To disappear is a matter of a higher necessity. You mustn't let biology control your disappearance. Disappearing means passing into an enigmatic state which is neither life nor death. Some animals know how to do it, and some primitives, who, before they die, slip out of sight of their kin.

This much was clear: your death was not going to be a big thing. Instead, we would view it as a metamorphosis, and in no way would this enigmatic state, into which we had both passed, *couple oblige*, spell the end for us. Mastering the real universe had never really mattered for you – that, moreover, must have helped you to 'let go' – and for a long time you had tried to initiate me into the High Stakes of Symbolic Exchange, that mad dream of the possible reversibility of, among other things, death in life and life in death. So when Death did finally present itself, well, neither you nor I were caught unawares... You, you'd always 'had dealings' with death, it was even your strength, and me, as usual, I pedalled behind... literally as well as figuratively, because it's you who were my strength.

How many times, in the Compiègne forest, during one of our many cycling escapades, had you tried out Jarry's ten-man-bicycle trick on me? It amused you to play the dead-man-who-continues-to-cycle-from-inertia; me, I spun the metaphor out along the cycle paths. Dead or alive, after all, it wasn't the most important thing. Only one thing counted: being together... and we were. The three of us were in training, without realising.

The same goes for deathly and pataphysical rigidity, as long as the mind stays alert and metaphysical. I was ready to follow you anywhere. Down that path like any other. I still am, more than ever. Your death doesn't exist.

One morning, in your final year, you had even written on the big mirror in the bedroom in felt tip pen: 'Existence isn't everything, it's really the least of things.'

It made me wonder, and this time, exceptionally, I asked you to explain yourself. Normally, I preferred leaving things in suspense, leaving them the choice, the time to reveal themselves at the right moment. You didn't like people forcing you into the obscenity of meaning... And, great card player that you were, you shuffled the cards and cut them again, and I was taken in. I agreed with you that existence wasn't much... a proposition, if that. Take it or leave it.

(Oh, the joy of giving into you, Jean! Admitted or secret, it was always at the end of our discussions. You never disappointed me, not once. I'd gladly have profited from it more, given how much I loved that sense of letting go, that surrender – so pleasurable, having nothing left to give, no further reserves... But I was wary, because you never surrendered, not even when your defences were down, and I never knew exactly what to stick to with you.... I only knew that I stuck to you, that you were my dearest hypothesis, my most beautiful illusion, and that I didn't want to lose you: I blundered. Moreover, it's funny, but I got the impression that everyone blundered, with you... doubtless for the same reasons).

Be that as it may – you must have had enough of existing – on 6 March, you chose to cross that wretched mirror... and I found myself back to square one, Jean!

Since then, long months have passed. As if *nothing* had happened. And I did practically *nothing* but repeat to myself: 'Existence is *nothing*, death doesn't exist.' And then one day, that *nothing* spoke to me of you, and I understood. I understood that you'd made off that way, and that was how I'd find you again... Everything came back to me. All those times you had whispered to me, about this *nothing*, that we could *also* see a happy destiny in it, as long as we allowed it the force of poetic illusion, as long as we turned it into the rule of the game... The same radical uncertainty – ours – the same absolute non-sense, which spoilt everything for us, could also deliver us from the end.

So that was where you had hidden it, this strength which stays with me today? In this unthinkable lightness of being and in this *nothing* which allowed you to leap over your shadow... imperceptibly?

So, out of preference, do nothing – what was there to do, anyway? – leave this *nothing* alone... *leave it alone and it'll come home*... without losing the famous 'sacred horizon of appearances' from view. Those all-powerful appearances which alone protect us from reality and allow us to transfigure it... Since my destiny was to seduce you, Jean, and let myself be seduced by you, seeing as it's that way, it makes me happy, oh how happy – I have never stopped trying to please you, and will not stop now! Seduction, seduction, I hold onto you, you hold onto me... and so much for the *barbichette*![1]

I was lucky enough to be there until the end, to be there for the last hours of your life. So I could see and know that you had *never* flinched before any enemy – neither inner nor outer – and that in a way you were part of your own beautiful death, succumbing to your own inertia, making use of the cancer to disappear. I saw you rush *smiling* into *your* own emptiness. And this form of sequence or chain reaction, this 'fatal strategy', marvellous, mysterious, and intangible (like everything which escapes the law of reason) offers itself up to me today as a strange, sublime attraction which I do not mean to resist and which, moreover, I shall make off with, right under everybody's noses!

Only the gods know how much love, how many riches and pleasures you gave me during those years of shared life together.... But you and I, we knew that what was essential was elsewhere, in a magic equation, black, cosmic magic, capable of warding off and diverting *all that as well as its lack*, a equation which made us play on until we were dizzy, all our rivalries, all our complicities. It was our own game, into which everything 'real' entered alive, so from the point of view of your secret rule, your death today seems like a new gesture of seduction...

One day you described seduction as a 'narrow escape, outside the body, of much lighter molecules, which know only one line of flight: that of the void'. That's literally how you left...

You knew how to establish our relationship on the hallowed ground of the game, the duel, the challenge, and I'm proud to have been able to meet the challenge for so long. Giving up today would mean betraying you. Jean, I want to continue our game of seduction *in exchange for* reality. Our story was based neither solely on your physical being nor on the quality of our desire. So, even if your last metamorphosis means readjusting the rules somewhat, please know that I don't intend to stop playing... the game will always be bigger than the player.

Nowadays, being accepted as a victim is one of the rights of man. Being accepted as a widow could be a right for the woman you devastated by your disappearance. But by suffering, I was searching for you in vain... What's left, then, is the joy, the joy of our secret, the joy of having been your wife, the joy of thinking you, the joy of seducing you, now and always, so as to divert you from the truth of your death, and, in return, to divert me from the truth of my widowhood.

To do this, we must not lose the secret. Not break the pact. Profit from having discovered the rule of the game, and stay in this unreal and enchanted world where all natural determinations have been abolished, including those of life and death...

Rituals, feasts, and friends are all essential for play to continue. Silly rituals or sensible rituals, magic rituals, always arbitrary but all abolishing sense and parodying the real, and protecting us from the encroachments of time by virtue of their 'eternal return'... a game which fate can only end up by going along with.

Moreover, what is it even doing, here, at a time like this?

Jean, it's you who thinks me, and I'm your magic spell. Unless it's the other way round?

Your work, so powerful and poetic, lets us into so many other worlds: it would be such a mistake to try and defend it! We should simply borrow it and share it – that's all. Ease into it, feel comfortable in it, and wait for it to give back a hundredfold.

In any case, as for me, I've chosen to play, live, and laugh with it, as I did with your much-loved incarnation. I've chosen to play with the complicity, the absence, the illusion, and the distance you imposed in order to get away from this world – the world of the impossible exchange – before you chose, finally, to leave it.

* * *

To all those of you who have been my accomplices – at least for the time of this reading – and kept me going in this 'other world' I have dragged you into, after him: Thank you.

Translated by Philippa Lewis

Note

1. Translator's note: The *jeu de la barbichette*, literally 'game of the small beard', refers to a traditional French children's game in which two players face each other, holding each other by the chin, and reciting a rhyme. They must stay in this posture as long as possible. The first to move, laugh or smile is the loser.

Index

Note: Locators in **bold** type indicate figures or illustrations.

A bout de souffle (Godard), 165, 167
Abélès, M., 153, 157
Adler, P. S., 108
Adorno, T. W., 170
Adotevi, S., 191
advertising
  aesthetic idealisation in, 88
  brands' increasing use of nostalgia, 99
  Hovis' nostalgic campaigns, 83–8, 90–1, 93
aesthetic, goal of the backward-looking, 65
aesthetics, baroque, 96–8
aesthetics of the imperfect, 54
Agfacolour, 172
Aldrin, P., 156
American Civil War, 123
An American Tragedy (Dreiser), 171
analogue film, use of aesthetics in *Californication*, 33–4
analogue nostalgia, and the aesthetics of virtual ruins, 34–6
Anders, G., 29
Antietam, 123
antithesis, definition, 97
Arcana 1996/2008 (Schmid), **66**
Ariel Pink, 77
Arndt, J., 5, 10
ARTE
  'brown soup' productions, 154
  Ce qui me manque (*What I Miss*), 153–6, 158
  counter-nostalgia, 157–8
  and European identity, 153–8
  founding and purpose, 153
  Histoire Parallèle (*Parallel History*), 152–5
  Karambolage, 153–4, 158
  media as time machine, 155–7
  nostalgia policy, 154–5
  and post-war reconciliation, 153
  'Summer of ...' series, 152
  war as flagship product, 154
The Artist (Hazanavicius), 1
Atia, N., 10
Atlas Group, 217, 219
Augustine of Hippo, 51
authenticity, vintage label as sign of, 75

'B for Larry' (Baselitz), 207
Back to Black (Winehouse), 73
backward-looking aesthetic, goal of the, 65
Baden, D., 106
Baker, W. E., 107
Banks, Joseph, 216
baroque aesthetics, in Citroën DS advertising campaigns, 96–8
Barroso, Jose Durão Manuel, 157
Barsley, M., xciiin2
Barthes, R., 47, 65, 97
Bartholeyns, G., 12–13, 51–68
Baselitz, G., 18, 203–11
Basioudis, I. G., 108
Battlestar Galactica (ABC), 134
Baudrillard, J., 2, 19, 30, 54, 101, 223–8
Baumeister, R. F., 87
BBC, 9, 85–6, 119, 129, 134
Beaglehole, J. C., 216
the Beatles, 73
Benjamin, W., 35, 44, 65, 67, 142, 148, 149
Bergala, A., 165, 171
Berg, O., 148
Bergson, H., 3, 31, 194, 199
Berkowitch, A., 108

229

Berlin Childhood around 1900 (Benjamin), 142
Berliner, D., 5, 54
Betamax, 42
Beti, M., 191–2, 195, 197
Beumers, B., 54
Beverly Hills 90210 (Fox), 134
Biddinger, M., 31, 45
Birago Diop, 191
Bishop, C., 28
Bizzarri, Alvaro, 180–1
   see also *Il treno del Sud*
black-and-white, and historical documentary films, 169–70
Blight, D., 122–3, 124
'Blighty' channel, 118
Blitz template
   business as usual discourse, 121
   in media treatment of London bombings, 120–2
   the 'Blue Flower, ' xxxvin2
Boardwalk Empire (HBO), 1, 129
Bogdanovich, P., 169, 173
Böhme, H., 27, 35
Böhn, A., 29
Böker, W., 186
Bolter, J. D., 28–9, 31
Bolzinger, A., 5, 7–9, 131, 133
Bonjour Tristesse (Preminger)
   colour and Frenchness, 173–4
   communication of Preminger's views on European post-war society, 164
   formalism of Preminger's strategy of colour, 165
   French success, 173
   Godard on, 163
   influence on Godard's *A bout de souffle*, 165–6
   mathematical themes, 168
   and Preminger's post-war return to Europe, 167
   presentation of Europe, 174
   presentation of France, 173
   presentation of sunburnt skin, 164, 166, 174
   remastered version, 164
   Seberg gazes into the camera, **168**
   synopsis, 167
   Technicolor material, 163
   title's evocation of nostalgia, 167
   use of colour and black-and-white, 163–4, 166, 168–9
Bordwell, D., 28
Bourdieu, P., 39
Bouty, I., 108
Boy on Bike advert (Hovis), 83
Boyd, J., 72
Boyer, R., 2
Boym, S., 2, 5, 29, 60, 73, 100, 129–32, 134, 142
Braudel, F., 214
Brinkley, David, 136
British Empire, 122
Brody, R., 165
Broken News (BBC), 119
Brown, A. D., 105–6, 121
Brown, S. D., 120–1
'brown soup' productions, ARTE's, 154
Buache, F., 179
Buck-Morss, S., 148
Burns, L. D., 105, 107
Buscombe, E., 164
Byng-Hall, J., 47

Cahiers du cinéma (Godard), 165
Calder, A., 93
Caldwell, J. T., 136
Californication (Showtime), 28, 32–4
Camacho, Emilie, 223
'Camp 1940' (Senghor), 196
Canetti, E., 205–7
Caranicas, P., 34
Cardamone, G., 187
carpe diem, 100
cars
   Baudrillard on the utopian value of, 101–2
   as perfect embodiment of the past, 102
   as triggering factors for nostalgia, 95
Casetti, F., 180
Cashman, R., 142–3
Cassin, B., 5, 199–200
Castelnau, Henriette-Julie de, comtesse de Murat, 8
Castelnuovo-Frigessi, D., 180, 183–4, 188

Cati, A., 39
Cavell, S., 161, 165
Cayrol, Jean, 170
Ce qui me manque (*What I Miss*) (ARTE), 153–6, 158
Césaire, A., 191, 193, 197, 199
Chalfen, R., 39, 41, 47
Chaney, D., 93
Chants d'Ombre (Senghor), 192
Charpy, M., 66
Chase, M., 140
Chassanoff, A., 32
childhood, 85, 93, 131, 162, 195, 216
Chivers Yochim, E., 31, 45
church, 84, 86, 91
Cinema in the Digital Age (Rombes), 34–5
cinematic historiography, colour and, 160–3
cinephilia, 35
Citroën DS
  heterotopian perspective, 102
  legendary status, 95–6
  location in Floch's semiotic square of the automotive sector, 101
Citroën DS advertising campaigns
  analysis, 95–104
  anti-retro message, 96
  baroque aesthetics, 96–8
  contradictory message, 97–8
  descriptions, 96
  Floch's analysis, 103
  interview pseudo-context, 98
  paradoxical effect of the core ambiguity, 100
  treatment of archived images, 99
Civil Rights Movement, 145
Clarke, Spencer, 77
classic film look, fetishist status, 34
Coastal drive, The Allure (Notorious JES), **61**
Cohen, A., 152, 156
Cohen, M. J., 213
Cold War, 203
Coleman, J. S., 108
collective memory, 77, 118, 122, 217
colonisation, 191, 193, 198
colonisation/colonialism *W, 191, 193, 195, 197–8

colour
  and cinematic historiography, 160–3, 170–2, *see also* film colour
Colour Consciousness (Kalmus), 165
commemoration, 119
commodity aesthetics, 89
commodity culture, temporal orientation, 213
concentration camps, filmed in colour, 170
consumer culture, 212–13, 215
contemporary perspectives on the past
  contempt, 212–16
  enigma, 217–22
  nostalgia, 216–17
Cook, P., 54
Cook, S. D., 114
Corrente, M., 187
counter-memories, 145, 147
counter-nostalgia, ARTE's, 157–8
Crewe, L., 52
Cronkite, Walter, 136
Crowds and Power (Canetti), 205
cultural objects, tactile dimension, 43
Culture and Imperialism (Said), 192
Cutcher, L., 105, 114
cut-up techniques, 70

Dachau, filmed in colour, 170
The Dailies (Demand), 220, **221**
Daily Express, 85
Dakowska, D., 156
Dallas (CBS), 134
Damas, L. G., 191
Dames, N., 10
Davies, J., 10
Davis, F., 2, 5, 54–5, 72
Davis, G. F., 107
Dayan, D., 109, 133
De Baeque, A., 165
Deleuze, G., 3, 98–9
Dell'Ambrogio, M., 179
DeLong, M., 44
Demand, T., 212, 219–22
depression, 9
Derrida, J., 78
Desperate Housewives (ABC), 137
Desrosiers, M., 33

232 Index

Dezalay, Y., 152, 156
Diagne, S. B., 194–5, 199
Di Chio, F., 180
'Die Ärhe' (Lüpertz), 211
digimodernism, 76
digital cinema, fetishist status of the classic film look, 34
digital home movies
 dematerialisation, 44
 screening experience, 43
 see also home movie making
digital images, processing example, 58
digital retro photography
 adding emotional value, 57–60
 apps marketing, 62, 64
 and the backward-looking aesthetic, 67
 convergence of vintage style enabling events, 54
 impact on temporality, 67
 key apps, 52
 Memories of San Clemente Pier, Dragonfly, Arizona, **53**
 mythologising effect of intentionally aged images, 54
 the past as an aesthetic experience, 65–7
 resurgence of still life, 62
 rise of a mimetic technology, 52–5
 and self-induced nostalgia, 55–7
 simulating photographic imperfection, 51
 time regained and the nostalgia market, 60–4
 when digital becomes analogue, 51–2
digital technology, and sampling, 76
digital television channels, as archives, 118
digitisation, and the relationship between family images and family memory, 42–3
Dika, V., 7, 135, 180
disease, 6–7, 161, 183, 185–6, 216
Dissertatio Medica (Hofer), 183
Doane, J., 5, 140
Doane, M. A., 30, 35
Dorbowski brothers, 62
Doss, E., 122

Doutriaux, Claire, 156
Dove-Viebahn, A., 139
Downton Abbey (ITV), 129, 216
Dr. Who (BBC), 134
Dreiser, T., 171
Dudley, A., 172
Dumont, H., 179
Dunkirk, 119
Duyvendak, J. W., 5, 9, 132, 134

earworms, 71, 73
Eastman, George, 171
Eco, U., 29
Edgerton, G. R., 19, 137, 147
Ehrenreich, B., 147
Eisler, Hanns, 170
Eliade, M., 208
Eloge de l'amour (Godard), 165–6
emotional value, adding through digital retro photography, 57–60
Endrigo, S., 185, 188
Eno, Brian, 78
Eros and Civilization (Marcuse), 142
Esquenazi, J.-P., 133
Ewig, I., 209–10

Facebook, 54, 215
Faces of Europe, 157
family photos
 digitisation and the dematerialisation of, 43
 location of conversations about, 43
Farbenlehre (Goethe), 161
FCLIS (Federation of Free Italian Colonies in Switzerland), 179–80, 186–7
Felix in Exile (Kentridge), 218
Ferraro, James, 77
Ferreira, C., 41, 43
Ferro, M., 154–5
fetishist status, of classic film look, 34
film colour
 Godard's argument, 172
 historical tension, 172
 historicity of colour relations and, 165
 and the horror of history, 171
 in newsreel of Nazi Germany, 170
 physio-psychological effects, 161–2

Index 233

post-war perspective, 172
Preminger and Godard's use, 166–7
and reality of atrocities, 170
use of in advertising, 165
use of in home movie formats, 171
Flaherty, M. G., 67
flashback
  in *Bonjour Tristesse*, 163, 166, 169
  diegetic vs extra-diegetic forms, 162
  in *Eloge de l'amour*, 165–6
  episodes of in nostalgic television series, 135
  function and aesthetics, 161–2
Fleming, Victor, 162–3
flickr, 56, 58
Fligstein, N., 107
Floch, J.-M., 101, 103
Flückiger, B., 33
Forbat, S., 220
Ford, Henry, 213, 216
Foucault, M., 102, 145
Fraser, J. A., 144
Fréchuret, M., 210
Friedrich, C. D., 206, 211
Friends (NBC), 135
Frith, S., 74–5
Froger, I, 45
Froger, M., 45
Fujiwara, C., 164, 167

Gabriel, Y., 105, 114
Game of Thrones (HBO), 132
Ganito, C., 41, 43
Garçon, F., 154
Garnier, V., 204, 207, 210
GDR (German Democratic Republic), artistic policy, 203
generational memory, and the mass-media culture, 72
genres, life-cycle, 75
German identity, place of trees in, 206, 208
gezellig, 86
Gilbert, A., 219
Gilroy, P., 118, 122
Glass, C., 121
Glazer, P., 140
global warming, 213
Gobineau, A. de, 199

Godard, J.-L., 163, 165–6, 170–3
Goffman, E., 46
golden age of pop, 71
Good Bye Lenin (Becker), 10
Grainge, P., 6
'The Great Friends' (Baselitz), 205
Gregson, N., 52
Grendi, E., 180
Griswold, W. G., 43
Grusin, R., 28–9, 31
Guffey, E. E., 27
Gunning, T., 30, 164
Gye, L., 43

Halbwachs, M., 43, 118
halcyon days, 54
Hansen, M. B., 149
Hansen, M. T., 108
Happy Days (ABC), 136
Hartemann, A., 16, 152–8
Hartog, F., 4, 66
Hatufim (Il, Channel 2), 132
Haug, W. F., 89
'haunting melodies' phenomenon, 72–3
Heckscher, C. C., 143
Heer, J., 140
Heimweh, 2, 7, 180, 183
Heinemann, B., 44
Hennion, A., 72
Herodotus, 155
'Heroes' (Baselitz), 204–5
Hesmondhalgh, D., 62
heterotopia, 102
Hipstamatic, 52, 62, **64**
hipsters, 44
Hirsch, F., 164
Histoire Parallèle (*Parallel History*) (ARTE), 152–5
Histoire(s) du cinéma (Godard), 170
historiography, cinematic, *see* cinematic historiography
history
  embodied in Nike TV advertisements, 214
  Ford's dismissal, 214

hits, 72–3, 76, 152
  definition, 71
  emotional perspective, 73
  temporal perspective, 72
Hodges, D., 5, 140
Hofer, Johannes, 7–8, 133, 183, 187
Holdsworth, A., 7, 134
Hollan, J. D., 43
Holocaust miniseries (NBC), 118
holograms, 79
Homeland (Showtime), 132
home movie making
  in the age of VHS, 42
  in the digital age, 42–4; *see also* digital home movies
  and family self-awareness, 40
  and feelings of belonging, 45–6
  nostalgic home movies, 44–6
  patriarchal perspective, 40
  the Super 8 experience, 40–2
homesickness
  expression of in *Lost*, 131
  historical perspective of in the military, 8
  as initial meaning of nostalgia, 131
  in medical discourse, 9
  relief of through social media, 9
  serial, 130–3
  symptoms, 8
Hopper, E., 135
Horace, 100
Horton, D., 86
Hoskins, A., 15, 19, 118–24
Hosties Noires (Senghor), 192
The Hour (BBC), 129
Hovis, nostalgic advertising campaigns, 83, **84**, 85–8, 90–1, 93
How I Met Your Mother (CBS), 135
Hugo (Scorsese), 1
the human brain, and the hits experience, 72
Humphreys, M., 105–6
'The Hunter in the Forest' (Friedrich), 206
Huntley, Chet, 136
Hutton, P., 88
Huyssen, A., 3, 118

hypnagogic trend
  definition, 77
  in pop music, 74, 77–9

iconography, 65
idealisation, 33, 45, 74, 84, 86–8, 91–2, 98, 131, 141
IG Farben, 172
Il treno che viene dal Sud (Endrigo), 185
Il treno del Sud (Bizzarri)
  Bizzarri's reasons for making, 187
  and the character of migrant nostalgia, 186–8
  character of the protagonist's nostalgia, 185–6
  inspiration for soundtrack and title, 185
  personal nature, 181
  protagonist, 181
  protagonist's symptoms of migrant nostalgia, 184
  Swiss and Italian perspectives on nostalgia, 183–4
  synopsis, 181–3
  theme, 180
indexicality, and analogue nostalgia, 34–5
Instagram, 45, 54
Internet, 72, 76
Introduction à la métaphysique (Bergson), 194
iPhonography, 52
Irele, F. A., 192–3, 196
Italian migrants, in Switzerland, 179
ITMA (BBC), 85–6

Jackson, Michael, 119
Jameson, F., 2, 4–6, 142, 144, 148, 161, 163, 213
Jankélévitch, V., 5, 95, 103, 104, 192, 198
Jaspers, K., 131
Jenkins, H., 7, 30
Jones, D., 63, 68, 191, 194
Josserand, E., 14, 105–15

Kalmus, N., 165
Kammen, M., 140
Kandinsky, W., 209

Kant, I., 8, 131
Karambolage (ARTE), 153–4, 158
Katz, E., 19, 133
Kavanagh, T., 93
Keenan, D., 77
Keightley, E., 3, 5–7, 13, 19, 83–93, 103
Kellaris, James, 71
Kennedy, John F., 147
Kentridge, W., 212, 218
Kessous, A., 6, 105, 114
Kiefer, A., 206
Kingdom of Childhood, 192
Kirby, A., 76
kitsch style, 77
Kitzinger, J., 120
Koc-Menard, S., 108
Krauss, R. E., 36
Kwon, S.-W., 108

La Barba, M., 7, 17, 179–89
Labianca, G., 108
Lampel, J., 107
Lang, Fritz, 173
Lasch, C., 5, 217
late-modern syndrome, 88
Lavoie, V., 52
Leary, M. R., 87
Le Goff, J., 4, 100, 122
Le voyage dans la lune (Meliès), 160
Lennon, John, featured in Citroën DS ad, 96–100, 102–3
Lennox, C. S., 108
Les plaisirs et les jours (Proust), 72
Levin, T. Y., 32
Lipsitz, G., 145
lo-fi design, 70
Lo stagionale (Bizzarri), 187
lomography, 51
London bombings, Blitz template in media treatment of, 120–2
Losi, N., 184–5, 188
loss of traces, Benjamin's, 44
Lost (ABC), 131–2
Lowenthal, D., 2–3, 5, 140
Löwy, M., 197–8
Luhmann, N., 153
Lüpertz, M., 203, 210–11

Mad Men (AMC)
  concept, 139
  corporate paternalism in, 143
  female social resistance in, 145–6
  form of nostalgia expressed in, 140
  historic positioning, 143
  male social resistance in, 146–7
  narrative and interrelated montage in, 135
  nostalgic vision of social and gender roles, 141
  as paradigmatic example of television nostalgia, 129–30
  period of time covered by, 136–7
  portrayal of sexism, 145
  presentation of a period of 'lost' American innocence, 144
  repeated disorientation of the audience's nostalgic expectations, 144
  social dissent in, 145
Maeder, D., 137
Magic City (Starz), 1
Maier, C., 140
Major, J., 213
The Making of Memory (Rose), 218
The Man in the Gray Flannel Suit (Wilson), 140
Mannerism, Baselitz references, 205
Manovich, L., 34, 215
Marchetti, D., 152, 156
Marcus, D., 2, 5, 137
Marcuse, H., 142, 148
Marinetti, 216
Marks, L. U., 28, 34
mashup, 70
Mayenfisch, A., 179
Mazé, C., 156
Mbembe, A., 195–6
McCabe, D., 105, 107
the media
  Blitz template treatment of London bombings, 120–2
  paucity of literature linking nostalgia and, 105
  replacement of political events by mass-media culture, 72
  role of templates in 'containing' the catastrophic, 120–1

the media – *continued*
  spaces and times for nostalgia, 5–11
  as time machine, 155–7
mediatisation, 119, 122–4, 135
melancholia
  and ARTE's 'brown soup'
    productions, 154
  definition, 122
  nostalgia and the state of, 9
  postcolonial, 118, 122
Meliès, G., 160
memorial arc, twentieth-century, 119
*Memories of San Clemente Pier,
  Dragonfly, Arizona* (Turner), 53
memory
  colour and, 161–3
  mediatisation of, 122
  and nostalgia, 3–5
  sensory qualities of, 91
  time and the concept of, 3
memory boom
  and the 2005 London Bombings,
    120–2
  candidates for drivers, 119
  commemoration as defining public
    mode, 118
  and the new structure of
    memorialisation, 122–3
  the start, 118
Le Mépris (Godard), 173
Meredith, K., 52
Merewether, C., 217
'Message' (Senghor), 195
Meyer, A. D., 107
migrant nostalgia
  character of in *Il treno del Sud*, 186–8
  concept analysis, 179
  and cultural creativity, 187
  and mental health, 183
  see also Il treno del Sud
the military, historical perspective of
  homesickness in, 8
Miller, D., 52
Milner, G., 30
mimesis, 3
mimetic technology, digital retro
  photography as, 52–5
Mink, G., 153
mise-en-abyme, 62

Mizruchi, M. S., 107
mnemonic imagination, 92
mobile phone photography, as leader
  of Western visual retromania, 52
mobile phones, and the enabling of
  vintage style, 54
'Model for a Sculpture' (Baselitz), 210
modernity, Sayre and Löwy's critique,
  197
Monroe, Marilyn, featured in Citroën
  DS ad, 96–100, 102
Moran, J. M., 39
Morozov, E., 215
Moudelino, L., 192
Mounier, E., 196
Münsterberg, H., 161
Murrow, Edward, 136
Myung-Ho, C., 108

Napoleon, 206
Nathan, T., 72
Nazi Concentration Camps
  (Stevens), 170
Nazi propaganda, 204
Négritude
  shaping of the movement, 191, *see
  also* Senghor's Négritude
Négritude et Condition Africaine
  (Irele), 196
Nerval de, G., 103
networks as media study
  context, 107–8
  discussion and conclusions, 113–15
  emotional repertoire findings,
    110–13
  instrumental repertoire findings,
    109–10
  interpretive repertoires, 109
  literature review, 108
  methods, 108–9
Neumayer, L., 153
The Newsroom (HBO), 136
'New Types' (Baselitz), 204
New York Office (Hopper), 135
Niemeyer, K., 1–20, 93, 99, 105,
  129–37, 139, 223
Nietzsche, F., 160, 174, 214
Nighthawks (Hopper), 135
Nike, 62, 214

Nora, P., 3, 99
nostalgia
  brands' increasing use of as source of inspiration, 99
  clash between two types of, 9–10
  cures for, 9
  dangerous longing for the mythical past, 140
  definitions, 1, 8, 58
  denial of in Citroën DS advertising, 97
  effective formula to encourage, 65
  etymology, 7, 131, 183, 216
  focus of literature, 10
  Hofer on the source of, 183–4
  introduction in medical nosology as a typically Swiss disease, 183
  literature review, 5–6
  the mediality of, 29
  in an organisational context, *see* organisational context of nostalgia
  paucity of literature linking the media and, 105
  prefabricated, 129
  reflective, 60, 83
  regressive, 84, 88, 92
  restorative vs reflective, 60
  Senghorian experience of, *see* Senghor's *Négritude*
  as stimulus for social and political change, 148
  Swiss and Italian perspectives, 183–4
  symptoms, 8
  as traditional companion to progress, 2
  triggering factors, 95
  two aspects of, 132
  wartime, 90–1, 93
nostalgia wave, examples, 1–2
nostalgic advertising campaigns, Hovis, 83–8, 90–1, 93
nostalgic television series
  flashback episodes, 135
  homecoming and longing, 133–4
  reruns and remakes, 134
  and television journalism, 136
nuclear family life, 40, 86–7, 91
Nuit et Brouillard (Resnais), 170

Oasis, 73
obsolescence, and retro-cultures, 27–8
Odin, R., 39, 41
Odyssey (Homer), 131
Office at Night (Hopper), 135
Oh, H., 108
old memories, 84–5, 87, 90–1
Old Photo Pro, 62
On Collective Memory (Halbwachs), 118
O'Loughlin, B., 118, 121
organisational context of nostalgia
  literature review, 105–6
  networks as media, *see* networks as media study
'Orphée Noir' (Sartre), 199
ostalgia, 6
Owen-Smith, J., 105, 107

Packer, G., 213
Pan Am (ABC), 1
Parallel History (Histoire Parallèle) (ARTE), 152
Parikka, J., 27, 30
'Paris, Capital of the Nineteenth Century' (Benjamin), 142
Park, C. W., 108
the past
  consumer appeal, 90
  contemporary perspectives, *see* contemporary perspectives on the past
paternalism, 143
Paterson, M., 44
Peterson, R. A., 74
photography
  birth of the lo-fi movement, 51
  Sontag on, 64
  see also digital retro photography
Pic Grunger, 65
Pickering, M., 5–7, 13, 83–94, 103
A Place in the Sun (Stevens), 171–2
Planchais, J., 155
Plasketes, G., 45
Poetic Transfer of a (Serious) Situation (M. Baudrillard), 223–7
Poison Pill, 107
Polaroids, 1

political change, nostalgic elements of popular culture as stimulus for social and political change, 148
political events, replacement by mass-media culture, 72
Poncet, E., 72
pop culture
 defining, 71
 golden age of, 71
 historical perspective, 74–5
 relation of to its own past, 73–4
 sampling, 76
pop music
 hypnagogic trend, 77
 nostalgic aesthetics, 77–9
Populaire (Roinsard), 1
postcolonial melancholia, 118, 122
posthumous albums, 74
post-scarcity culture, 119, 122, 124
'The Postwar Struggle for Colour' (Dudley), 172
Potter, J., 109
Potts, J., 18, 212–22
Powell, W. W., 105, 107, 144
prefabricated nostalgia, 129
presentism, 4, 66, 153, 157–8
progressive rock, 74
progress, nostalgia as traditional companion to, 2
prosopopoeia, 99
Proust, M., 72, 161
Puig de la Bellacasa, M., 44

Raad, W., 212, 219
Radical Nostalgia (Glazer), 140
Radiohead, 76
Ranz de Vaches, 9
Ratcliffe, M., 44
'R. Crumb Effect, ', 33
Reagan, Ronald, 140
recording, metaphysics of, 30–2
reflective nostalgia, 60, 83
The Refusal of Time (Kentridge), 218
regressive nostalgia, 84, 88, 92
Reik, T., 72
Reiley, K., 44
reruns, 134
Resnais, Alain, 170–1
restorative nostalgia, vs reflective, 60

Retro Camera, 62
retro-cultures, obsolescence and, 27–8
retro design, 1
retromania in pop music
 critical history of pop culture, 74–5
 hits, obsession, recollection, 71–4
 nostalgic aesthetics, 77–9
 sampling, 76
Retromania (Reynolds), 73
retro photography, digital, *see* digital retro photography
retrotyping, 83, 88, 90–3
Révolte et Mélancolie (Sayre/Löwy), 197
Revolution (the Beatles), 74
Reynolds, S., 2, 13, 27, 29, 52, 68, 71–3, 76
Ricciardi, T., 179
Richard, F., 5, 134
Ricoeur, P., 3, 5, 135
Risso, M., 183–4, 186, 188
rituals, 10, 133–4, 227
Robnik, D., 35
rock, idealisation of, 74
Rodowick, D. N., 35
Rombes, N., 34–5
Rosa, H., 3, 36, 67, 99
Rosen, P., 30
Rose, S., 218, 220
Ross, A., 143–4
Rostain, S., 154
Routledge, C., 10
Roux, E., 6, 105, 114
Rushdie, S., 162–3, 169

Said, E., 192
sampling, and retromania in pop music, 76
Sartre, J.-P., 199
Sayre, R., 197–8
Schabacher, G., 135
Schaub, M., 179
Schein, E. H., 114
Schifres, A., 154–5
Schlappner, M., 179
Schmid, Joachim, 65–6
Schrey, D., 12, 27–36
Scorsese, Martin, 171
Scott, Ridley, 83
scratching, xxxvin1

Seberg, Jean, 163, 165, 167
Sedikides, C., 10, 106
See It Now (CBS), 136
self-parodist entropy, 75
Senghor, L.-S., 17, 191, 193–4, 197, 199, 201
Senghor's *Négritude*
  and Bergsonian intuition, 194
  characteristic anti-values, 198
  concept analysis, 191–2
  creation and nostalgia in as basis for a postcolonial utopia, 196–200
  emphasis on rhythm, dance and life, 199
  expression of ethical underground stance, 192
  function, 193, 197
  and the 'Kingdom of Childhood, ', 192–6, 199
  and nineteenth century European racialist doctrines, 195
  purpose, 198
  tensions, 194
  underground potential, 195
  understanding the romantic undertone of the anti-modern and anti-capitalist values, 197–8
Sennett, R., 143
September 11 terrorist attacks
  haste for memorialisation, 123
  media's struggle to establish suitable template, 123
  media treatment, 120–1
  serial homesickness, 130–3
Serres, M., 29
Sertoglu, C., 108
Shandler, J., 118
Shaw, C., 140
Shusterman, R., 76
Shutter Island (Scorsese), 171
Silicon Valley, 213
Silverstone, R., 120, 133
Simpson, D., 118
Sit, R. Y., 43
The Skaters, 77
skeuomorphs, 1
Skype, 9
Slater, D., 89
slavery, 191, 193, 195

Snagge, J., 93
Sobchack, V., 30
social media, 215
  and the enabling of vintage style photography, 54
  Facebook, 54, 215
  flickr, 56, 58
  hunger for the present, 215
  Instagram, 45, 54
  and the nostalgia boom, 2
  and relief of homesickness, 9
  Twitter, 215
  YouTube, 213
Sontag, S., 39, 64
Sony, 42
Soyinka, W., 195
Spanish Civil War, 140
Spigel, L., 7, 137
St. Joan (Preminger), 167
Steinle, M., 154–5
Sterling, B., 27
Sterne, J., 27–8, 31
Stevens, George, 170–2
Stiegler, B., 78
still life, resurgence, 62, **63**
Stoddart, S., 140
Strangleman, T., 105, 107
Sturken, M., 118
The Sun, 120
'Sunday Best, ' Hovis advert, **84**
Super 8 home movies
  aesthetic status, 41
  choosing for its charming imperfections, 45
  gendered perspective, 40–1
  granularity, 41
  screening as important family celebration, 43
Switzerland
  Italian migration story, 179–88; *see also Il treno del Sud*
  xenophobic movement, 179
Syberberg, Hans Jürgen, 211
Synthetic, 62
Szendy, P., 71–2

Tacitus, 206
Tannock, S., 6, 140–2
Technicolor, 162–3, 165, 168, 172, 174

Index

Teilhard de Chardin, P., 197, 199
television
   as important symbol for family life, 137
   as time machine, 130
television advert, Britain's favourite, 83
television news, 213
television series, revivals, 2
Televisuality (Caldwell), 136
Tempels, Fr. Placide, 199
temporality
   crisis of, 2
   and digital retro photography, 67
   and the hits experience, 72
   and Senghor's *Négritude*, 193
temporal structures, social nature, 99
textual ruins, analogue's malfunctions as, 35
Thorburn, D., 7, 30
Tierney, J., 10
time
   as semelfactive and irreversible, 95
   subjective perception, 67
Tobner, O., 192, 197
Tortajada, M., 179
touch-screen technologies, 44
Toussaint Louverture (Césaire), 193
Towa, M., 191
Toy Story 3 (Pixar), 60
'Trap' (Baselitz), 207
'The Tree I' (Baselitz), 206
trees, place of in the German identity, 206, 208
tribute bands, 74
Trodd, T., 220
Truffaut, François, 173
Tuan, Y.-F., 87
Turbeville, Deborah, 65
Turner, J., 53
Turner, V., 157
Twitter, 215

Ulead VideoStudio 6, retro interface, 45
utopia, nostalgia and, 101

valuation types, Floch's, 101
Varikas, E., 200

Vertigo (Camacho), 223
Video 8, 42
Viennet, D., 5, 134
Vietnam War, 123, 136, 181–2, 186
vintage images, subject matter, 60, 62
vintage label, as marketing tool, 75
Vintage photo booth vendor at the San Bernardino County Fair (Notorious JES), **61**
vinyl records, 33, 35, 44–5, 73, 75
Virilio, P., 3, 124
Visages d'Europe (*Faces of Europe*) (ARTE), 157
The Walking Dead (AMC), 132
The Wall (Pink Floyd), 119

war
   as ARTE's flagship product, 154
   and the destruction of the European ideal, 206
   filmed in colour, 170–1
   and the German colour film industry, 172
   as pictorial style, 65
   as template for terrorist attacks reporting, 120, 123
wartime nostalgia, 90–1, 93
'The Ways of Worldly Wisdom' (Kiefer), 206
WeHeartIt.com, 60
Wenger, K., 154
Wentz, D., 15–16, 129–37, 139
Westphal, J. D., 107
Wetherell, M., 109
Whitman, M. V. N., 143–4
Wholey, D. R., 105, 107
Wildschut, T., 10, 106
Williams, R., 52
Wilmut, R., 93
Wilson, J. L., 5, 54
Wilson, S., 140
Winehouse, Amy, 73
Winter, J., 118
The Wire (HBO), 77
Wittgenstein, L., 47
The Wizard of Oz (MGM), 162, 169
The Wizard of Oz (Rushdie), 162–3, 169
Wohl, R. R., 86

The Wonder Years (ABC), 131, 134
'Woodmen' (Baselitz), 208
working-class idyll, in Hovis
   advertising campaigns, 85–6
World Wars, and ARTE programming, 153–4

Yanow, D., 114
Ybema, S., 106, 114

Yerushalmi, Y. H., 3
'Yesterday' channel, 118
Yin, R. K., 108
YouTube, 213

Zajac, E. J., 107
Zanier, L., 186, 189
Zawadzki, P., 157
Zimmermann, P. R., 8, 39–40

Printed in Great Britain
by Amazon